The Process
of Change in
Early Modern Europe

Essays in Honor
of Miriam Usher Chrisman

The Process of Change in Early Modern Europe

*Essays in Honor
of Miriam Usher Chrisman*

Edited by
PHILLIP N. BEBB & SHERRIN MARSHALL

Ohio University Press
Athens

Ohio University Press books are printed on acid-free paper. ∞

LIBRARY OF CONGRESS
Library of Congress Cataloging-in-Publication Data

The Process of change in early modern Europe: essays in honor of
    Miriam Usher Chrisman / edited by Phillip N. Bebb & Sherrin Marshall.
        p.   cm.
    Includes bibliographies and index.
    ISBN 0-8214-0900-X
    1. Europe—History—1492-1648. 2. Reformation—Germany. 3. Chrisman, Miriam
Usher. I. Chrisman, Miriam Usher. II. Bebb, Phillip N., 1941- . III. Marshall, Sherrin.
D231.P74 1988   88-19497
940.2—dc19   CIP

TABLE OF CONTENTS

ACKNOWLEDGEMENTS

The editors express their appreciation to the Center for Reformation Research, and William Maltby in particular, and to the Society for Reformation Research, especially Thomas Brady, Jr., for assistance in the publication of this book.

We also thank Donald, Abbott, and Nicholas Chrisman for tangible and intangible support. Holly Panich and Helen Gawthrop aided us in the entire publication process; their sensitivity and skill were greatly valued.

Finally, we note our debt to friends and colleagues, whose encouragement and enthusiasm inspired us throughout.

Miriam Usher Chrisman:
In Appreciation

BY PHILLIP N. BEBB
& SHERRIN MARSHALL

*R*ejecting all forms of what he called idealistic con-
structions, preconceived theoretical frameworks
which historians attempted to impose on their
material, Usher came to stand for a position of empir-
ical realism based on research and analysis.[1]

These words characterize Abbott Payson Usher, perhaps the
single, most creative influence on the life of Miriam Usher
Chrisman. Usher, of old New England stock, had a distinguished career as a scholar. An early exponent of the New
Economic History, Usher concerned himself with "basic meth-
odological problems," which he sought to clarify in more than
sixty-five publications, most of which appeared while he was a
professor at Harvard University.[2] His balance of the roles of family man and scholar imprinted itself on his younger daughter's
personality, and she was able to devote the same care to her
family and career.

Miriam U. Chrisman was born in 1920 at Ithaca, New York,
where her father taught at Cornell University. Her academic
career closely resembled that of her father. She began with a
government major, receiving her A.B. degree with highest
honors from Smith College in 1941. She went on to earn three
master's degrees: one in economics from the American University
in 1948, another in education from Smith in 1955, and a third in

history from Yale in 1959. She also received her doctoral degree in history in 1962 from Yale University, where she worked under the direction of Hajo Holborn.

While acquiring these degrees, Chrisman led a full life. In 1936, she lived in Germany, and in 1939 in France.[3] After graduating from Smith, she became a research assistant for the National Resources Planning Board, where she remained until its demise in August 1943. Immediately thereafter, she became a research assistant for the National Planning Association. Both the Resources Planning Board and the Planning Association emanated from the New Deal Era, the former as part of the National Industrial Recovery Act of 1933, the latter originally as part of the National Economic and Social Planning Association founded in 1934. The goals of both organizations were similar: to project options for the utilization of resources during and after the war.[4] In both cases, Chrisman engaged in research that centered on a high degree of public awareness, one that she continues to evince.

Late in 1943, when she was twenty-three, Chrisman married a physician, a recent graduate from the Harvard Medical School and a lieutenant in the United States Navy.[5] O.Donald Chrisman has remained a main support and major inspiration in his wife's activities. While Donald interned at Boston City Hospital, Miriam taught at the Tenacre School in Wellesley. When he transferred to a residency in orthopedic surgery at Johns Hopkins Hospital, she taught at the Bryn Mawr School in the same city. She also earned a master's degree in economics. Upon Donald's return to Amherst College and Cooley-Dickinson Hospital in Northampton, Massachusetts, Miriam taught at the Northampton School for Girls.

Chrisman changed her occupation during the early 1950s. In 1950, Nicholas Ramsey, her first child, was born, followed by D. Abbott in 1952. Those who know her will find it no surprise that Chrisman remained at home during their most formative years: she has always regarded her first obligation as her family. There is little wonder that she introduced History of the Family courses and a graduate seminar on this topic at the University of Massachusetts, because she holds that the principal unit of social change is the family and changes take generations.

Her belief in the fundamental importance of the family extends to her own familiar practices and projects. A few examples must suffice. When she formally returned to academia at Smith, first as a student, then as a part-time instructor in history in

1955-1956, she was almost always present when her children were home. When she began to attend Yale University on a part-time basis, she traveled to New Haven on Wednesdays, making sure to write Nicholas and Abbott postcards they could read at lunch. A different practice was the creation of a family constitution; once a year family members drew up an agreement that everyone signed. Abbott recalls one rule that was rarely violated: there would be no fighting between the boys after 5 o'clock in the afternoon, when their father returned home. Another family project, still enjoyed, was the creation and maintenance of large flower and vegetable gardens, an interest Miriam may have acquired from her father. But perhaps the best example is found in the preface to *Lay Culture, Learned Culture; Books and Social Change in Strasbourg, 1480-1599*, dedicated to her sons, in which she wrote, "My husband . . . has been the pillar of the whole project."[6]

Because of her belief in the equality of all human beings, Chrisman did not become part of the more ardent behavior of the feminist movement.[7] She reached back to a definition of feminism in the 1930s and particularly the 1940s where it was assumed during World War Two that women could contribute to political and intellectual life. Chrisman was more interested in integrating the work of women and men than creating separate categories.

Perhaps because of her family, Chrisman's view of history is remarkably consistent. She received her doctorate at forty-two, the same age at which she joined the University of Massachusetts-Amherst. Her first book, based on her dissertation and dedicated to her husband, was *Strasbourg and the Reform: A Study in the Process of Change*.[8] Although her first book, it is a mature work, in that by this time in her life she had already developed a cohesive view of history. Unlike those who produce early in life and whose views change, Chrisman was not subject to such adjustment.

The scholarship of the subject of this collection has dealt with three interrelated themes, summarized by part of the title of this book, the process of change. It is important to bear in mind that she completed her dissertation in the year that saw publication of Bernd Moeller's *Reichsstadt und Reformation*, which brought so much attention to the relationship between the Reformation and the German imperial cities. As such, Chrisman's *Strasbourg and the Reform* became one of the first American

3

responses to the Moeller thesis. Her concern with the cities, especially Strasbourg, represents the first theme.[9] The second is a mixture of social and intellectual history dealing with the question of who communicated what to whom.[10] Chrisman's astonishing achievement in this area is *Lay Culture, Learned Culture* and the companion list of almost six thousand books on which it is based, *Bibliography of Strasbourg Imprints, 1480-1599*.[11] Included in this category are a number of articles published in the last decade.[12] The final theme is social groups and family history, and her edited collection *Social Groups and Religious Ideas in the Sixteenth Century*,[13] including her article on the urban poor[14] and recent work on family history.[15]

The care with which Chrisman presents her scholarship is also reflected inside and outside the classroom. Until she retired, she taught large numbers of students through carefully thought out lectures, syllabi, and readers that she edited. Her travels gave her firsthand experience that she could translate to her students.[16] And she was effective outside the classroom as well. For example, in the student strikes at the University of Massachusetts during the Vietnam conflict, Chrisman taught large audiences about the history of Southeast Asia. Her approach is that one better apprehends the current reality by the study of history.

A model of Chrisman's approach to her historical avocation is found in her private account of her visit to the Soviet Union in 1985. Previous to and throughout the trip, she involved herself in the study of Russia's past and present. In a report on the trip, she refers to U.S. foreign policy and her hopes that it will never be based on an idea that the country contains sufficient discontent to overthrow the government. She recalled that the Decembrists of the nineteenth century constituted such a group of dissidents, yet more than half were executed. Citing Maxim Gorky's *Autobiography*, she writes that most astute Russians distrust foreigners, and they seek only to endure. In this vein, she concludes her account with the observation that survival has been the goal of the individual.

Many of Chrisman's academic and personal interests are reflected in this manuscript. Observations cross centuries and cultures as she ponders geography, architecture, commerce, and agriculture. Two illustrations make the point. At the Hermitage Museum in Leningrad, perhaps the most beautiful city she has seen in Europe, she encountered an exhibit on the Altai nomadic

Miriam Usher Chrisman. *Courtesy of D. Abbott Chrisman.*

Abbott Payson Usher, 1883-1965. *Courtesy of D. Abbott Chrisman.*

Miriam Usher Chrisman with Nicholas (left) and Abbott (right), 1954.
Courtesy of D. Abbott Chrisman.

Donald and Miriam Chrisman, 1984. *Courtesy of D. Abbott Chrisman.*

culture in central Asia, whose artifacts dated from the fourth-fifth centuries B.C. She writes, "I have been worrying around with these nomads for at least twenty-five years . . . the gold objects are breathtaking . . . and the textiles were the finest early textiles we have ever seen." The second example is perhaps more poignant, in that it reflects her own interests as well as serves as a heuristic device. In Bukhara, she encountered a procession that returned a baby, traditionally born in the maternal grandparents' house, and its mother to the father's house. Music, gifts, and merriment accompany the procession. Chrisman writes that "I was delighted by the procession because it is very similar to [the one] to escort the bride to the groom's house in prehistoric Greece . . . [I describe] in the history of the family course."

Miriam Usher Chrisman has led a remarkably full life as wife, mother, scholar, educator, associate, and friend. She has served the historical profession in many ways, and she has been rewarded by her election as president of the Society for Reformation Research, an organization she currently aids as American editor for the *Archive for Reformation History*. In recognition of her service, she was awarded the Prix d'Honneur by the Society of Friends of Old Strasbourg in 1983 and made an honorary Doctor of Humane Letters at Valparaiso University in 1984. Indeed, she has been and continues to be an inspiration for many, especially in her concern to get younger people actively involved in the profession.

If every good life returns to its origins, Chrisman's life brings to fruition her father's life, and her extension is found in her sons. In this connection the maturity that characterized her work is to be found in her first book on Strasbourg. The preface began with a series of questions on the process of change. Later, in her acknowledgements, she writes, "I owe a very special debt to my father, Abbott Payson Usher. In conversations over a long period of time we pursued the nature of ideological change and the moment of invention, and his own work profoundly influenced my own thought and work."[17]

NOTES

1. *The National Cyclopedia of American Biography*, 50 (1970): 223.

2. Ibid. Usher was the son of Edward Preston Usher and Adela Louise Payson. He received his A.B. in 1904, A.M. in 1906, and Ph.D. in 1910, all from Harvard. Even though he taught at Cornell and Boston University, his name was still associated primarily with his alma mater. After retirement in 1949, he taught both at the University of Wisconsin-Madison and Yale, two schools that would play influential roles on the careers of his descendants. His daughter's connection to Yale will be discussed, and her son Nicholas was on the faculty at the University of Wisconsin.

3. It is quite possible that these two experiences ultimately influenced Chrisman's choice to work in Strasbourg, since this city serves both German and French interests.

4. The major difference between these two is that the first board is public and the second is private. See Philip W. Warken, *A History of the National Resources Planning Board, 1933-1943* (New York, 1979); Marion Clawson, *New Deal Planning: The National Resources Planning Board* (Baltimore, 1981); and James S. Olson, ed., *Historical Dictionary of the New Deal: From Inauguration to Preparation for War* (Westport, Conn., 1985). The National Planning Association announced in 1943 that "the basis of America's post-war economy should be private enterprise"; government, agriculture, labor, and business sectors must plan together. See *Business Week* (July 31, 1943):42-43.

5. See *Marquis Who's Who Dictionary of Medical Specialists*, 22 ed., vol. 2 (1985-1986), 1974.

6. New Haven, 1982, xvi. Many thanks to Abbott, Nicholas, and Donald Chrisman for use of the personal reference in this paragraph.

7. On the other hand, she was not immune to the issues involved. Chrisman wrote one of the first important articles on how the lives of women came to be changed by the Reformation. See "Women and the Reformation in Strasbourg 1490-1550," *Archive for Reformation History* 63(1972):143-68. In this, she wrote, "The Reformers advocated marriage of the clergy as a means of ending the separation of the clergy from the rest of the community. Indirectly this led to a justification of the married state and familial life which, in turn, gave women new significance" (p. 143).

8. New Haven, 1967.

9. See also her *Urban Society and the Reformation* (St. Charles, Mo., 1976).

10. A. G. Dickens and John Tonkin, *The Reformation in Historical Thought* (Cambridge, Mass. 1985), 303.

11. Both are published at New Haven: Yale University Press, 1982.

These were begun in the 1960s when she was one of the first to utilize computers. See the review by Tom Scott and Chrisman's response in the *Archive for Reformation History* 75(1984):309-16.

12. "L'impremerie à Strasbourg de 1480 à 1500," in *Strasbourg au coeur religieux du XVIe siècle: hommage à Lucien Febvre, actes du colloque international de Strasbourg, 25-29 mai 1975*, ed. Georges Livet and Francis Rapp (Strasbourg: Libraire Istra, 1977), 539-50; "Matthias Schuerer, Humaniste-Imprimeur," in *Grandes Figures de l'humanisme alsacien: courants, milieux, destins* (Strasbourg: Libraire Istra, 1978), 159-72; "Lay Response to the Protestant Reformation in Germany, 1520-1528," in *Reformation Principles and Practice, Essays in Honour of A. G. Dickens*, ed. Peter N. Brooks (London, 1980), 35-52; "Les publications historique à Strasbourg, 1480-1599," in *Horizons europeens de la reforms en Alsace: Das Elsass und die Reformation im Europa des XVI. Jahrhunderts. Mélanges offerts à Jean Rott pour son 65e anniversaire*, ed. Marijn de Kroon and Marc Lienhard (Strasbourg, 1980); and "From Polemic to Propaganda: The Development of Mass Propaganda in the Late Sixteenth century," *Archive for Reformation History* 73(1982):175-96; "Polemique, bibles, doctrine: L'édition protestante è Strasbourg, 1519-1599," in *Bulletin de la Societe du Protestantisme Français* (July-August 1984):319-44; and "L'imprimerie et l'evolution de la culture laique è Strasbourg, 1480-1599," in *Revue d'Alsace* 3(1985):57-77.

13. With Otto Gründler ("Studies in Medieval Culture," vol. 13, Kalamazoo, Mich., 1978).

14. Ibid, "Urban Poor in the Sixteenth Century: The Case of Strasbourg," 59-67.

15. "The Influence of Religion on Family Life: Catholic, Jewish and Protestant," *Halcyon, A Journal of the Humanities* (1983):19-39; and "Family and Religion in Two Noble Families: French Catholic and English Puritan," *Journal of Family History* 8(1983):190-210.

16. During her travels, Chrisman lived and studied in Belgium, France, England, Turkey, Greece, Italy, Africa, Iran, India, Thailand, Japan, Peru, Bolivia, Ecuador, Switzerland, China, and Russia. Of course, she is always identified with Strasbourg.

17. *Strasbourg and the Reform*, xi.

■ Introduction

The Process of Change in Early Modern Europe: Urban Society, Intellectual Development, and Family Life

SHERRIN MARSHALL

T homas Brady, Jr., has reminded us of the "need for synthesis" in study of the Reformation. Viewing the Reformation as a process of change, as Miriam Usher Chrisman did in her pioneering study of Strasbourg, encouraged her to examine later the ways in which ideas influenced that process. Her perceptions of how urban society, intellectual development, and family life interacted with one another enable us to better understand the coming of the Reformation, the atmosphere in which it thrived, and in fact, the entire milieu of sixteenth-century Europe. Just as Chrisman's work has influenced study of these themes and reflected them, essays in her honor verify the connections among them. No one can be considered in isolation; through their synthesis we can help reconstruct the sixteenth-century world in its complexity.

The Reformation succeeded in a variety of urban settings where a wealth of ideas and ideals flourished. This ferment helped bring the Reformation and facilitated its spread. Jean Rott's catalogue shows that intellectuals such as the Strasbourg humanist Thomas Wolf, Sr., accumulated a library of nearly three hundred volumes during his lifetime. This collection, inventoried in 1512 following Wolf's death, demonstrates the broad intellectual interests of a pillar of the church in Strasbourg just prior to the coming of the Reformation. Rott notes that when Miriam Chrisman first surveyed this library, she concluded that about 46 percent of its contents were devoted to juridical and legal works, hardly surprising in view of Wolf's various functions as procurator of the Strasbourg ecclesiastical courts, provost of "Old Saint Peter's," the Strasbourg collegial chapter, and canon of the Cathedral at Worms. Twenty percent of his library was devoted to canon law alone, for example. What Chrisman and Rott consider more remarkable, however, is the broad range of humanist works that they have identified. It is significant that Wolf's library was broadly international and included the works of humanists from Italy to the Low Countries. Humanist writings were the single most important intellectual development to bring about the Reformation, and such works had an impact on their readers that was translated into action after Luther came to the fore.

As Phillip N. Bebb points out in his essay on the Nürnberg *sodalitas*, many patrician Nürnbergers not only studied in Italy but became what he terms *humanist practioners*. These included not only the scions of the merchant families, but other family members—such as Charitas Pirckheimer, sister of the humanist Willibald, herself abbess of St. Clara's cloister—and the friends who composed the circle of the *sodalitas Celtica*. Bebb demonstrates the broad span of this group, which brought together members of the governing council of the city, other patricians, and representatives of the religious establishment, of whom the best known was Johan Staupitz. In other words, these were the influential citizens of Nürnberg. Bebb therefore concludes first that the creators of the Reformation were not always the young, as Bernd Moeller and Lewis Spitz have maintained. Bebb also reminds us that because of their economic connections, the Nürnbergers were in contact with humanism as an international movement, as well as that within the German Empire. The interaction of Nürnberg and Saxony in 1517 seems particularly notable in this context. In a variety of locales, a kind of broad circle of international humanism was created and replicated, which nourished and strengthened more localized groups.

Like Bebb, Susan Karant-Nunn concludes that certain assumptions about the early years of the Reformation are in need of revision. She focuses on "What Was Preached in German Cities in the Years of the Reformation: *Wildwuchs* versus Lutheran Unity." By examining a range of sermons preached by the well-known clergy, such as Carlstadt, as well as those of less renowned preachers, Karant-Nunn demonstrates that preaching in this period of flux was eclectic and action oriented. At least as important, she considers the evidence available on sermons that were preached but not actually printed, often because "they departed too greatly from tolerated teaching." Only a small fraction of sermons actually made their way into printed collections. In her affirmation of Franz Lau's conclusion that the early Reformation was a time of *Wildwuchs*, a period of "rapid and disorderly growth of the evangelical movement," Karant-Nunn not only suggests that the conclusions of Bernd Moeller on this subject might be reconsidered but also recognizes the fundamentally humanistic elements in these early sermons.

Many historians feel that humanistic tenets not only provided a theoretical and ideological impetus for the Reformation but also purport to see in humanism the origins of sixteenth-century toleration theory. Hans R. Guggisberg has been an influential spokesman for this viewpoint in the past. In his essay, Guggisberg offers a view of Sebastian Castellio's family that traces the familial contacts that supported his life and work. The circle in Lyon of what Guggisberg terms *Castellionists* was guided by a "nucleus of Sebastian's relatives." This group included Marie Roybet, widow of Castellio's brother, Michel. Michel had been imprisoned in 1557 for printing Castellio's tract on predestination and married Marie after his release. She, in turn, had already been widowed once; her first husband was also a printer. After Michel's death the following year, she wrote Castellio to reaffirm her support of him and his work. This example is one of a number that Guggisberg utilizes to demonstrate the ways Castellio was bound into a broad supportive network of family and friends. Such a network provided sustenance of every sort for him in his sometimes perilous lifetime and aided his children after his death. The family had been modest in its origins and Castellio's prominence did not bring them a lasting rise in status, despite his best efforts to inculcate his children with the fruits of a humanist education and a pious upbringing.

Castellio never found the toleration for himself, his humanist beliefs encouraged him to advocate for others such as Michel

Servetus. A kindred spirit was the Spanish Marrano Samuel Usque, whose volume *Consolations for the Tribulations of Israel* is the subject of Jerome Friedman's essay. Usque represented a large group who suffered long for what Friedman describes as their "carefully nurtured exterior religious ambivalence." The Spaniard Usque in fact was a contemporary of Castellio's; his writing, like Castellio's, owed much in a constructive sense to Renaissance humanism while providing a response to religious persecution.

Samuel Usque's remarkable apologetic aimed to create "a Marrano argument against Christianity which actually used that religion's own concepts against itself in order to defend the Jewish integrity of those who . . . willingly left the Jewish religion." Friedman stresses the eclecticism of Usque's views, which borrowed freely from a variety of religious persuasions, and concludes that his "composite of so many varied ideas demonstrates the extent to which ideas moved from one group to another and how easy it was to create belief systems to suit almost any occasion and to satisfy almost any conceivably specific religious church, sect or group." Influential friends sustained Usque, just as Castellio relied on a supportive network: Usque's work was dedicated to Dona Gracia Nasi, perhaps the most important Marrano patroness.

Usque's arguments might have found a wider audience earlier in the century. By the time he wrote, in the mid-sixteenth century, the "euphoria of the early Reformation years," when "Luther appealed to the Jews to heed the evangelical message and be reunited with the Christians under the one true messiah had given way to rampant persecution by Catholic and Protestant alike," as R. P. Hsia observes in "Printing, Censorship, and Antisemitism in Reformation Germany." Hsia emphasizes the impact of Luther's pamphlets on the "transmission and reception of antisemitic ideas" and stresses that these tracts summarizing Luther's views were widely available. The essay demonstrates the juxtaposition of humanism and Lutheranism was by the end of the century an uneasy fit. Hsia examines the sixteen-work booklist of the minor Dortmund printer Arnd Westhof between 1575-1603 and itemizes humanist texts, distichs by Cato, Greek poetry, and catechismic and devotional literature, as well as antisemitic diatribes.

A renewed struggle for supremacy, cloaked in an expressed

desire for parity between Catholics and Lutherans, seemed threatening to Dortmund Lutherans in the 1590s. This, in turn, caused them to turn their wrath toward the Dortmund Jews. It was possible to exercise control over at least this enemy, and the Jews accordingly were expelled from Dortmund in 1596. As Hsia notes, "in excoriating the Jews, by declaring them enemies of the 'true Christian religion,' the Lutherans were also asserting their identity against Catholic counterattack." Although the more powerful and vocal Jewish community of Frankfurt appealed successfully to the Emperor Rudolf II, who ordered the Dortmund city council to confiscate and destroy all copies of Luther's inflammatory pamphlet, in fact Rudolf's edict was ignored. Whether in Spain or Germany, the fate of the Jews depended on whose pawn they might be in the struggle for power between the majority groups.

The printing press was the preeminent weapon in this power struggle. Use of a computer enabled Miriam Chrisman to provide a statistical analysis of the Strasbourg printing industry from 1480-1599 in *Lay Culture, Learned Culture*. Mark U. Edwards, Jr.'s contribution here examines the polemical (or controversial) literature of Catholics and Protestants and suggests that computerized statistical analysis demonstrates the domination of the Protestants. Edwards also provides additional substantiation for the effective use of the printing press in the first half of the sixteenth century.

Statistical analysis has been used in recent years by both social and intellectual historians. Ellis L. Knox, writing on "Occupation and Social Status in Early Modern Augsburg," balances his analysis between tax records and legislation directed for or against guild workers, the *Handwerker-Akten*. Used in conjunction, these sources demonstrate that social position within the guilds had many nuances and that, as Knox observes, "the social fabric was more complex and more dynamic than the broad categories of citizen and foreigner, patrician and commoner." Wealth and class, in Knox's opinion, are not equivalent, and status varied greatly according to one's guild affiliation.

Certain trades also served to define the practitioner's respectability. Such trades or crafts included those that operated under servitude or serfdom as well as those that were suspect because they tacitly encouraged, or at least ignored, immoral practices. The former included those who served feudal lords: for example, huntsmen, foresters or wardens. The latter included the keepers of bathhouses. In 1638, notes Knox, the Barbers and Bathhouse Keepers Guild was split, since barbering had become more respectable and its practitioners had no desire to continue their affiliation with a group as denigrated as bathhouse keepers.

During the early modern period, suggests Merry E. Wiesner in the introduction to her essay "Paternalism in Practice," city governments became increasingly concerned with maintaining morality and order along with economic and physical security." Wiesner observes that whereas, in the later Middle Ages, prostitution had been regarded at least as a necessary evil, in the course of the sixteenth century prostitutes moved from a marginal position in the community to one that was totally outside it. First, it was decreed that prostitutes were obliged to wear special clothing, often a yellow band or veil. Then, they were restricted from appearing in public. Many guilds decreed that their members were forbidden to associate with prostitutes. Finally, by the second half of the century, various German cities began to close their brothels. These decrees did not end prostitution but did create an environment in which prostitutes could now be singled out and punished rather than tolerated.

A number of these essays have thus regarded the ways in which Reformation society and the early modern state came to define conformity. First among these was of course religious conformity. While Guggisberg and Friedman both discuss those who stood outside the pale and Hsia delineates some of the ways in which antisemitic measures served to alleviate other religious tensions, L. Jane Abray examines the fate of French-speaking refugees in Strasbourg throughout the sixteenth century. Even when the official city policy hardened after 1563 and allowed less free religious expression, Strasbourg "rarely refused to shelter religious refugees" and in fact emphasized compromise whenever possible. Again, as we have seen in other essays, this policy was frequently built on humanistic principles: Abray discusses the renowned Latin school, which was founded in Strasbourg in 1538 and provided a focal point for humanist education. In sum, even in times of religious stress and upheaval, toleration could be experienced not only in theory but in reality.

This was true in large measure only for the early years of the Reformation. In every instance, the passage of time caused orthodoxy to be defined and redefined. *Wildwuchs* gave way to doctrinal struggles and the need felt by each religious group to maintain hegemony over its particular geographic area and its particular clientele. Just as religious eclecticism became unacceptable, the social structure also became increasingly rigidified and brought increasingly under the control of the state, as was the case with religion. The backdrop that witnessed the tightening of state and local control in religious terms provided impetus for efforts at the tighter control over social groups, such as the prostitutes.

The extent to which this repressively legalistic articulation succeeded is another question. Throughout western Europe, the heritage which had brought the Reformation remained vital enough to influence and counterbalance the more rigidly structured forces that sought to control and repress. The process of change might be offset by the endurance of continuity, but the forces set in motion during the Reformation years could not be undone.

Several of these contributions, then, see the process of change much as Miriam Usher Chrisman has regarded it: lasting change, to Chrisman, occurs in increments over a period of several generations. As Reformation historians, we focus inevitably on the monumental changes that occurred within a very short period of time. Other perspectives, often interdisciplinary in their nature, serve to illuminate the ways in which changes in mentality develop and create a lasting impact.

The Reformation's Fate in America: A Reflection

THOMAS A. BRADY, JR.

I
n a few fields of European history, American scholars have made a lasting, collective impact on international scholarship. One such field is Renaissance Italy, where the American achievement since about 1950 has been simply spectacular. Another is Reformation Europe, of which Steven Ozment has recently written, "There is no field of historical study today that is more alive with change and fresh ideas than that of Reformation Europe."[1]

As a field of historical studies, the Reformation is very young. Few university departments of history offered it as a regular subject until the post-World War Two era, fewer yet offered it as a graduate field, and with very few exceptions, the leading Reformation scholars in America were professors of divinity. The only important exception, Cornell University historian Preserved Smith (1880-1941), seems to have had a little enduring impact on Reformation scholarship.[2] The other Americans prominent in Reformation studies before 1945 were almost all church historians or theologians, such as Arthur Cushman McGiffert, Williston Walker, John T. McNeill, and Roland H. Bainton. The occasional exception, such as Robert Herndon Fife, a Columbia University professor of German literature, also had no permanent impact on the field.[3]

Between the immediate postwar era and today, by contrast, the Reformation has assumed a relatively well-defined place in the curricula of the American universities and colleges, particularly in the discipline of history.[4] The beginning of this growth is noted in a recent survey:

> The emergence of American scholarship to a promi-
> nence rivaling that of Germany was signaled as early
> as 1946 with the foundation of the American Society
> for Reformation Research, and that society's col-
> laboration with its German counterpart to revive the
> journal *Archiv für Reformationsgeschichte*.[5]

The pioneers of this emergence were the scholars who had labored to lead Reformation studies away from closely defined denominational interests and toward both the broader world of historical scholarship and Christian unity.[6] This struggle—in which John T. McNeill, Roland Bainton, and many others pioneered—gained power from German immigrants, especially Wilhelm Pauck, who combined the traditions of German Protestant scholarship with a profound sense of the crisis of modern Christianity and a zeal for Christian unity.[7] These scholars laid the foundations for a broad concern in contemporary American Reformation studies for the delineation of Reformation thought as a whole.[8]

The concern for comprehensiveness and depth of historical perspective on the Reformation received a whole new dimension at the hands of another immigrant, Dutch historian Heiko A. Oberman (1930-). The early phases of his vastly productive scholarship aimed to establish that the Reformation, properly understood, represents the victory of the soundest streams of late medieval thought, properly understood.[9] To this broad emphasis, Oberman has more recently added an emphasis on the "social history of ideas," by means of which he strikes a bridge to a younger, quite different line, the social history of the Reformation. In their recent survey of Reformation historiography, Dickens and Tonkin remark on "the immense breadth of American writing [on the Reformation], especially in social history."[10] History as the outcome of broad social movements may seem an understandably attractive approach for American scholars, given the importance of democratic ideals to the political culture of "a country as ecumenically minded as it is confessionally diverse."[11] In some respects, perhaps, the approach may reach back to Preserved Smith, but in other respects there is a profound discontinuity between his psychologizing and the orientations of recent social history, which tend to be either behaviorist or Marxist.[12] One of the characteristic features of the new social history of the Reformation is its concentration on the early Reformation movement in the cities, especially in south Germany.[13] For twenty years, young American historians have been a fixed presence in the archival readings rooms at Nuremberg, Strasbourg, and Zurich.[14]

This American affinity for the urban reformation affords a valuable clue to some enduring elements in American intellectual life. According to a vital belief of modern liberalism, cities are the nurseries and schools of liberty, and belief in the kinship of Reformation and liberty is old in America, where the dominant culture is Protestant in origin and liberal in disposition.

The story of the Reformation as the first great step toward liberty served as a foundation stone of the dominant American Protestant view of history for more than a century. It was not an orthodox view, for orthodoxy had been faithful to the Protestant reformers' esteem for truth above liberty, but a fruit of the weakening of Calvinist orthodoxy. The new, progressive vision saw America as the completion of the ascent of humanity, which the Reformation had begun, toward true liberty. The story may have sounded radical when voiced by Joseph Priestley (1733-1804) against orthodoxy in the late eighteenth century,[15] but a century later it had itself become the orthodoxy of the American Protestant bourgeoisie.[16] No one ever proclaimed this view more triumphantly than did Boston historian John Lothrop Motley (1814-1877), when he rose on December 16, 1868, to address the New York Historical Society on the theme "Historical Progress and American Democracy." As when the artesian wells of the western United States

> are sunk through the sod of the prairies, through the loam, through the gravel, through the hard-pan, which is almost granite, until at last, 1,000 or 1,500 feet beneath the surface, the hand of man reveals a deep and rapid river coursing through those solitary, sunless depths. . . . And when the shaft has reached that imprisoned river, . . . the waters, remembering

the august source . . . whence ages ago they fell, leap upwards to the light with terrible energy, rising in an instant far above the surface of the current to delight and refresh mankind. . . . Such was the upward movement out of intellectual thraldom which we call the Reformation when the shaft of Luther struck the captive stream.[17]

In America, the dogmatic coupling of the Reformation with the progress of liberty and the identification of America as the place where history realized what the Reformation had but promised was hardly doubted until the second third of the twentieth century. Secure in its sense of being the vanguard of history, the American Protestant bourgeoisie was spared, for a time, the terrible crisis of confidence that came to European Protestants in World War One, when two great representatives of Protestant civilization, England and Germany, flung themselves upon each other in a contest to maintain, or acquire, world empire.[18]

The crisis of American liberal Protestantism began before the onset of the Great Depression. In 1927, Missouri-born theologian Reinhold Niebuhr (1892-1971) announced that "a psychology of defeat, of which both fundamentalism and modernism are symptoms, has gripped the forces of religion."[19] The Depression completed the collapse of liberal Protestantism's faith in history as the story of liberty and progress, on which Niebuhr's *Moral Man and Immoral Society* pronounced the verdict in 1932.[20] The crisis and its aftermath, which lingered on into the post-1945 era, could not fail to affect the way the Reformation was taught in America, for the Protestant Reformation had always formed a landmark, a kind of postbiblical covenant, in the visions of American Calvinism, both in its orthodox and its secularized liberal forms. By the postwar era, two new competitors emerged to vie for the role of the enduring heart of the historical Reformation: the sects or "Anabaptists," on the one hand; and Luther's personal struggle and theology, on the other. It is possible to describe this development in terms of historiographical evolution alone, but the new views—opposed views, for the sects had been Luther's bitterest foes—were made necessary by a deep failure of the historical vision that had united the Protestant Reformation with the mainstream of American history to form the gushing artesian well of Motley's striking image. It is all the more striking, therefore, that this

20

process in American Protestantism had been both prefigured and influenced by a similar development in German Protestantism.

In German Protestantism, the issue of the Reformation and the modern world had been squarely joined by the outbreak of World War One. On the one hand, the Augsburg-born theologian Ernst Troeltsch (1865-1923) criticized German Lutheranism for its social backwardness, the consequence, he thought, of an incomplete passage from the church-shaped culture of medieval Europe.[21] By contrast, the sect-born Protestant traditions of western Europe—especially the Calvinists, Baptists, and other groups in Britain—had adapted more swiftly and creatively to modern social forces. Troeltsch also rejected an understanding of Christian history in terms of ideas alone, the usual method of church historians, and argued for the mutually shaping interaction of religion and social forces.[22]

The countermoment to Troeltsch's critique appeared in an attempt to reinterpret the meaning of the Reformation by focusing on the theology of the young Luther as its central, normative moment. Its chief exponent was Karl Holl (1866-1926), though he was building on a mildly modernist Lutheran theology already a generation old. This "Luther renaissance" gained edge and force from World War One's disastrous implications for European Protestantism.[23] Troeltsch and Holl—both Swabians, born a year apart—had traveled in much the same liberal Christian circles before the war. Whereas the Great War merely strengthened Troeltsch's conviction about Germany's stunted development, however, it drove Holl to find in Luther the central clue to the meaning of modernity: the liberation of the conscience. To some extent, probably, the parting of the ways reflected the attentions of Troeltsch and Holl to different flanks of German Protestantism. Troeltsch, a politically engaged man, saw that German Protestantism was losing its masses to Social Democracy, while Holl believed that "Catholicism, from which we shall never get free, is our worst enemy."[24] The two men also disagreed about the possible sources of renewal: whereas Troeltsch, with his emphasis on social institutions as the meeting point for social forces and religion, recommended study of and borrowing from western European and American Protestantism, Holl sought new life in the theology of the young Luther.

German Protestant theology, spread through the pens of German-American and German emigré writers, poured into

American Protestantism during the middle third of the twentieth century. With it came the materials for two new interpretations of the Reformation, one based on Troeltsch's church-sect typology, the other on the German "Luther renaissance."

Ernst Troeltsch's agenda, while clear enough to his leading American interpreter, H. Richard Niebuhr, lost much critical force in its application by Americans to Reformation history. Troeltsch's chief work appeared in Olive Wyon's translation in 1931, and his polemical flattery of Calvinism and the sects seemed perfectly tailored to traditional Protestantism's self-esteem. The crisis of liberal Protestantism, however, opened the door to a curious twisting and flattening of Troeltsch's ideas. Since the 1920s, engaged scholars, mostly Mennonites, had been struggling to rehabilitate the historical reputation of the Anabaptists. The crisis in mainline Protestantism permitted the transfer of Troeltsch's teaching on the sects from the Congregationalists, Baptists, and other "free churches" to the Anabaptists and their descendants, who now were seen to represent the authentic sixteenth-century revival of true Christianity. This was a serious misuse of Troeltsch, who had seen church and sect not as contraries but as maximizations of the two fundamental tendencies of Christianity, universalism and individualism, both of which had been active at all times, though in different proportions, in the Christian past.[25] The admirers of the Anabaptists, by contrast, took the two types for opposites and professed to find in the "radical Reformation" of the German sects the roots of a more truly Christian route to the modern world.[26] Troeltsch's typology was thus reduced to a narrow, mechanical device for marking out a new route from the Reformation, via the Anabaptists, to modern America, though at the expense of abandoning most of the rest of the Reformation. By the early 1970s, this venture, having failed to identify Anabaptism's "essence," began to go the way of all other idealist histories of Christianity.[27]

The second attempt to fill the gap in the Reformation's American profile, left by the ebbing self-confidence of American liberal Protestantism, drew strength from the imported Luther renaissance. The roots of this reception lie in the interwar era, but the birth of its main phase may be dated to 1946, when Wilhelm Pauck, himself a central link to the glory days of the German Luther renaissance, wrote that the American Protestant churches are only now slowly beginning to realize that the fresh knowledge of the Reformation, and particularly of Luther's work, which modern historical scholarship has made available, might become a source of a revival of the Protestant faith.[28]

At that time, America had produced very little in the way of contributions to Luther scholarship in the vein with which Pauck was familiar, the line that had roots in the Luther anniversary experience of 1883 in Germany and had come to maturity during and after the Great War.

The original American reception of the Luther renaissance planted two lines of thought.[29] One held that Martin Luther, far from remaining captive to medieval, church-dominated culture, as Troeltsch had alleged, initiated the socially progressive treatment of this-worldly life in this-worldly terms. The other line held that by rejecting the scholastic and humanist answers to the fundamental problems of religion, both captive to the past, Luther "broke through" to an understanding of the human situation directly relevant to the modern condition.[30] For both lines of interpretation, Luther's appearance formed the central, most meaningful event of the European Reformation. Superficially, perhaps, the view that Luther's "ten-minute speech" at Worms in 1521 "altered the shape of Christendom and changed the course of human history,"[31] does not differ so much from Motley's image of Luther as the well-digger's drill bit. The mood, however, of the American Luther renaissance is entirely different, for the somber atmosphere of late twentieth-century American Christianity does not permit a triumphant celebration of Protestant America's achievements.

The American reception of the new views of Luther and the Reformation depended on the crisis of American Protestantism, true, but it also reflected a related phenomenon, the emergence of ecumenism in American Christianity. At first, this spirit embraced only Protestantism's need for renewal, but then something more surprising occurred: Roman Catholic support for the new way of seeing Luther's thought as the central theme of the Reformation. The prior history of American Roman Catholicism, at least in the present state of our knowledge, provides few clues to this turn of events, for which the prehistory must be sought, again, in Germany.

The recruitment of German Catholic scholarship for the Luther renaissance depended on the abandonment of the Catholic search, best represented by the work of Hartmann Grisar, for the roots of the Reformation in Luther's psychic constitution and disorders and its replacement by an acknowledgement of Luther's role as a sincere, devout, Christian reformer, who attacked a church that was mired in corruption and increasingly irrelevant to the world. This step came in the work of Joseph Lortz, whose *Reformation in Germany* (1939-1940) confessed the church's need in Luther's time of a thoroughgoing reform.[32] Although Lortz, to be sure, did not simply adopt the views of Karl Holl, he shared with Holl's disciples a belief that, in Lortz's words, "Luther was the Reformation."[33] He also shared their admiration for German counterrevolutionary nationalism, for some of the leading representatives of the German Luther renaissance were to be found among what Klaus Scholder has called "the folkish theologians."[34]

The American reception of the Luther renaissance was hardly shaped by German counterrevolutionary nationalism, but, though its roots still lie in obscurity,[35] it clearly reflects the growing integration of the Lutherans and Catholics into American life.[36] The reasons why Lutherans might greet a Lutherocentric view of the Reformation need no explanation. For the Catholics, however, it may be suggested that this view made the Reformation chiefly an issue between the Christian denominations rather than part of the definition of what was or what was not American. The reception of the Luther renaissance thus helped to relieve the threat to American Catholicism's hard-won Americanism, posed by the old Reformation-and-liberty ethos. The new view also suited better the historical memories of the Lutheran and Catholic populations, both largely children of the post-Civil War migrations, who joined hands against the limping Calvinist vision of Protestant America as the standard-bearer of liberty and progress in world history.[37] If this seems a conservative Europeanization of America's history, in another sense it is a sign of Americanization, for the alliance of Lutheran and Catholic scholarship recapitulates what the Puritans had once asserted: the New World will solve the problems created by the Old. Their worlds, however, are by no means identical with the Puritans' two worlds, and generations of civic education cannot make Plymouth Rock and Salem, Roger Williams and Jonathan Edwards, the Burned-Over District and Cane Ridge, or Cowpens and Chancellorsville important parts of Christian history as seen from either a Lutheran or a Catholic point of view.

The bifurcation of the Reformation's image in the post-1945 era, therefore, had both American and European roots. Neither alternative, the celebration of Anabaptism or the Luther renaissance, could win and hold command of Reformation studies in America. Both views aimed to revise earlier American verdicts on the Reformation, such as that of Preserved Smith, in favor of more positively Christian ones; but at the same time, the centers of research in the field were moving into the secular atmosphere of the universities. By the 1960s, when the discipline of church history was declining in the divinity schools, Reformation studies were flourishing in university departments of history.[38] One price of this growth, however, was the need to justify study of the Reformation in ways unconnected with their importance, noted by Pauck, for the renewal of Protestantism in particular and Christianity in general. This need is part of the background of the social history of the Reformation as a field of study in America.

Social history is neither what is left, after religion and religious ideas are extracted from history,[39] nor is it a history "disdainful of all but statistical evidence and the condition of the masses."[40] It is rather "the study of the human past in terms of the groups through whose interrelations a given society gets its living and reproduces its structure and its culture."[41] From this standpoint, the Reformation's influence is studied in terms not of Reformation ideas as such but of the institutions, ideas, hopes, experiences, and prejudices of the many generations of European and American Protestants who held or rejected them, modified and adapted them, and lived and died by them. Only as mediated in these ways do the ideas take on historical life.

The social historians' restoration of the mediating forms and phases between sixteenth-century Europe and contemporary America resembles, in two ways, the liberal vision of nineteenth-century Protestant America. First, it seeks the roots of the dominant American religion and culture in the fertile ground of international Calvinism and all its kith and kin. Second, it tries to find the old thread by searching in the city, the social milieu that has so long been held, from Sismondi to Weber and beyond, to have been liberty's nursery, kindergarten, and school.[42]

25

The immediate stimulus to American scholarship on the urban reformation in particular came, once again, from Germany to America. In 1962, a study of the urban reformation by Bernd Moeller was published, in which he detected in the southern cities "an especially clear congruence between an urban-oriented theology and a corporate urban self-consciousness" that was missing in the Franconian and northern cities, where Lutheranism predominated.[43] This insight led him to appreciate the south German urban reformation's revitalization of the communal, popular political forces against the dominant trend toward oligarchy. He summed up the significance of this other, southern, urban, non-Lutheran reformation for the German future in his closing sentence: "In the form of modern, Anglo-Saxon democracy, however, despite many changes and intellectual accretions, a piece of medieval German civic life returned to Germany."[44] Thus, Moeller restored the continuity between the south German roots of Protestantism and American democracy via Geneva, France, Scotland, and England, and his work exercised "a tremendously vital influence" on Reformation research in both Germany and America.[45]

American interest in the German-speaking urban reformation produced one major work of synthesis, Steven Ozment's *Reformation in the Cities*, in 1975.[46] His theme is that the Reformation was a movement for religious liberation and enlightenment, which took its rise in the southern cities and whose early leaders are to be understood as "freedom fighters." Against the celebration of the sects and the American Luther renaissance, Ozment embraces the entire spectrum of the Reformation movement in this concept of liberation. His restoration of the early Reformation's unity of outlook, which may be the book's most lasting contribution, recaptures some of the vision of American liberal Protestantism's great vision of the Reformation as a great step in the drive toward liberty.

Ozment's book is atypical of, but also complementary to, the main American current of scholarship on the urban reformation, because its author comes to the subject not from urban history but from late medieval spirituality and thought, bringing a new perspective on the connection between theology and social history. More typical is the monograph on a single city, which may account for the lack of influence of this line of scholarship—or of any line of scholarship on the Reformation—on the

26

general picture, mostly by social scientists, of the transformation of Europe in the sixteenth century.[47] Mostly, this failure stems less from the peculiarly "parochial," the term is E. William Monter's, character of the American research on the Reformation than from the waning receptivity of the social sciences in America to historical scholarship of any kind. It is nonetheless true that almost a quarter of a century after Moeller's fruitful sketch, no one, except for Ozment, has offered a general interpretation of the urban reformation.[48]

It is easy to forget now, when we reflect on our need for synthesis, that in the first half of the 1960s it was a fairly new thing for American historians of the Reformation era to work in European archives. The graduate students studied mostly with professors who knew little or nothing about archives, and until the Foundation (now, Center) for Reformation Research began its course on Reformation paleography in 1963, there was no place in America where a neophyte could prepare for work in European archives. Perhaps, Reformation scholars took a "parochial" turn, when they turned to local archives and to social history, but it is difficult to see how, after the long concentration on ideas alone, a sense of the Reformation as a historical movement could have been recaptured in any other way. It is more than twenty years since the first American author set out to embrace the Reformation as a global social event in one local setting, as a "process of change." The year was 1965, the setting was Strasbourg, and the author was Miriam Usher Chrisman.

NOTES

1. Steven E. Ozment, "Introduction," in *Reformation Europe: A Guide to Research*, ed. Steven E. Ozment, (St. Louis, 1982), 1.

2. A recent survey refers to only two of Smith's publications on the Reformation (one neutral and the other negative), A. G. Dickens and John Tonkin, *The Reformation in Historical Thought* (Cambridge, Mass., 1985), 218, 279. See Lewis W. Spitz, "Luther in America. Reformation History Since Philip Schaff," in *Luther in der Neuzeit. Wissenschaftliches Symposion des Vereins für Reformationsgeschichte*, ed. Bernd Moeller, Schriften des Vereins für Reformationsgeschichte, no. 192 (Gütersloh, 1983), 160-77, who writes that "in all these works Smith reflected his liberal and social biases, not taking the religious and

theological components so seriously as he should have, though he understood them quite well" (pp. 165-66).

3. Spitz, "Luther in America," 167.

4. In this respect, see Miriam U. Chrisman's brief obituary of Roland H. Bainton and Harold J. Grimm in *Archive for Reformation History* 76(1985):5.

5. Dickins and Tonkin, *Reformation*, 211. In 1985, it dropped the *American* from its title.

6. Ibid. Of special interest here is John T. McNeill's *Unitive Protestantism: A Study of Our Religious Resources* (New York, 1930), a remarkable combination of historical scholarship and ecclesiastical program. In the same vein belongs the work of Quirinus Breen (1896-1974) of the University of Oregon; on whom see Quirinus Breen, *Christianity and Humanism. Studies in the History of Ideas*, ed. Nelson Peter Ross (Grand Rapids, Mich., 1968), xi-xvi.

7. This comes to the fore with special urgency in his essay, "The Central Question in the Minds of Contemporary Protestants," in Wilhelm Pauck, *The Heritage of the Reformation*, rev. ed. (Glencoe, Ill., 1961), 287-301.

8. See Spitz, "Luther in America," 170.

9. See ibid., 171; Dickens and Tonkin, *Reformation*, 210, 307.

10. Dickens and Tonkin, *Reformation*, 319; and, for what follows, see 300-307.

11. For a very different estimate, see Ulrich Kremer, *Die Reformation als Problem der amerikanischen Historiographie*, Veröffentlichungen des Instituts für europäische Geschichte Mainz, no. 92 (Wiesbaden, 1978), esp. 224-25.

12. This connection is spotted by Spitz, "Luther in America," 166, who writes of Smith's "liberal and social biases."

13. On the present state of research, see Kaspar von Greyerz, "Stadt und Reformation: Stand und Aufgaben der Forschung," *Archiv für Refomationsgeschichte* 76(1985):6-63; and Hans-Christoph Rublack, "Is There a 'New History' of the Urban Reformation?" in *Politics and Society in Reformation Europe, Essays for Sir Geoffrey Elton on his 65th Birthday*, eds. Tom Scott and E.I. Kouri (London, 1987) 121-41. (My thanks to Professor Rublack for a copy of this study in typescript.)

14. In the bibliography compiled by Greyerz, "Stadt und Reformation," 49-63, Americans wrote nearly half of the items in languages other than German.

15. See Hartmut Lehmann, "Die Entdeckung Luthers im Amerika des frühen 19. Jahrhunderts," in Moeller, ed., *Luther in der Neuzeit*, 152-53.

16. Kremer, *Die Reformation als Problem*, 28-31. A comparative history of this idea in the various Protestant cultures of Europe and North America would be extremely valuable.

17. John Lothrop Motley, *Democracy: The Climax of Political Progress and the Destiny of Advanced Races: An Essay*, 2d ed. (Glasgow, 1869), 23.

18. For example, the writings of A. C. McGiffert (1861-1933), who represented the pinnacle of liberal Protestant Reformation scholarship from the 1890s into the early 1930s, betray no scrap of doubt that the Reformation inaugurated the movement toward the spiritual and political liberty of the modern world. Kremer, *Die Reformation als Problem*, 46-59.

19. Quoted by Martin Marty, *Righteous Empire: The Protestant Experience in America* (New York, 1970), 236. See also Kremer, *Die Reformation als Problem*, 18-19.

20. For the publication and the reactions to it, see Richard Wightman Fox, *Reinhold Niebuhr. A Biography* (New York, 1985), 136-47.

21. All accounts of Troeltsch and his work in English have been made obsolete by the recent "Troeltsch renaissance" in West Germany. See esp. Horst Renz and Freidrich Wilhelm Graf, eds., *Troeltsch-Studien. Untersuchungen zur Biographie und Werkgeschichte* (Gütersloh, 1982). The easiest access to Troeltsch for English-speakers is provided by Robert Morgan, "Introduction: Ernst Troeltsch on Theology and Religion," in *Writings on Theology and Religion*, trans. and eds. Robert Morgan and Michael Pye (Atlanta, 1977), 1-51.

22. See Dickens and Tonkin, *Reformation*, 273-76. The reception of Troeltsch in America, like that of Max Weber, mangled his thought in a idealist-functionalist direction, a distortion the current Troeltsch revival will do much to correct. Elsewhere, Troeltsch's affinity to historical materialism was always recognized. See, for example, *Leo Kofler, Zur Geschichte der bürgerlichen Gesellschaft. Versuch einer verstehenden Deutun der Neuzeit*, 4th ed., Soziologische Texte, no. 38 (Neuwied-Berlin, 1971), 13-14 (originally published in 1948).

23. For references, see Thomas A. Brady, Jr., "Luther's Social Teaching and the Social Order of His Age," in *The Martin Luther Quincentennial*, ed. Gerhard Dünnhaupt, (Detroit, 1985), 285, n. 6. Recent accounts of Holl tend to repeat the older ones, and there will be no "Holl renaissance" until two tasks are accomplished: the publication of whatever papers remain to illuminate his biography; and a systematic comparison of the studies in his celebrated Luther volume with their prewar antecedents. I rely in the main on Otto Wolff, *Die Haupttypen der neueren Lutherdeutung*, Tübinger Studien zur systematischen Theologie, vol. 7 (Stuttgart, 1933), 318-84. In English, there are the introductions to two translations edited by James Luther Adams and Walter F. Bense: Karl Holl, *What Did Luther Understand by Religion?* (Philadelphia, 1977), 1-14; and Karl Holl, *The Reconstruction of Morality* (Philadelphia, 1979), 9-30.

24. Holl to Paul Gennrich 1921, quoted by Johannes Wallman,

"Holl und seine Schule," *Zeitschrift für Theologie und Kirche*, Beiheft 4(1978):9.

25. The secular historians were considerably more critical. See Kremer, *Die Reformation als Problem*, 74 (Preserved Smith), 124 (Carlton J. H. Hayes). Possibly, the reception of Troeltsch was also distorted by the influence of Werner Stark's superficially similar ideas. Dickens and Tonkin, *Reformation*, 277-78.

26. See, e.g., Franklin H. Littell, *The Origins of Sectarian Protestantism: A Study of the Anabaptist View of the Church* (New York, 1964), 154. The argument that the Anabaptists were both more Christian and more modern than the Protestant reformers was already present in the McGiffert's interpretation of the Reformation. See Kremer, *Die Reformation als Problem*, 52.

27. See James M. Stayer, Werner O. Packull, and Klaus Deppermann, "From Monogenesis to Polygenesis: The Historical Discussion of Anabaptist Origins," *Mennonite Quarterly Review* 49(1975):83-121; James M. Stayer, "Reflections and Retractions," in *Anabaptists and the Sword*, rev. ed. (Lawrence, Kans., 1976), xi-xxxiii.

28. Wilhelm Pauck, "Luther and the Reformation," in *The Heritage of the Reformation*, 17. Nearly a quarter (pp. 12-16) of this essay is devoted to Reinhold Niebuhr. On Pauck, see Kremer, *Die Reformation als Problem*, 211-18.

29. Besides Pauck, a Westphalian, should be mentioned Prussian scholar George W. Forell, on whose work see Kremer, ibid., 191-97.

30. I refer to the writings of Harold J. Grimm and Lewis W. Spitz, respectively, for which see ibid., 91-100, 197-202. I do not mean to suggest that their views are the same, and the differences are suggested by a contrast between the pair "religion and society," which is the title of a Festschrift for Grimm (note 39), and the pair "religion and culture," which was posed by Spitz' most important work, *The Religious Renaissance of the German Humanists* (Cambridge, Mass., 1963), 293.

31. Lewis W. Spitz, *The Protestant Reformation, 1517-1559*, vol. 3, *The Rise of Modern Europe*, (New York, 1985), 75.

32. Dickens and Tonkin, *Reformation*, 199-207, who point out that the roots of this change reach back to the latter part of the Great War.

33. Quoted in ibid., 205.

34. Klaus Scholder, *Die Kirchen und das Dritte Reich, vol. 1, Vorgeschichte und Zeit der Illusionen 1918-1934* (Berlin, 1977), 125-30. It is worth noting, that the evolution of German Catholic views of Luther, from Luther the disturbed personality (Grisar) to Luther the German prophet against Rome (Lortz), had been anticipated, apparently for very similar reasons, in the career of a prominent Catholic scholar of the previous century, Johann Ignaz von Döllinger (1799-1890). Dickens and Tonkin, *Reformation*, 181-83.

35. Which is complete for the Catholic side but not, fortunately,

for the Lutheran side. See Myron A. Marty, *Lutherans and Roman Catholicism. The Changing Conflict: 1917-1963* (Notre Dame-London, 1967).

36. Spitz, "Luther in America," 165, summarizing Kremer's findings: "Catholic and Lutheran historiography were no longer culturally isolated and benefitted from the Luther renaissance and the popularity of Crisis theology."

37. This is the most important lesson of Kremer, *Die Reformation als Problem*, especially 218-25.

38. So much so that the latter have subsequently begun to furnish the divinity schools with historians.

39. Which seems to have been approximately the view of Harold J. Grimm, for which see Phillip N. Bebb, "Reformation History and Social History: The Contribution of Harold J. Grimm," in *Pietas et Societas: New Trends in Reformation Social History. Essays in Memory of Harold J. Grimm*, eds. Kyle C. Sessions and Phillip N. Bebb, Sixteenth Century Essays and Studies, vol. 4 (Kirksville, Mo., 1985), 1-10.

40. Spitz, *Protestant Reformation*, 2.

41. Thomas A. Brady, Jr., "Social History," in Ozment, ed., *Reformation Europe*, 161.

42. See Hans-Christoph Rublack, "Forschungsbericht Stadt und Reformation," in Bernd Moeller, ed., *Stadt und Kirche im 16. Jahrhundert*, Schriften des Vereins für Reformationsgeschichte, no. 190 (Gütersloh, 1978), 9-26.

43. Greyerz, "Stadt und Reformation," 6.

44. Bernd Moeller, *Reichsstadt und Reformation*, Schriften des Vereins für Reformationsgeschichte, no. 180 (Gütersloh, 1962), 76.

45. Greyerz, "Stadt und Reformation," 7.

46. Steven E. Ozment, *The Reformation in the Cities: The Appeal of Protestantism to Sixteenth-Century Germany and Switzerland* (New Haven, 1975). See Rublack, "Forschungsbericht," 23-24; Dickens and Tonkin, *Reformation*, 306-307.

47. E. William Monter, "Reformation History and Social History," *Archive for Reformation History* 72(1981):7. (Cf.) Heiko A. Oberman, "Reformation: Epoche oder Episode," *Archiv für Reformationsgeschichte* 68(1977):88, who remarks in an aside that ("on the other hand, studies on the introduction of the reformation into a city, the authors of which are utterly innocent of theology, are no longer just chimeras.") "Arbeiten über die Einführung der Reformation in einer Reichsstadt ohne jede theologiegeschichtliche Ahnung sind dagegen bereits nicht mehr nur eine reine Chimäre."

48. See Rublack's "Is There a 'New History' of the Urban Reformation?"

The Library of
the Strasbourg Humanist
Thomas Wolf, Senior (+ 1511)

JEAN ROTT

T homas Wolf, Sr.,[1] born ca. 1445, was the son of Andrew Wolf, a rich peasant from Eckbolsheim near Strasbourg, and Enneline Hell, whose brother John was canon (1419) and later dean (1467-1481) of the collegial St. Thomas chapter at Strasbourg.[2] He studied at Erfurt (1460/1), Basel (1466/7), and Bologna (1470/5), where he was promoted as a doctor in canon law on May 6, 1475.[3] He then returned to Strasbourg, where he worked as procurator at the ecclesiastical courts and was consulted by the municipal government.[4] Meanwhile, he had secured several benefices in the Strasbourg diocese, beginning with a canonry, which he had already held in 1465, when he also became canon of Young St. Peter's, another rich collegial chapter of Strasbourg. Some years later, he also entered the third collegial chapter of the city, Old St. Peter's (1482), whose provost he was from 1484 to his death. In addition, he was canon of the cathedral of Worms and of the collegial chapters of Seltz and of Neuwiller in Lower Alsace,[5] because of his connections with influential men at the papal court, such as the famous Alsatian curialist and master of the pontifical ceremonies, John Burcardi. But he was also acquainted with humanists like Rudolf Agricola, Peter Schott, Jr., and other prominent learned men at Strasbourg: Geiler, Brant, Wimpheling, and so on. Being a very clever canonist, he was much consulted as middleman,[6] arbitrator,[7] or supervisor,[8] but he also seems to have been an efficient opponent to the efforts of Bishop William III of Strasbourg to reform his clergy in 1509.[9]

33

He used his wealthy revenues partly for the studies of his nephews Amandus (+ 1504) and Thomas Wolf, Jr., partly for the buildings and decoration at Old and Young St. Peter's, partly for the reconstruction of his canonical court at Young St. Peter's and of a contiguous house he had purchased from the abbey of Marmoutier, and not least for the collection of a large and interesting library, which he released in his will[10] to his son John, who studied at Bologna in 1498.[11] He died of hydropsy on August 12, 1511,[12] and was probably buried at Old St. Peter's.

His funeral had just taken place, when his brother Caspar, who was angry that he had not been mentioned in the will, occupied the courts of the deceased with a dozen mercenaries. Caspar seized the keys, expelled his brother's servants, took away the silver plate and the letters of credit, and began to live well, eating and drinking and selling a great part of the grains and wine hoarded by the wealthy doctor. This brought about a long trial before the Reichskammergericht between Caspar and the executors of Thomas' will, during which the Senate of Strasbourg played a dubious part.[13] As part of the trial, an inventory of the movables left by Thomas, among them his books, was made in summer 1512.[14]

His library amounted to about three hundred volumes,[15] mostly bound folios, a large number for these times. A first approach to their contents was given in 1982 by Miriam Usher Chrisman in her masterwork *Lay Culture, Learned Culture: Books and Social Change in Strasbourg 1480-1599*, (pp. 61, 332, 335). Chrisman pointed out that 46 percent were legal works necessary to the functions of Wolf, but that he also had a good number of humanistic books, and that in several cases he had two or even more copies or editions of a treatise. When the volumes were registered, they were not in their old place anymore, but had been moved to another of Wolf's houses, so that the original arrangement had been completely disturbed, and the listing of the different tomes of one work was dispersed throughout the inventory. This list seems to have been dictated by a notary to a colleague; care was taken in many cases to respect the spelling of the title, which helps to tentatively identify the editions.

As mentioned earlier, nearly half of Wolf's collection pertained to his duties as a lawyer, especially as procurator in canon law, to which 20 percent of the whole was devoted.[16] Besides that, the percentage, rough as the others, of religious books was relatively small (16 percent), a proportion which is significant for the more worldly than spiritual interests of this master-pluralist.[17] But for insight into intellectual life in Strasbourg around the year 1500, the high proportion of classical, humanistic, historical, and medical works (39 percent) is much more relevant and allows us to have a glance into the main concerns of Thomas Wolf, Sr.[18] Is it not revealing, for instance, that he, who was an impassioned builder, had in his library not only the treatise of Vitruvius (n. 138) but also that of Leon Baptista Alberti (n. 172)? Like his juridical books, these other works were imprints, if we can rely upon our hypothetic identifications, largely North Italian, especially Venetian. This, of course, is due to his relatively long sojourn in Bologna, but it assumes also that either of his nephews during their lengthy studies in Bologna or another agent in Venice provided him regularly with new books, according to his instruction.

However, it would be more interesting to ask what his influence was on the development of the humanistic ideas of the Strasbourg scene of his time. Yet, one faces a disconcerting lack of sources. To what degree did he share his books with his friends? To what extent did he discuss the content of his volumes during the colloquies held in his fashionable canon-court near Young St. Peter's? How much did he encourage the efforts of humanistic Strasbourg printers like Schürer, Knobloch, or Schott?[19] Given the scarcity of documents on the topic, these questions are easier to raise than to answer.[20] For the moment we must be content with the inventory of his library.

NOTES

1. Not to be confused with his homonymous nephew Thomas Wolf, Jr., (1475-1509), known as a humanist author (cf. Charles Schmidt, *Histoire littéraire de l'Alsace à la fin du XVe et au commencement du XVIe siècle*, II. Paris, 1879, 58-86). The best biographical sketch on Thomas Wolf, Sr., is that of F. Rapp: *Réformes et Réformation à Strasbourg. Eglise et société dans le diocèse de Strasbourg (1450-1525)*, (Paris, 1974), 302-304; see also G. Knod in *Allgemeine deutsche Biographie* XLIV, (1898), 51-54. My hearty thanks to Katia Peterschmitt, who so gently revised my article written in "dictionary English."

2. Thomas had at least three brothers: Andrew; John, who was

first *scultetus* of Eckbolsheim, then a clergyman, and died as dean of Old St. Peter's; and Caspar, who was captain of the mercenaries of the city of Strasbourg and raised to nobility by Maximilian I.

3. Gustav C. Knod, *Deutsche Studenten in Bologna* (Berlin, 1899), 642, n. 4277.

4. On January 7, 1486, he received the citizenship of Strasbourg with the task of counseling the magistrate in all things except those contrary to ecclesiastical law and to persons or institutions to whom he was linked (Charles Wittmer and J. Charles Meyer, *Le livre de bourgeoisie de la ville de Strasbourg 1440-1530*, II [Strasbourg, 1954], 416, n. 3737).

5. He was also chaplain of a prebend in the great choir of Strasbourg Cathedral and was assigned several rectorates in local parishes of the diocese, either according to the ordinary procedure or by apostolic provisions.

6. In 1493, he intervened in the quarrel between regulars and seculars at Strasbourg.

7. In 1501, he was asked to mediate in the controversies on the Immaculate Conception between Dominicans and Franciscans.

8. In 1506, he helped to supervise the election of the new bishop of Strasbourg, William III von Honstein.

9. See the bishop's letter to the General Vicary of the diocese on August 28, 1511: Archives du Bas-Rhin, G 1444, n. 2.

10. Written on July 29, 1510, and available in three contemporaneous copies: Archives du Bas-Rhin, G 4222, n. 6 (two copies), and Archives du Chapitre St. Thomas (AST: in the City Archives of Strasbourg), Suppl. 1 a. He left his property at Worms to the cathedral there and bequeathed the major part of his estate and rights in Strasbourg city and diocese to the chapters of Old and Young St. Peter's. His executors were Laurentius Hell, dean and probably his relative, Ulrich Bertsch, canon, John Monschein, also canon, and John Oberlin, vicar, all of Young St. Peter's.

11. Cf. Knod, *Deutsche Studenten*, 641, n. 4276.

12. This is the most reliable date: Philippe-André Grandidier, *Nouvelles oeuvres inédites* II (Colmar, 1898), 596-99; other sources give August 14 or 16.

13. AST Suppl. 1, p (38 fols.), the list of the silver plate and of most of the letters of credit seems to be lost. In spite of the extravagance of Caspar Wolf and his accomplices, a year after the death of Thomas, nearly 2000 quarter-casks of grain and more than 1200 hl. of wine in 28 barrels remained; as did more than 20 beds with straw mattresses, sheets, cushions (one with an embroidery showing the wolf preaching to the geese), numerous benches, chairs, tables, plenty of kitchen tools, 18 chests full of clothes, liturgical vestments, and so on.

14. On this much entangled affair see AST Suppl. 1 b-u; Archives du Bas-Rhin, G 1444 1-5; Archives municipales de Strasbourg, II 123 (VDG 115-116) 32-33A.

15. There are 283 "items" of books in the inventory (among them 43 manuscripts); but nos. 277, 278, 279, and 282 do not specify either the number of volumes or their content; for 3 manuscripts the subject is not indicated (nos. 70, 143, 222), and 2 items I cannot identify: so that only 274 volumes can be relisted according to their subject matter. In 7 items, the name of the author is given but not the title of the work (nos. 2, 39, 98, 158, 160, 163). The number of works amounts at least to 294 (nos. 52, 118, 152, 207, 240 contain two authors; and 138, 174, 202, three) but certainly went beyond 300, because nos. 33, 161, 212, 229, 232, 235, 243 read *cum aliis* or *ceteris opusculis* without any further specification. On the other hand, Wolf had 2 copies of Ambrosius' *Opera*, Aulus Gellius, Ausonius (?); 5 works Bartolus, Clavasio, *Decisiones Rotae*, *Digestum vetus*, Perottus' *Cornucopia*, Raymond de Pennaforte, Serapion, Spagnuoli's *Parthenice*; and 3 works of Tudeschis. Moreover, he had 3 copies of the *Sextus Decretalium; 4 of the Clementinae* and Boich's *Distinctiones*; even 5 of the *Decretales*.

16. Law composed 45 percent: law in general, 8.7 percent; civil law, 16.3 percent; canon law 20 percent (see the arrangement by subjects).

17. Religious topics composed 16 percent: Bible, 3.7 percent; Church fathers and scholastics, 4 percent; worship, 3.7 percent; curates's manuals composed 4.6 percent.

18. Classics composed 13.5 percent: literacy and philosophical works, 5.5 percent; philology, 1.4 percent; geography and history, 4.4 percent; science and medicine, 2.2 percent. Works by humanists composed 15.4 percent: Italian humanists, 11.8 percent; Cisalpine humanists, 3.6 percent; literature, 10.3 percent; grammar and philology, 5.1 percent. Medieval and contemporaneous geography and history composed 3.3 percent. Medieval and contemporaneous science and medicine composed 6.8 percent. This gives another general approach: literature and philosophy composed 15.8 percent; grammar and philology, 6.5 percent; geography and history, 7.7 percent; science and medicine, 9 percent.

19. See M. U. Chrisman, *Lay Culture*, 92-102.

20. Perhaps more information will be provided by the imminent publication of the *Correspondence* of Jacob Wimpheling prepared by Otto Herding and Dieter Mertens.

THE LIST OF THOMAS WOLF, SENIOR'S BOOKS
(AST Suppl. 1 p. fol. 17 r-24 v)

We owe most identifications to the skill and well known courtesy of Miriam Usher Chrisman, who researched them twelve years ago primarily by consulting the *Catalogue* of the printed books of the British Museum Library. Her statements were augmented by quotations, mainly from the *Gesamtkatalog der Wiegendrucke*, the *Catalogue des livres imprimés de la Bibliothèque Nationale de Paris*, and other sources. But, six unidentified manuscripts remain (nos. 38, 47, 67, 184, 254, 273) and six unidentified imprints (nos. 42, 57, 83, 233, 266, 281).

The books are presented here as follows: in the original, each was cited *Item*, but I have used numbers; then the text of the inventory; after the = is the identification of the manuscript or of the edition, with author's name (if necessary, in case his name is not obviously mentioned in the inventory), title (also if necessary), place and year of publication (reference to catalogue or bibliographies: see no. refers to another part of works issued in two or more volumes that were never listed together in the inventory; cf. no. refers to a similar work mentioned in the inventory or elsewhere.

Abbreviations

BMC . . ., c. . . . = *British Museum, Catalogue of Printed Books*, number of the volume and the column.

BN . . ., c. . . . = Paris, *Bibliotheque Nationale, Catalogue des livres imprimés*, number of the volume and the column.

Besta = Enrico Besta, *Storia del diritto italiano*, I, 2: *Fonti. Legislazione e scienza giuridica* (Milano, 1925).

Chrisman = Miriam Usher Chrisman, *Bibliography of Strasbourg Imprints, 1480-1599* (New Haven and London, 1982).

GKW = *Gesamtkatalog der Wiegendrucke*, number of volume and notice.

Hain = Ludov, Hain, *Repertorium bibliographicum*, number of notice.

Ms. = Manuscript

Polain = M. Louis Polain, *Catalogue des livres imprimés su quinzième siècle des Bibliothèques de Belgique*.

Ritter = Fr. Ritter, *Répertoire bibliographique des livres imprimés en Alsace aux XVe et XVIe siècles. IIe partie: Livres du XVIe siècle qui se trouvant à la bibliotheque Nationale et Universitaire de Strasbourge*.

BOOKS IN THE LIBRARY

Folio 17r

1. Item Panor. super quarto et quinto Decretalium [*Paulus Leopard in the margin*: Abb.] = Tudeschis (Tedeschi), Nicolaus de, archiepiscopus Panormitanus, alias Abbas Sioulus: Lectura. . . . Nuremberge 1477 (BMC 242, c. 159).

2. Alex. de Ymmo. = Tartagni, Alexander, de Imola: work and edition not identifiable.

3. Consilia Bauerij = Baveriis, Baverius de: Consilia medica, Bononie 1489 (BMC 12, c. 1197: GKW 3, 3739).

4. Repertorij Bertachini tercia pars = Bertachinus, Joannes: Repertorium (utriusque juris), Venetiis 1494, or Mediolani 1499-1500 (GKW 4, 4158, 4160); see nos. 102 and 124.

5. Bar. super 2a parte Digesti noui = Bartolus de Saxoferrato: Venetiis 1493 or 1499 (BMC 12, c. 254; GKW 3, 3576, 3577, 3580).

6. Platinus = Platini Plati: libellus de carcere, s.l. and a., or Mediolani 1483 or 1484 (Hain 13070-73).

7. Angeli de Aretio super titulo de lectionibus Instituti. = Gamilionibus, Angelus de, de Aretio; Lectura super titulo de actionibus Institutionum, Lovani 1475, or Tolosae 1480 (BN 56, c. 1235).

8. Consilia Baldi = Ubaldis, Baldus de [hereafter quoted, Baldus]: Consilia [pars 1a or 2a] Brixie 1490 (BMC 243, c. 21); see no. 49.

9. Sermo sextus de membris generationis etc. = falcutius, Nicolaus, Florentinus: (De conservation sanitatis) Sermo sextus . . ., Papie [1481-1484], or Venetiis 1491 (GKW 8, 9704, 9705); see nos. 17, 71, and 86.

10. Castigationes Pliniane = Barbarus, Hermolaus: Romae 1492 (BMC 11, c. 85; GKW 3, 3340).

11. Grammatica Francisci Venturinnj = Florentiae 1482 (BMC 247, c. 516).

12. Pratica Johannis Arculanj = Venetiis 1493 (BMC 166, c. 553).

13. Juuenalis = Satirae, numerous editions 1470-1501 (BMC 120, c. 131-35). B Folio 17 v.

14. Yasdoneus germanicus = Wimpheling, Jacobus: Isidoneus . . ., Argentinae 1497, or s. l, and a. (Ch. Schmidt, *Histoire littéraire de l'Alsace* II, 320-321).

15. Ausonij Poemij (!) poete etc. = Ausonius, Poenius: Epigrammata, Venetiis 1494 or 1496 (BMC 8, c. 714; GKW 3, 3031, 3032).

16. Interpretationes noue Ludowicj Bologninj 2a pars = Bononie 1497 (GKW 4, 4625); see no. 104.

17. Sermo primus de conservatione sanitatis etc. Nicolaj Floretinj = Falcutius; see no. 9.

18. Johannes de Ymmola super 3m librium Decretalium = Venetiis 1499 or 1500 (Hain 9140, 9141).

19. 1 permenten buch continet primo sententiam Azonis super C etc. = Azo Portius: Summa super Codice et Institutis, several editions 1482-1499 (BMC 9, c. 145; GKW 3, 3144-48).

20. 1 grosz bappiren geschryben buch, Ana. super V Decre., wisz inn pretter gebunden = Ms. = Anania, Joannes de: Lectura super quinto Decretalium (cf. print Mediolani 1490; Hain 941).

21. Lectura Angeli de Perusio super secundo Codicis vsque ad finem C. = Ubaldis, Angelus de, de Perusio; Lyon 1479? (BMC 243, c. 19).

22. Dominicus de Sancto Geminiano super 2°Vj, ist blo inge-

bunden = (Lectura) super secumda parte Sexti libri Decretalium, Mediolani 1480-1481, or Venetiis 1485-1486 or 1491 (BMC 54, c. 467; GKW 7, 8649, 8650, 8654); see no. 28.

23. Lectura prime partis Barto. = Bartolus: work and edition not identifiable.

24. Quartum scriptum sancti Thome = Thomas de Aquino: Opus quarti scripti (super libros Sententiarum Petri Lombardi, 1. IV), Moguntiae 1469, or (Cologn) 1480 (BMC 237, c. 528).

25. Sextus = (Bonifatius VIII papa): Liber sextus Decretalium, numerous editions 1465-1500 (BMC 206, c. 334-38; GKW 4, 4848-4905).

26. Decretum = Gratianus: Decretum, numerous editions 1471-1509 (BMC 90, c. 740-44).

27. Prima pars cons. domini Pauli de Cast. = Paulus de Castro: Consilia, Venetiis 1489 (BMC 182, c. 100); see no. 48.

28. Domini Dominicj de Sancto Geminiano super prima parte Sextj librj Decretalium lectura = see no. 22.

Folio 18r

29. Consilia Angeli = Gamilionibus: Consilium de actionibus, Venetiis 1473, and others (Besta, 864, no. 6).

30. Lectura domini Angeli de Aretio super Institutionum liber = Gambilionibus: Spire 1480 (BMC 81, c. 683).

31. Abbas super 3° = Tudeschis: Lectura super tercio Decretalium libro, Nurembergk 1485 (BMC 242, c. 159).

32. 3a pars Speculatoris = Duranti, Guillelmus: Speculum judiciale, Rome 1474, or Bononiae 1474, or Mediolani 1478 (GKW 7, 9150-9153); see nos. 61 and 75.

33. Lectura Bartholi de Saxoferrato super auten.cum ceteris = Lectura super Autenticis et super tribus libris Codicis Venetiis 1492 (GKW 3, 3485).

34. Consilia Ludowicj Romanj = Pontanus, Ludovicus, de Roma: Venetis 1493 (BMC 192, c. 772).

35. Ein rot ingebunden buch, est 3a pars speculj historialis fratris Vencencij etc. = Vincentius Bellovacehsis: (Augsburg) = 1474 (BMC 249, c. 251); see nos. 69 and 117.

36. Domini Francisci de Accolitis super 2° libro Decretalium scriptura = Accoltis: Bononie 1481, or Papie 1496 (BMC 1, c. 661).

37. 1 swartz ingebunden buch, incipit Johanninia hec dicetur etc. = Barbatia, Andreas: Johannin hec dicetur repetitio (on Decretales 1.3, cap. 18), Bononie (1475?) (GKW 3, 3379).

38. 1 geschriben buch, incipiens: Quoniam vita breuis etc., halb gelb ingebunden = Ms. = ?

39. Abbas Siculus etc. = Tudeschis: work and edition not identifiable.

40. Abbas super 2a parte primj librj Decretalium = Tudeschis: Basilee 1488 (BMC 242, c. 157).

41. Secunda pars Abbatis super primo = Tudeschis: numerous editions 1473-1501 (BN 183, c. 662-66).

42. 1 swartz halb ingebunden buch, cuius titulus: De eo qui fecit murari quendam murum commune et fecit in eo trabes immitti = ?

43. Deci. Rote = Decisiones Rotae, Venetiis 1496 (GKW 7, 8207, 8208).

44. Abbas super 2° Decret. etc. = Tudeschis: Rome 1480 (BMC 242, c. 158).

45. Bar. super secunda Digesti veteris = Bartolus: Venetiis 1493 or 1500 (GKW 3, 3603, 3604).

46. Abbas super secunda 2i = Tudeschis: Secunda pars super secundo Decretalium, Venetiis 1488 (BMC 242, c. 158); see no. 95 and 97.

47. 1 roth permenten geschriben buch, incipiens: Hoc edicto etc. = Ms. = ?

48. 2a pars d. Pau. de Castro consiliorum = see no. 27.

49. Consilia Baldj = Baldus: Consilia (pars 2a or 1a); see no 8.

50. Francisci de Zabarellis super Clementinis = Venetiis 1481, or 1487, or 1497, or Thaurini 1492 (BMC 262, c. 766).

51. Lectur Jo. de Ymmola super prima parte Inforciatj = Venetiis 1475 (BMC 117, c. 103).

52. Pratica Johannis Mathei de Gradj = Ferrariis de Gradibus, Joannes Matthaeus de: Practica . . . cum textu . . . Rasis, Papie 1497 (BMC 166, c. 513; GKW 8, 9832).

53. Jacob. Alpharot. super vsibus feudorum = Alvarottus, Jacobus: Consuetudines feudorum, Venetiis 1477, or (Lyon 1478), or Papie 1498 (BMC 4, c. 338; GKW 2, 1589-92).

54. Alex. de Ymmola super 2a parte Digesti veteris cum apostillis = Tartagni: Mediolani 1507 (BN 182, c. 828).

55. Lectura Bar. de Saxoferrato super Codice = Bartolus: editions 1471-1500 (GKW 3348-3505: la pars; 3506-22: 2a pars; 3523-35: super tribus ultimis libris Codicis).

56. Tabula notabilium dictarum (!) Abbatis Siculj = Diaz de Montalvo, Alonzo: Repertorium sive tabula notabilium questionum, articulorum, dictorum Nicolai . . . Abbatis Siouli (Nurnberg ca. 1495) (GKW 7, 8310).

57. Tractatus usurarum super C. = ?

58. Ein wisz ingebunden buch: Repertorium questionum et materiarum Heinrici Bouic = Bouhic or (Boich), Henricus: Distinctiones super = libris Decretalium, pars 6a: Repetorium . . ., (Lyon) 1498 (GKW 4, 4964).

59. Bartho. super prima parte Digesti veteris = Bartolus: several editions [1471/72] 1489 (GKW 3, 3581-88).

60. Barth. super 2a Inforciatj = Bartolus: Venetiis 1493 or 1500 (GKW 3, 3641, 3644).

61. Secundo pars Speculj = Duranti, Guillelmus; see no. 32.

62. Consilia Alex. de Ymmola = Tartagni: Venetiae 1477 (BMC 234, c. 844).

Folio 19r

63. Sextus Decretalium, permentin 5 cf. no. 25.

64. Bar. super prima Digesti probably, veteris, cf. no. 91 = Bartolus; for editions see no. 50.

65. Inuentarium Speculatoris = Fredoli, Berengarius: Inventarium Speculi judicialis (Guillelmi Duranti), issued with the Speculum, Rome 1474 or Mediolani 1478; or separate Venetiis 1485 or Nuremberg 1486 (GKW 7, 9152, 9153, 9156, 9157).

66. Instituta cum ceteris, in pergameno = (Justinianus I): (Institutiones) Instituta, Venetiis 1494, or 1497, or 1503 (BMC 206, c. 51).

67. Liber scriptus, incipiens: Rta. de sponsalibus, ist wisz ingebunden = Ms. = ?

68. Andree Barbacij commentarij in titulum de judicijs = Barbatia; Bononie 1496 (GKW 3, 3363).

69. 1 rott ingebunden buch gedruckt: Speculum historiale fratris Vincencij de Burgundia = see no. 35.

70. Eyn rot ingebunden geschryben buch, bermenth, hat vszwendig funff spangen = Ms. = not identifiable.

71. Sermo tertius de membris capitis = Falcoutius; see no 9.

72. 1 blo geschryben ingebunden buch, incipiens: Gregorius episcopus = Ms. Gregorius IX papa: Decretales.

73. Inforciatus, permentin, geschriben = Ms. = (Justinianus I): Digestum Infortiatum.

74. ff. vetus, geschriben, permentin = Ms. = (Justinianus I): Digestum vetus.

75. Prima pars Speculj = Duranti, Guillelmus; see no. 32.

76. Philippus de Franc. super toto vtili tituli (!) de ap. extra = Franchis, Philippus de: Super . . . titulo de appelationibus . . ., several editions [1471/72]-1496, partly with the title Super utilissimo . . . titulo . . . (GKW 9, 10242-47).

77. Baldus super 2° Decretal. = Mediolani 1478 (BN 196, c. 747).

78. Baldj super vsibus feoudorum (!) = Boma [1475?], or Parme 1475 (BMC 243, c. 24; BN 196, c. 750).

79. Repetitiones plurime quorum titulos etc. = perhaps (Repetitiones, disputationes necnontracatus diversorum doctorum), Venetiis 1472 (BMC 201, c. 158).

80. Repertorium domini Petri Brixiensis, vszwendig zwey B. B. = Monte, Petrus de, episcopus Brixiensis: Repertorium utriusque juris, Patavii 1480 (BMC 163, c. 113).

81. 1 bapyrin Decretal gedruckt = Gregorius IX papa: Decretales, numerous editions 1470(?)-151° (BMC 206, c. 320-25).

82. Bar. super prima Inforciatj = Bartolus: Venetiis 1493 or 1499 (BMC 12, c. 253; GKW 3, 3625, 3628).

83. 1 grosz gedruckt buch bapyrin, incipit: Inter multa salutaria etc., hat vszwandig b. A. =

84. Liber impressus, incipiens: Rubrice juxta ordinem Decretalium; halb rot ingebunden = Decisiones Rote Egidii de Bellemere, Rome 1474, or Venetiis 1496 (GKW 7, 8209, 8210).

85. Lectu. domini Cini prima pars C. = Cinus de Sinibaldis, de Pistorio: Lectura super Codice, pars la, [Strasbourg ca. 1475], or Papie 1483 (BMC 223, c. 82; GKW 6, 7045, 7046).

86. Sermo quartus de membris spiritualibus et Sermo quintus de membris naturalibus = Falcutivus; see no. 9.

87. 1 bermentin geschryben Decretal = Ms. = Gregorius IX papa: Decretales.

88. 1 permenten geschryben Decretal = Ms. = the same.

89. Reportata domini Anthonij de Alex. et. super 2a. C. = Alexandro, Antonius de: Neapoli 1474 (GKW 1, 1226).

90. Franciscj Moneliensis de Genua in Archidiaconum super Decret. = In Archidiaconum (Guidonem de Baysio) super Decretis (Gratiani), (Venetiis) 1481 (BMC 78, c. 279; GKW 3, 3747).

91. Bar. super secund a parte Digesti ve. = Bartolus; see no. 45.

92. Andree Barbatcij in commentaria de fo. compe. = Commentaria in titulum de foro competenti, Bononie 1497 (GKW 3, 3362).

93. Clementine = (Clemens V papa): Constitutiones (Clementinae), numerous editions: separate 1460-1509 (BMC 206, c. 343-46); GKW 6, 7077-97); with Extravagantes 1476-1491 (GKW 6, 7098-7117).

94. Prima pars Abbatis super secundam (!) Decretalium = Tudeschis, Colonie 1477 (BMC 242, c. 157).

95. Abbas super prima 2i = Tudeschis: Prima pars super secundo Decretalium; see no. 46.

Folio 20r

96. Bar. super secunda Digesti noui = Bartolus: Venetiis 1493 or 1499 (GKW 3, 3576, 3580).

97. Abbas super 3a 2i = Tudeschis; see no. 46 and 95.

98. Prima pars Abbatis = Tudeschis: work and edition not identifiable.

99. Lectu. domini Barto. de Saxoferrato super Auten. = Bartolus: Lectura super Autenticis, several editions 1477-1490 (GKW 3, 3475-84).

100. Repertorium super Ymmola per dominum Baldum editum cum alijs consilijs et repetitionibus etc. = perhaps previous edition of: Repartorium super lectura Alexandri de Imola. Index. . . . denuo excusus, Lugduni 1535 (BN 182, c. 831-32).

101. Secunda pars Cini super C. = Cinus; see no. 85.

102. Repertorij Bertachinj secunda pars = see no. 4.

103. Bar. super prima C. = Bartolus: Super la Codicis, numerous editions 1471-1499, perhaps Venetiis 1492 or 1493 or 1499 (GKW 3, 3501, 3502, 3505).

104. Interprettiones noue Ludowioi Bolognini prima pars = Bononie 1495 (GKW 4, 4624); see no. 16.

105. Bar. super prima C. = Bartolus; cf. no. 103.

106. Andree Barbacij commentaria in ti. de var. obli. = . . . de verborum obligationibus. Bononie 1497 (BMC 11, c. 27; GKW 3, 3376).

107. Tractatus Bar. super tercio libro. C. = Bartolus: perhaps, Lectura super tribus (ultimis) libris Codicis, numerous editions (1471)-1495 (GKW 3, 3523-35)(?).

108. Jo. Fabri super Institu. = Faber, Joannes, Runcinus: Opus . . . super Institutionibus, Venetiis 1488 or 1492 (GKW 8, 9634, 9635).

109. Friderici de Senis = Petrucius, Fridericus, de Senis: Disputationes, questiones et consilia per titulos Decretalium, Rome 1472; or Questiones disputatae, Senis 1488 (BMC 188, c. 202).

110. Abbas super quarto et quinto = Tudeschis: . . . [Decretalium]. Venetiis 1473 (BMC 242, c. 159).

111. Decretales libri tercius, quartus et quintus distinctionum domini Heinrici Boic = Boic (h)(Bou (L)io), Henricus: Opus . . . distinctionum super = libris Decretalium, Legduni 1498 (BMC 24, c. 593; GKW 4, 4964).

112. Consilia Calderini = Calderinus, Joannes et Caspar: Venetiis 1497, or Mediolani 1497 (GKW 6, 5900, 5901).

113. Baldj super tribus primis libris Institu. C. = Baldus: Mediolani 1492 or 1504 (Besta 855, n. 3).

114. Bar. super Secunda C = Bartolus: Venetiis 1493 or 1500 (GKW 3, 3519, 3522).

Folio 20r

115. Liber de nouo codice faciendo, pergamenus, scriptus = Ms. = (Justinianus I): Codex.

116. Octo libri Ptholmej = Ptolemaeus, Claudius: . . . octo libros . . . geographiae, Rome 1490 (BMC 196, c. 336).

117. Liber undecimus Speculi historialis = Vincentius Bellovacensis: Speculum historiale, (pars secunda): see no. 35, Polain 4, 3942.

118. Sextus et Clementine = (Bonifatius VII papa): Liber sextus Decretalium + Clemens V papa: Constitutiones (Clementinae); numerous editions with this title, foremost Venetiis 1494-1500 (BMC 206, c. 338-39; GKW 4, 4889-4903).

119. Decretum = cf. no. 26.

120. Eyn rot ingebunden permenten geschryben buch, incipit: Johannes episcopus, constitutiones noue = Ms. = Clemens V papa: Constitutiones.

121. Liber Clementinj = the same. Liber Clementinarum, [Rome ca. 1478] (GKW 6, 7091).

122. Decretales = see no. 61.

123. Johannis de Ymmola super Cle. lectura = Opus . . . in Clementinas, Venetiis 1475, or 1480, or 1486, or 1492 (BMC 117, c. 102).

124. Repertorij Berthachini prima pars = see no. 4.

125. Instituta in pergameno = Venetiis 1494 (BMC 206, c. 51).

126. Cronica Nurenbergensis latinisch = Schedel, Hartman: Liber chronicorum, Nuremberge 1493 or 1497 (BMC 214, c. 296).

127. Bar. super prima Digesti noui = Bartolus: Venetiis 1403 (GKW 3, 3560).

128. Apparatus Decretalium pergamenus + Innocentius IV papa: Apparatus Decretalium, Venetiis 1481 or 1491 (BMC 111, c. 623-24).

129. 1 alt gesohr. latinisch evan. buch ingebunden = Ms. = Biblia: Evangelia.

130. Nouella Johannis Andree super sexto libro Decretalium geschryben = Ms. = (cf. editions 1476-1499, GKW 2, 1730-33).

131. Josephus de bello judaico = Josephus, Flavius: s.1 and a. (BN 78, c. 1276-77).

132. Repertorium vocabulorum poesis, historiarum = Conrad de Mure: Basilea (ca. 1470) (GKW 7, 7424).

133. De questionibus circa jurisdictionem = perhaps Baldus: Tractatus de questionibus; Parisius 1475 or 1477 (BN 196, c. 752-53)?

134. Pratica Sauonarole = Savonarola, Joannes Michael: Practica major, s. 1, 1478; or Practica de febribus, Venetiis 1496 (BMC 213, c. 614).

135. Consilia Montagnane = Montagnana, Bartholomaeus, senior: Consilia (medica), Venetiis 1497 or 1499 (BMC 162, c. 812).

136. Mesue cum alijs opusculis = Mesue (Yuhanna Ibn Masawai) cum additionibus. Venetiis 1491, or . . . cum expositione Mondini, Venetiis 1495 or 1497 (BMC 262, c. 674).

137. Q. A. Pedianus = Asconius Pedianus; Quintus Aurelius: Commentarii in orationes Cioeronis, Venetiis 1477 or (ca. 1492) (BMC 7, c. 752; GKW 3, 2739, 2740).

138. Vitrumnus (!) de architectura; panepiscemon (!) Angeli Policiani; Frontinus de aque ductibus = Vitruvius Pollio, Marcus: De architectura; + Politianus, Angelus: Penepistemon in priora analytica; + Frontinus, Sextus Julius: De aqueductibus; Venetiis 1496-1495 (BMC 249, c. 817).

139. Libri Eneidorum Virgilij in pergameno scripti = Ms. Virgilius Maro: Eneis.

140. Heynricus Boio geschryben, incipiens: Venerabilibus et dilectis etc. = Ms. = Boic (h): Disticationes super 1m librum Decretalium; cf. no. 111.

141. Recollecta domini Pauli de Castro, geschryben = Ms. = no print with this title; perhaps his Consilia; cf. nos. 27 and 48.

142. Operum Sanotj Ambrosij pars secunda, rot ingebunden = Basilea 1492 (BMC 4, c. 522; GKW 2, 1599); see nos. 155 and 175.

143. Liber scriptus continens varia collecta, wysz ingebunden = Ms. = not identifiable.

144. Liber scriptus ingebunden, continens varia jurie = Ms. = not identifiable.

145. Henricus Boic super 3 Decretalium = cf. no. 111.

146. Liber Plinij super historia naturalj secunda, rot ingebunden = Plinius (senior): numerous editions 1469-1507 (BMC 191, c. 495-97).

147. Aber syn geschryben buch latinus, incipiens: Quecumque in ecclesiasticis officijs etc., wyszingebunden = Ms. = Duranti, Guillelmus: Rationale divinorum officiorum.

Folio 21r

148. Liber scriptus de vita Christi, wisz ingebunden = Ms. = probably Sacchi, Bartholmaeus, de Platina: De vita Chrisi ac pontifium (cf. BMC 210, c. 750-51).

149. Liber scriptus, incipiens: Incipit prologus ad sententiam de casibus conscientiae etc., wysz ingebunden = Ms. = Angelus de Clavasio: Summa de casibus conscientia; cf. next no.

150. Summa Angelica, rot ingebunden = Clavasio; cf. preceding no.: numerous editions 1486-1509 (BMC 5, c. 490; GKW 2, 1923-46).

151. Opus Pandectarum = (Justinianus I): perhaps Pandectarum opus (quod Digestum vetus vocitamus), Nurenberge 1482 (BMC 206, c. 32).

152. Vocabularius Nestor Tortelius = Dionysius Nestor, Novariensis: (Vocabularium), Mediolani 1483, or Venetiis 1488 or 1496, or [Strasbourg] 1507 (BMC 53, c. 101) + Tortelius, Johannes: Commentarii de orthographia, several editions 1471-1493 (BMC 240, c. 330-31).

153. Margarita poetica, wisz ingebunden = Eyb, Albertus ab: Several editions 1472-1495 (GKW 8, 9529-37): Strasbourg edition 1503 (Chrisman, p. 30, C. 7.2.1 and p. 135, H 1.1.15).

154. Summa super titulis Decretalium, scriptus in pergameno = Ms. = perhaps Bartholomaeis, Henricus de, cardinalis (II) Ostiensis (cf. BMC 12, c. 131-32).

155. Operum Sancti Ambrosij pars tercia, rot ingebunden = see no. 142.

156. Cornucopie = Perottus, Nicolaus: numerous editions 1489-1508 (BMC 187, c. 119-20).

157. Junianus maius = Maius, Junianus, Parthenopaeus: De priscorum proprietate verborum, Neapoli 1475, or Venetiis 1482 or 1490 (BMC 150, c. 816).

158. Plutarchus = work and edition not identifiable.

159. Quintilianus = work and edition not identifiable.

160. Suetonius Tranquiilus = work and edition not identifiable.

161. Tullius de officiis cu, alijs = Cicero, Marcus Tullius: numerous editions 1465-1500 (GKW 6, 6914-74).

162. Salustius cum commento = Sallustius, Crispus: probably one of the numerous editions of his writings with Bellum Catilinarium cum commento Laurentii Vallensis (Valla), 1491-1502 (BMC 211, c. 872-74).

163. Laurencius Valla = work and edition not identifiable.

164. Epistole Marilij Ficinj = Venetiis 1495, or (Nurenberg) 1497 (GKW 8, 9873, 9874).

165. Episole Ciprianj = Cyprianus, Thascius Caecilius: Epistolae (and opera), several editions 1471-(ca. 1486) (GKW 7, 7883-87).

166. Thucidides 5 (Venetiis 1485?) (BMC 238, c. 727).

Folio 22R

167. Cornelius Celsus = Celsus, Aulus Cornelius: Medicinae liber, Venetiis 1497 (BMC 35, c. 1062; GKW 6, 6459).

168. Marci T. C. Tusculane questiones = Cicero: one of the editions Venetiis 1472-1502 (BMC 39, c. 583; GKW 6, 6890-98).

169. Epistole M.t.C. = Cicero: numerous editions 1467-1507 (BMC 39, c. 460-64; GKW 6, 6799-6879).

170. Tragedie Senece = probably Venetiis 1492 (other editions 1474-1506; BMC 219, c. 43-44).

171. Homeri Ylias = Brixie 1477 or 1497 or Venetiis 1502 (BMC 106, c. 115).

172. Leonis Baptiste de re edificatoria = Alberti, Leo Baptista; Florentie 1485 (BMC 2, c. 1338; GKW 1, 579).

173. Commentarij Pyrri Peroti in cornucopie etc. = Perottus, Pyrrhus: Venetiis 1494 (BMC 187, c. 120).

174. Opera agricolationum Columelle = Opus . . . Columellae, Varronis, Catonisque cum commentariis Philippi Beroaldi, Venetiis 1494 (BMC 42, c. 273).

175. Operum Sanoti Abrosij pars prima, rot gebunden = see no. 142.

176. Epistole Sancti Jeronimj = Moguntina 1470 (BMC 115, c. 872).

177. Cornucopie = cf. no. 156.

178. Isagoge Joannicij Galieni liber medicine, ist nit in bretter ingebunden = Joannicius (Hunai Ibn Ishak): Isagoge . . . cum commentario Galeni, Venetiis 1487 (BMC 109, c. 209).

179. Cyrugia magistri Gaidonis, rot ingebunden = Guido de Cauliaco: Cyrugia, Venetiis 1499 (BMC 94, c. 160).

180. Repertorium morale domini Geremie, geschryben, rot ingebonden = Ms. = Hieremias de Montagnone (cf. his Epytoma Sapientiae . . . Compendium moralium, Venetiis 1505 [BMC 162, c. 818]).

181. Nouella Super (!) Jo. Andree super 3 Decretalium = Venetiis 1489 (GKW 2, 1729).

182. Marcialis cum duobus commentis, blo ingebonden = Venetiis 1495 or 1498 (BMC 153, c. 815).

183. Expositio Psalterij, scriptus in pergameno = Ms. = perhaps Petrus de Herentale, Expositio . . . super librum psalmorum (cf. prints [Cologne] 1480; BMC 188, c. 220-20).

184. 1 dick wisz buch geschryben papirin incipienz; De acousationibus = Ms. = ? (cf. prints [Strasbourg] 1482 and 1485; Chrisman p. 93, B 7.1.2)

185. Theophrastus de plautis (!) = De historia plantarum, Tarvisii 1489 (BMC 237, c. 118).

Folio 22r

186. Felix Hemmerlin gedruckt = Opuscula et tractatus (Strasbourg 1497) (BMC 95, c. 514).

187. Liber scriptus continens Mercuriales Johannis Andree super regulis juris libro sexto cum alijs = Ms. = (cf. editions 1472-1492: GKW 2, 1734-40).

188. Liber scriptus, rot ingebunden, continens artem notarie et praticam curie Romane = Ms. (cf. Ars notaritus, editions ca. 1474-ca. 1500: GKW 2, 2636-61).

189. Formulare Curie Romans = perhaps Formularium instrumentorum ad usum Curiae Romanae, numerous editions 1474-1493 (GKW 9, 10217-24).

190. Satyre Franciscj Philelphj = Venetiis 1502 (BMC 73, c. 23).

191. Fasciculus medicine = Ketham, Johannes de: Venetiis 1495 (BMC 122, c. 602).

192. Apianus de bellis ciuilibus = Appianus Alexandrinus: Venetiis 1500 (BMC 6, 175; GKW 2, 2291).

193. Herodotus = Historiae, several editions 1474-[1500?] (BMC 102, c. 659-60).

194. Ausonius = perhaps Opera, Parmae 1499 (BMC 8, c. 714; GKW 3, 3094).

195. 1 wisz ingebunden buch Operum Sancti Ambrosij pars 3a = second exemplary of no. 142/155/175; see nos. 199 and 203.

196. Tractatus Bartho. de testi. et de insignijs et armis = Bartolus: De testibus + de insigniis, probably Parisiis 1475, following Baldus, Tractatus de questionibus (BN 8, c. 357).

197. Aulus Gelius = Gellius: (Noctium Atticarum commentarii), Venetiis 1489 or 1496 or 1500 (BMC 83, c. 430).

198. Commentarius Cesaris = Rome 1472 (GKW 6, 5865).

199. Operum Sancti Ambrosij pars secunda, wysz ingebunden = see no. 195.

200. De immortalitate animorum = Ficinus, Marsilius: Platonica theolgia de immortalitate animorum, Florentiae 1482 (BMC 72, c. 766; GKW 8, 8881).

201. Diuus Plato = Venetiis 1491 (BMC 191 c. 182).

202. Nonius Marcellus, Varro de lingua latina, Festus Pompeius = Nonius, Maroellus: de proprietate sermonum; + Varro, Marcus Terentius: . . . ; = Festus, Sextus Pompeius: De verborum significatione: Parmae 1480 (BMC 172, c. 706).

203. Operum Sancti Ambrosij prima pars wysz ingebunden = see no. 195.

Folio 23r

204. Nous decisiones Rote scripte = Ms. = Decisiones Rote (cf. editions [ca. 1470]-1496; GKW 7, 8197-8208).

205. Cyrurgia Petri de la Cerlata = Argellata, Petrus de: Venetiis 1492 (BMC 6, c. 689; GKW 2, 2322)

206. Secunda pars summe fratrie Anthonini = Antoninus Florentinus: Venetiis 1474 or 1477, or Spire 1477 (GKW 2, 2195-97).

207. Pratica Jo. Serapionis et pratica Platearij = Serapion, Joahannes (Yuhanna Ibn Sara-Biyun): Practica; + Platearius, Joannes: Practica; Venetiis 1497 (BMC 262, c. 678).

208. Julius Firmicus = Firmicus Maternus, Julius: (Mathesis) De nativitatibus, Venetiis 1497 (BMC 73, c. 432; GKW 8, 9980).

209. Textus Sententiarum = Petrus Lombardus: Basileae 1488 (BMC 188, c. 228).

210. 1 rot ingebunden buch, opera Virgilij cum commento = Virgilii opera cum quinque (BMC 219, c. 464), numerous editions 1475-1502, perhaps Venetics 1493, or 1495, or 1499, or commentariis, Argentin(e) 1502

211. Aulus Gelius = [cf. no. 197].

212. Liber Rasis ad Almansorem cum alijs opusculis = Rhazes: (Muhammad Ibn Zakariya): [Venetiis] 1497 or 1508 (BMC 166, 549-50).

213. Illustrium virorum epistole = (Lyon) 1499 (GKW 8, 9368).

214. Eutropius et Paulus Diaconus de historijs Italice provincie = Rome 1471 (BMC 69, c. 767).

215. Dialogus Gregorij = Gregorius I papa: Parisiis 1494 (BMC 91, c. 817).

216. Liber de ecclesiasticis scriptoribus, mit spangen = Trithemius, Johannes: Basileae 1494 (BMC 241, c. 533).

217. Justinus historious = Venetiis 1497 (BMC 241, c. 585).

218. Liber Leuiticus in pergameno scriptus = Ms. Biblia: Leriticus.

219. Liber Numerj in pergameno scriptus = Ms. Biblia: Numeri.

220. Paralipemenon (!) mit eym coperth stryfflecht = Biblia: Liber (I and II) Paralipomenon, edition not identified.

221. Parabole Salomonis, in pergameno scriptus = Ms. = Biblia: Liber proverbiorum.

222. Liber in pergameno scriptus, in quo scriptum est in principio: Hic liber est Inferioris Monasterij = Ms. = not identifiable.

Folio 23r

223. Collectio florum No. et ve. test. Ludo. Bologninj = Bologninus, Ludovidus: Syllogianton id est collectio florum . . ., Bononiae 1486 or 1496 (BMC 22, c. 1206; GKW 4, 4637, 4638).

224. Liber scriptus in pergameno, habet in principio: Duodecim prophete = Ms. = Biblia: Duodecim prophetae minores.

225. Breuiarius (Serapionis, corrected in) Serapianus = Practica dicta Breviarium, Venetiis 1477 (BMC 262, c. 678); cf. ? no. 207.

226. Epistole Francisci Philelphi = (Venetiis 1490) (BMC 73, c. 18): or Strasbourg 1495 or 1509 (Chrisman, p. 148, H. 1.3.3).

227. Liber Alexandri Aphrodisei, hat eyn bermenten coperth = Problemata, Venetiis 1488/89, or s.1 (1506?) (BMC 3, 341-42: GKW 1, 860); or Enarratio de anima, Brixiae 1495 (BMC 3, c. 344; GKW 1, 859).

228. Anthonij Mancinelli regule constructionis = Venetiis 1492 (BMC 151, c. 563).

229. Summa Orlandina cum ceteris opusculis = Rudolphinus de Passageriis, Rolandinus: Summa artis notarie, several editions 1480-1496 (BMC 208, c. 900; BN 131, c. 5).

230. Vocabularius predicantium = Melber, Joannes: several editions [1475?]-1504 (BMC 157 c. 426; Ritter 1563); Strasbourg editions 1482-1504 (Chrisman, p. 17, C 4.1.1.).

231. Exercitium puerorum grammaticale = numerous editions 1485-1506 (BMC 69, c. 891; GKW 8, 9496-9509).

232. Ruffi Festi Auiennij opera cum ceteris opusculis = Avienus, Rufus Festus: (Opera); + Aratus: Phaenomena: + Serenus, Quintus: de medicina; Venetiis 1488 (BMC 8, c. 1160; GKW 3, 3131).

233. Epythemata musarum nympharumque = ?

234. Facecie Pogij = Bracciolinus Poggius: Basilaea 1488, or (Spire 1490?), or Lipczk 1491 (BMC 25, c. 422).

235. Platina de honesta voluptate cum alijs opusculis = Venetiis 1503 (BMC 210, c. 755).

236. Spica Anthonij Mancinellj cum alijs opusculis = Venetiis 1492 (BMC 151, c. 564).

237. Liber continens Kalendarios scriptus et impressus = Ms. and prints = not identifiable.

238. Exercitium veteris artis = perhaps Exercitata veteris artis quae sunt Ysagoge Porphirii, Nuremberg 1494 (BN 141, c. 89), or Textus veteris artis s. Isagogarum Porphirii, predicamen torum Artistotelis . . . Item exercitata circa hoc . . ., Hagenawe 1501 (BMC 6, c. 1000; Ritter 1917

239. Enee Siluij de origine Behemorum ad Alfonsum = Pius II papa, Piccolomini: Historia Bohemica, (Basel 1490?) (BMC 190, c. 841).

240. Lamentationes et Apocalipsis = Biblia: Lamentations Jeremiae = Apocalypsis, edition not identified.

241. Textus Salustij scriptus in pergameno = Ms. = Sallustius Crispus, Caius.

242. Laurencius Valla in elegancijs = Elegantiae linguae latinae, numerous editions 1471-(1505) (BMC 246, c. 25-28).

243. Soliloquia abbatis cum ceteris opusculis = perhaps Pseudo-Augustinus: Liber soliloquiorum beati Augustini anime ad Deum, Winderperg 1484 (BMC 8, c. 567).

244. Pars estivalis, impressus breviarius, rot ingebunden = probably Breviarium Argentinee, (Strasbourg) 1478 or 1489 (GKW 5, 5259-61).

245. Breviarius, pars hiemalis = probably the same.

246. Baptiste Manthuanj de beata Virgine = Spagnuoli, Baptista, Mantuanus: perhaps Carmina ce beata Virgine, Daventriae 1506 (BMC 226, c. 695), or Strasbourg 1501 (Chrisman, p. 29, C 7.1.11); cf. no. 253.

247. 1 bethbuch per totum annum cum psalterio = not identified.

248. Ein geschryben bethbuch pars hiemalis, geschriben, bermentinn = Ms. = not identified.

249. Epistole Marij Philelphi gedruckt = Venetiis 1492 (BMC 73, c. 27).

250. Eyn responsorium bohlin bappirin ingebonden rot = perhaps Responsoria noviter cum notis expressa, Norimbergae, 1499 (Hain, 13879).

251. Ein bethbuch, pars hiemalis, in pergameno scriptus = Ms. = not identified.

252. Ex summa Raymundj rot ingebonden = Raymond de Pennaforte: Summa confessorum . . . metrificata, or Summula, several editions 1480-1508 (BMC 199, c. 332-33; BN 147, c. 228: Besta, p. 840).

253. Parthenice fratris Baptiste Manthsanj = numerous editions 1488-1500 (GKW 3, 3276-3303); cf. no. 24?

254. Rethorica de generibus dicendj, geschriben = Ms. = not identified.

255. Margaritha philosophica impressus = Reisch, Gregorius: Friburgi 1503 (BMC 200, c. 675; Ritter 1983).

256. Hypocrates de natura hominis = (Rome 1485?) (BMC 104, c. 237).

257. Orationes Beroaldj = Lugduni 1492, or Parrhisii 1499 (BMC 16, c. 160; GKW 4, 4145, 4146).

258. Regimen sanitatis Magnini Mediolanensis = Lovanii 1486 (BMC 150, c. 353) or Strasbourg 1503, (Chrisman, p. 230, S 1.3.5).

259. Eyn geschryben bethbuch mit eym kalender, permentin = Ms. = not identified.

Folio 24r

260. 1 alter psalter permentin = Biblia: Psalterium, not identified.

261. Ode Franciscj Philelphi = Brixiae 1497 (BMC 73, c. 22).

262. Stultifera nauis = Brant, Sebastianus: Basileae 1497 or Argentina 1497 (GKW 4, 5054, 5047).

263. Esaie in pergameno scriptus = Ms. = Biblia: Prophetia Isaiae.

264. Epistole Petri Schot Argentinensis = Lucubrationes, Argentine 1498 (BMC 216, c. 59).

265. Epistole Plinij = Plinius (junior): Bononiae 1498 (BMC 191, c. 48).

266. Dialogus de veris ac salutaribus animj gaudijs = ?

267. Grammatica (!) Francisci Nigri = Basileae 1500 (BMC 172, c. 90).

268. Liber de floribus poetarum etc. = Flores poetarum . . . pro instruendis pueris, (Firenze ca. 1500), or more probably Flores poetarum de virtutibus et vitiis, several editions [ca. 1475]-1490 (GKW 8, 10069, 10070-74).

269. Tractatus de imitatione Christi cum alijs = Kempis, Thomas a: Argentine 1487 or 1489, or U[m] 1487, or Lugduni 1489 (BMC 116, c. 532-33; Chrisman, p. 21, C. 5.1.6).

270. Gramatica (!) Nicolai Peroti = Parrhisiis 1504 (BMC 187, c. 120).

271. Liber Moysis in pergameno scriptus = Ms. = Biblia: Liber Moysis.

272. Tractatus de horis canonicis dicendis = probably Moesch, Johannes: (Basel) 1483, or Augustae 1489 (BMC 161, c. 878).

273. 1 cleins rots permentin gesohryben bochlin: Tractatus de sacra scriptura = Ms. = ?

274. Passio Tuberini impressus, klein bochlin = Tuberinus, Joannes: In beatum Symonen . . . passionis Christi . . . martirem, Tridenti 1482 (BMC 242, c. 62).

275. 1 bethbuch permentin, pars hiemalis, scriptus = Ms. = not identified.

276. Summa Raymundj geschrieben in permenth, ein clein roth buchlin = Ms. = cf. no. 252.

277. Item vil bermenten sextern gedruckt in eyner hantqueheln gebonden.

Folio 25r

278. Item zwey buschlin allerley sexternen geschryben vnnd gedruckt: sint nit natquelheln vnbunden.

279. Item funff korb mit allerley bocheren die nit in pretter begunden sindt, vnd sonst allerly plettce vnd sextern vnd briefen.

Folio 25r.

280. Ouch in der stuben: 1 tafel zu eym neyen almanach. . . .

281. 1 mappa mundi gefaszt. . . .

Folio 30r

282. Im husz vor der stuben: 1 gemelts langs ledel mit eym deckel wie ein dach, darin etlich bocher.

Folio 31r

283. Im summerhusz im hof: 1 grosser futerkasten . . . (darin) . . . 1 pirmenten geschryben meszbuch.

ALPHABETICAL LIST OF AUTHORS AND ANONYMOUS WORKS

LIST BY SUBJECT ARRANGEMENT

56

Imola: Super 3 m librum
Decretalium, 18; Syper
Clementinas, 123
Innocentius IV, Pope, 128
Petrucius, 109
?? R (. . .) ta de sponsalibus,
67 Ms.
Sancto Geminiano, 22 + 28
Tudeschis: Super 2a 1i
Decretalium, 40, 41; sup. 2
Decretal., 44; sup. 1a 2i
Decr., 94, 95; sup. 2a 2i
Decr., 46; sup. 3a 2i Decr.,
97; sup. 3 Decr., 31; sup. 4
and 5 Decr., 1, 110; sup.
1a? [perhaps 1i Decr.], 98;?
39
Zabarellis, 50
Civil law:
Texts:
Justinianus I: Codex, 115 Ms.;
Digestum vetus, 74, 151;
Infortiatum, 73 Ms.; In-
stitutiones, 66, 125
?? Hoc edicto, 47 Ms.
Treatises:
Alexandro, 89;
Alvarottus, 53
Ars notariatus, 188 Ms.
Azo, 19
Baldus: Super usibus
feudorum, 78; Super
tribus primis libris Institu-
tionum, 113
Barbatia: do foro competenti,
92; de verborum obliga-
tionibus, 106
Bartolus: Lectura super
Codice, 55; super 1a Cod.,
105; sup. 2 a Cod., 114;
sup. 3 Cod., 107; super 1a
Digesti veteris, 59 and
(64?); sup. 2a Dig. vet., 45
and 91; sup. 1a Dig. novi,
103 and 127; sup. 2a Dig.
novi, 5 and 96; sup. 1a Infortiati, 82; sup. 2a Infort.,
60; super Authenticis, 33
and 99; de testibus et de
insigniis, 196; sup. 1a ??,

23; Bologninus: Inter-
pretationes, 16 + 104
Cinus, 85 + 101
?? De eo qui fecit murari
quendam murum
communem, 42
Faber, 108
Gambilionibus: De
actionibus, 7; Lectura
super Institutionibus, 30
Imola: Super 1a Infortiati, 51
Tartagni: Super 2a Digesti
veteris, 54
?? Tractatus usurarum, 57
Ubaldis, A. de, 21
General:
Andreae: Mercuriales, 187 Ms.
Baldus: Consilia, 8 + 49; (Reper-
torium super Imola), 100: de
questionibus (?), 133
Baveriis, 3
Bertachinus, 4 + 102 + 124
Calderinus, C. and J., 112
?? de accusationibus, 184 Ms.
? de questionibus, 133
Gambilionibus: Consilia, 29
Monte, 80
Paulus de Castro: Recollecta,
141 Ms.; Consilia, 27 + 48
Pontanus, 34
Repetitiones, 79
Rudolphinus, 229
Tartagni, 2; Consilia, 62;
Repertorium, 100
Varia collecta [juris?], 143 Ms.
Varia juris, 144 Ms.

Religion:

Biblical texts:
Apocalypsis, 240
Esaie, 263 Ms.
Evangelia, 120 Ms.
Lamentationes, 240
Levitious, 218 Ms.
Moysis, 271 Ms.
Numeri, 219 Ms.
Parabole Salomonis, 221 Ms.
Paralipomenon, 220
XXI Prophetae, 224 Ms.

Church fathers:
  Ambrosius, 142 + 155 + 175;
    195 + 199 + 203
  Augustinus (Pseudo5), 243
  Cyprianus, 165
  Gregorius I, Pope, 215
  Heronymus, 170
Curates' manuals:
  Antonius Florentinus, 206
  Clavasio, 149 Ms.; 150
  ?? Dialogus de veris ac
    salutaribus animi gaudiis, 266
  Duranti: Rationale, 147 Ms.
  Herentals, 183
  Johannes de Turrecremata, 183
  Kalendarii, 237
  Kempis, 269
  Melber, 230
  Moesch, 272
  Raymundus de Pennaforte, 276
    Ms.; 252

?? Tractatus de sacra scriptura,
  273 Ms.
Scholastics:
  Petrus Lombardus, 209
  Thomas de Aquino, 24
Prayer books:
  Betbuch, 247; Ms. 5 248, 251,
    259, 275
  Breviarium, 244, 245
  Missale, 283 Ms.
  Psalterium, 260
  Responsorium, 250

Dubious subject matter:
  ?? Inter multa salutaria, 83
  ?? Quoniam vita brevis, 38 Ms.

Not identifiable subject matter:
  Mss. 70 and 222 (and 143)
  Imprints 227, 278, 279, 282

Humanism and Reformation: The Nürnberg *Sodalitas* Revisited

BY PHILLIP N. BEBB

*T*hey were enthusiastically on his side from the time the theses were posted; they declared their unity with him and made his cause a matter of party principle. By their applause and their complementary efforts they drove him forward, carrying his name into town council chambers and into the halls of princes as well. In this way Luther finally became a factor in the calculations of the politicians, although not on any large scale before 1520. The humanists were the one united group of men to stand behind Luther in the first years.[1]

In this manner Göttingen professor Bernd Moeller describes a relationship between humanism and the early years of the Lutheran Reformation. Although many humanist adherents withdrew their support after Luther's ideas crystallized, those who remained were generally younger than the reformer. The Reformation, consequently, seems to be a "rebellious movement of the younger generation against the older."[2]

American scholars have attempted to verify the soundness of Moeller's thesis. Lewis W. Spitz of Stanford University, for example, analyzes the generational problem involved in the development of the German Reformation.[3] This problem was posed by Luther himself "who, perceiving quite early that the

Gospel made very little headway among the older men, wondered why." For a variety of reasons, Spitz maintained that adherence to evangelical principles was an attachment of youth: "The Reformation was revolutionary, cutting deeper than had humanism, and breaking more decisively with the past. A young man's movement." These young revolutionaries were part of what Spitz declared was the third generation of humanism in the North, people who wanted to change society not merely criticize it. "The younger humanists of the third generation were impatient for change and became the men, who, with Luther, made the Reformation."[4]

The views of Moeller and Spitz are corroborated by Hans J. Hillerbrand of the City University of New York. In discussing the early years of the Reformation in his recent work *The World of the Reformation*, Hillerbrand maintains that not only were the humanists the fount from which Lutheran ideas flowed but that those who imbibed those ideas were young: "the common characteristic of the advocates of the new theology was youth. . . . Virtually all were young men in their 20s and 30s when the controversy broke out, a fact that helps to explain the vitality of the new faith. The Reformation was a movement of youth."[5] Since young men were rarely members of governing councils in the free imperial cities, Hillerbrand appears logically correct when he states that city councils were "retarding forces," hindering the introduction of Reformation practices in their communities. Instead, agitation for religious change came from more popular, working elements within the cities. The attitudes of governing councils opposed this change. "The fact is that they did not and, on the contrary, strove to thwart the propagation of the new faith."[6]

Moeller, Spitz, and Hillerbrand present provocative and interrelated theses that are important for understanding the process by which the Reformation developed. Yet, specific studies may qualify their generalizations. The present examination attempts to do this by investigating the humanist *sodalitas* in Nürnberg.

The role played by Nürnberg's humanist circle in the development of the Reformation in the city has been stressed by most commentators.[7] With few exceptions, however, these historians proceed to characterize only the leading lights of the circle—such as Willibald Pirckheimer, Albrecht Dürer, Lazarus Spengler, and Christoph Scheurl—and to indicate their relationship with the government of Nürnberg and Martin Luther. The maturity and educational background of the group and its social and economic bases have been described only in general terms. These shall be examined more clearly.

Chronologically, this study concentrates on the period from 1517 to 1520, those few years when the major issues associated with the Lutheran Reformation were elaborated. It does not extend beyond 1520 for three reasons. First, historians have already pointed out the extensive control exercised by the city council (*Rat*), composed of members of the oldest and wealthiest families in the city, with respect to the city and the territories over which it claimed jurisdiction.[8] This "sovereignty" was well established by the end of the end of the second decade of the sixteenth century.[9] Thus, by 1525 when a religious colloquy was held, the result of which was the city's official adoption of Lutheranism, the council's proclamation was a mirror of its political, military, and juridical power. Second, the process of church reform in Nürnberg has already been discussed in terms of institutional changes.[10] Although the city's adoption of Lutheranism was not official until 1525, the Reformation had been at work for quite some time prior to that year. Finally, the council was inclined toward Luther by 1520 because afterwards it appointed only his followers to the important administrative posts and preaching positions in the city's parish churches.[11] It is true of course, as Gerald Strauss says, that Lutheran preachers dominated the council's religious advisers by 1523 and that the city's decision to stop all non-Lutheran preaching dates from this year.[12] Yet, the introduction of Lutherans into the spiritual life of the city obviously occurred prior to that year.

One must look to the years before 1520, therefore, to see how the city's disposition toward Luther's reforms developed. The bases for this inclination are to be found within the Nürnberg humanist circle. Hence, this essay will examine briefly the history of the Nürnberg circle; its composition in 1517-1520, its relationship to the city's government, and its connections to Wittenberg and electoral Saxony; and, finally, the movement toward Luther before the final ban of excommunication was placed on him.

Throughout most of the fifteenth century, the intellectual climate in Nürnberg did not seem to favor the development of humanism[13] because of two conditions. In the first place, because the city contained no university, it lacked the institutional base that might offer a stimulus to classical linguistic and ethical studies. Second, the prominent citizens were primarily concerned with commercial and economic conditions, since the city's geographic position made it a center of commercial and military networks, from North to South and East to West.[14] Yet, the wealth of many of these citizens enabled them to send their sons abroad to be educated. A relatively large number of young Nürnbergers went to Italy, chiefly northeastern Italy, to receive their education and acquire business and legal techniques that they would then employ in family firms. In the course of their studies, some came under the influence of humanism. Thus, in April 1487, when Conrad Celtis received the crown as poet laureate of the empire in Nürnberg, and later, when he lived and worked in the city, he found a coterie of like-minded individuals with whom he communicated his humanistic concerns.[15]

Nürnberg humanism, therefore, developed its native origins from the circle associated with Celtis, the *sodalitas Celtica*.[16] Members of this group—such as Hartmann Schedel, Johann Pirckheimer and his son Willibald, Sebald Schreyer, Peter Danhauser, Sixtus Tucher, and Dietrich Ulsenius—were scholars and patrons. What is striking, as Lewis W. Spitz notes about local humanist societies spawned by Celtis, is "how many members were laymen, especially professional people like doctors and lawyers."[17] A similar professional membership will be encountered in the succeeding decades.

Although Celtis did not remain long in the city, characteristically, he was itinerant, the interests he stimulated aided the growth of an educational reform movement that pressed for the creation of a new secular school. The council's decision in 1496 to open such an institution, called the poet's school (*Poetenschule*)[18] and offering instruction in classical languages and letters, had two major effects on the future of humanism in Nürnberg. First, after Celtis refused the proffered directorship, Heinrich Grieninger was brought in from Munich to accept it. Grieninger, a humanist who had studied in Italy, possessed a good knowledge of Latin literature, knew Greek and Hebrew, and edited a Latin grammar in 1500.[19] Certainly one of the more illustrious students of this school was Georg Burkhard, known as Spalatin, who later became an important official for Elector Frederick the Wise.[20] Second, the existence of the school threatened the already established educational interests in the city: the private tutors and four Latin schools. Both their hostility to the poet's school, which helped cause its abolition in 1509, and their readjustments to counter its raison d'être advanced humanism. For example, Sebastian Sperantius, Celtis's friend, was brought to one of the Latin schools. His successor was Johannes Cochlaeus, a prominent humanist who ultimately became Luther's bitter foe.

Thus, there were humanist practitioners in Nürnberg, albeit no longstanding humanist tradition, and some of them were to be found in the city's religious institutions. The most obvious example was the scholarly and saintly Charitas Pirckheimer, sister of Willibald and abbess of St. Clara's cloister from 1503. She was held in high esteem by those who came in contact with her. Celtis even dedicated a Latin ode and his edition of Roswitha to her.[21] Although the most prominent, however, Charitas was not the sole religious representative. Others that might be included were Georg Pirckheimer, prior of the Carthusian monastery; Benedict Chelidonius in the Benedictine monastery of St. Egidius; and the priors of the city's two parish churches, Erasmus Toppler and Melchior Pfinzing of St. Sebald; Lorenz Tucher, Sixtus Tucher, and Anton Kress of St. Lorenz.

Although humanistically inclined Nürnbergers could be found in the city in the first years of the sixteenth century, the ground they prepared was not fertile enough to bring forth the Reformation issue. With few exceptions, notably those of the Pirckheimers and other patricians and their relatives, there was no central locus of humanist activity. Prior to 1516-1517, no group is mentioned as meeting periodically; the first such group is associated with Johann von Staupitz and the city's Augustinian monastery.

Staupitz, Luther's theological adviser, sometime dean and biblical professor of the theological faculty at the newly established University of Wittenberg, was elected vicar general of the Observant branch of the Augustinian Hermits in 1503. The Nürnberg chapter belonged to this wing, and along with the chapter at Erfurt, it resisted Staupitz's administrative attempts to merge the Observants with the provincial order.[22] Staupitz's efforts occasionally resulted in his presence in Nürnberg.

It is possible that Staupitz's visits after 1512 were enhanced by the residence of a former Wittenberg colleague, Christoph Scheurl (1481-1542). A native Nürnberger, Scheurl studied in Italy for eight years, and after receiving his doctorate in Roman and canon law at Bologna, he accepted an appointment to the faculty of law at Wittenberg in 1507.[23] Although he remained in the employment of the Elector of Saxony until his return to Nürnberg in 1512, Scheurl's acquaintance with Staupitz predates the Wittenberg experience. The vicar general had been in Italy in the first years of the sixteenth century, and the two must have met then, for he attended Scheurl's graduation in 1506. Certainly, the ties between the two were solid, as evinced by Staupitz's "letter of friendship" to Scheurl's father in 1511 and the lawyer's invitation to the theologian to visit Nürnberg late in 1516.[24] Staupitz's acceptance and his presentation of a series of Advent sermons, followed by a second visit early in 1517 during which he gave the Lenten sermons,[25] resulted in a closer relationship between the city, the Augustinian monastery, and finally Martin Luther.

On January 2, 1517, Scheurl wrote to Luther inviting him to become a member of a Nürnberg group of humanists meeting in the Augustinian monastery.[26] The lawyer said he was moved to write because of Staupitz's "table talk" with some prominent citizens during the preceding month.[27] While it is likely that Scheurl knew Luther at Wittenberg—Luther began teaching moral philosophy there in 1508—this letter was the first one known to pass between them.

In a letter to Staupitz, Scheurl included the names of members of the humanist circle.[28] In addition to himself, Scheurl cited Anton Tucher (1457-1524), Hieronymus Ebner (1477-1532), and Caspar Nützel (1471-1529), the three most powerful men in Nürnberg's government; further, Hieronymus Holzschuher (?-1529), Andreas (1453-1531) and Martin Tucher (1460-1528), and Sigmund (ca. 1478-1547) and Christoph Fürer (1479-1537),—all presently members of the government or, as patricians, eligible to be elected; finally, Lazarus Spengler (1479-1534), the council secretary, Albrecht Dürer (1471-1528), and Wolfgang Hofmann (?-1522/23), a man who appears to be an agent of the Fugger firm in Nürnberg.[29]

By itself, the list included some of the most influential men in the city; but it was not complete. To it must be added the names of Willibald Pirckheimer (1470-1530), probably the best known of the group[30] Wenceslaus Linck (1483-1547); Wolfgang Volprecht (?-1528), the preacher and prior of the Augustinian monastery in the city; and George Beheim (1448-1520), the provost at St. Lorenz, one of the parish churches.[31] Other names might be added as well, such as Charitas Pirckheimer, Georg Spengler, and Jacob Welser,[32] but there is little evidence that they attended sessions and their inclusion on the list would be basically honorific.

According to this membership, the Nürnberg humanist circle contained about sixteen individuals, of which birthdates exist for thirteen. The average age of these thirteen in 1517 is over forty-seven years, and this figure probably would not change much if the birthdates of three remaining members were known. Thus, in terms of age the group would not appear to be subject to the temptations of youth. Its established social position also would seem to incline it toward a conservative approach in questions of church reform.

All sixteen were well established in terms of social and economic position in Nürnberg society. Seven of them (Andreas and Anton Tucher, Ebner, Christoph Fürer, Holzschuher, Nützel, Pirckheimer) were members of the governing council of the city, election to which was closed virtually to all but patricians; and three of these seven (Anton Tucher, Ebner, Nützel) occupied the top three posts within the council. Since the government was composed only of thirty-four men with power,[33] about one-fifth of its membership was found in the humanist circle. Of the remaining nine humanists, two (Sigmund Fürer, Martin Tucher) were patricians engaged in business in 1517 but would become councilors within the next few years. Two more were employed directly by the council, Spengler as secretary and Scheurl as legal adviser. Three of the final five (Beheim, Linck, Volprecht) had posts within the city's religious institutions, administered by the council; the fourth (Hofmann) was a wealthy merchant, and the last, Dürer, was an artist who had transcended the bounds of an artisan background.

In addition to its age and status, perhaps the most striking characteristic of this group was its education. The twelve or thirteen who were born in Nürnberg came from economically prosperous families, and about one-half of these received a traditional education in business and law. Moreover, about one-half of the total acquired a formal university education; and two, Linck and Scheurl, held theological and legal doctorates, respectively. Whereas some attended German universities at Heidelberg,

Ingolstadt, and Leipzig, the Italian ones at Pavia, Padua, and Bologna also were well represented. Most prominent in reviewing their educational background, however, is the role played by legal studies. At least one-half of the circle had studied law formally.

Thus, there existed in Nürnberg a group of individuals distinguished by age, status, and education. Moreover, and as a result of their economic prosperity, these men had contacts with friends and relatives residing in the most advanced European centers of economic activity. Nürnbergers were found throughout Germany, in France, Switzerland, Italy, Spain, Bohemia, Silesia, and elsewhere, and this, in part, accounts for an extensive correspondence to and from the humanists.[34] At the same time, the official position of many members of the group within the government and a fear that their personal communications might be made public restrict many of these letters to only the most general observations[35] these communications, therefore, must be used with caution.

Particularly close, however, and not solely in an economic sense, was the relationship between Nürnberg and Saxony, electoral and ducal. Spengler, Beheim, and Linck had attended the University of Leipzig, and Staupitz (after whom the circle called itself the *sodalitas Staupitziana*)[36] had aided Elector Frederick in staffing the new University of Wittenberg. Both Linck and Scheurl had taught at the university, and Scheurl had been a legal adviser to the Saxon princes and an assessor at periodic courts held in Leipzig and Altenburg.

Personal ties also existed between Elector Frederick, Dürer, and Anton Tucher. In 1496, when Frederick visited Nürnberg, for example, he commissioned Dürer's first paintings, one of which was a portrait of the prince. Further commissions followed, and some maintain that the artist became Frederick's favorite painter.[37] On the political side, the elector had direct relations with the city government. In 1508, as an example, when he was attending the imperial council of regency meeting in Nürnberg, Frederick stayed with Tucher,[38] who had been chosen leader of Nürnberg's government in 1505. They had been acquainted for some time, and Scheurl, who began the Tucher genealogy late in the 1530s, mentioned that Anton was instrumental in the lawyer's appointment to Frederick's university.[39]

These links represent a key to Nürnberg's reformation, especially those with electoral Saxony via Frederick; his influential secretary, chaplain, and former student in Nürnberg, Georg Spalatin[40] and with the faculty of the University of Wittenberg and the Augustinian monks in that city. Through Frederick, Spalatin, and members of the university and religious communities, the Nürnbergers kept abreast of developments in Saxony. Conversely, to cite only one example, Anton Tucher was the council caretaker (*Pfleger*) of the Augustinian monastery in Nürnberg; thus, he provided a connection between the humanists, the council, the monastery, and Saxony.[41]

The relationship between Nürnberg and Saxony is emphasized by events that occurred during autumn 1517. After Luther had posted his Ninety-five Theses, Ulrich Dinstedt, an Augustinian canon in Wittenberg, sent them to Nürnberg, where Caspar Nützel translated them from Latin into German for publication.[42] Scheurl, the recipient of the Theses, in turn sent copies of them to his friends Johann Eck in Ingolstadt and the humanists Kilian Leib at Rebdorf and Conrad Peutinger at Augsburg.[43] Later, Scheurl wrote to his Augustinian friend, Caspar Güttel, that "Pirckheimer, Anton Tucher, and Wenceslaus Linck all admire and treasure Luther's views."[44] In the same letter, Scheurl mentions that Eck was willing to travel miles just to debate Luther.

The successive names by which the Nürnberg humanists referred to themselves indicate, in large measure, their inclination toward the ensuing Reformation. Generically, they called themselves the *Augustiniana* but modified this through time, becoming the *sodalitas Staupitziana, sodalitas Linckiana*, and *sodalitas Martiniana* in honor of Staupitz, Linck, and Luther.[45] This progression points out the path taken by the circle from early 1517, after Staupitz had concluded his Advent sermons, to late 1518, when Luther visited Nürnberg on his way to Augsburg and his meeting with Cardinal Cajetan. Immediately after the meeting, Linck began to preach on the Beatitudes (Matthew 5:3-9) as the subject of his Advent sermons, and these were published the following year. Both collections of sermons, Staupitz's and Linck's, indicate a receptiveness by the congregations to which they preached, as well as a great deal about the religious views of the humanist circle.

Although it is difficult to gauge accurately the degree to which a formally written treatise corresponds with an oral sermon, there is no reason to doubt that Staupitz's and Linck's published sermons differ much from their spoken words. Moreover, it is not necessary to show theological agreement on the part of the Nürnberger humanists of views subsequently associated with the Reformation; rather what seems important is their acceptance of ideas that they thought supported their interest. Since this is so, detailed examination of sermon content is not necessary. Yet, in both Staupitz and Linck, it is clear that themes of justification, opposition to works righteousness, and salvation were central to their arguments.

Staupitz's Advent sermons of 1516 were printed early in 1517. Issued in Latin and also in a German translation by Scheurl, they were dedicated to Hieronymus Ebner.[46] In the dedicatory epistle, Staupitz wrote that during Advent "by preaching Christ, I have applied myself to give an elucidation to the decree of eternal predestination."[47] He then proceeded in twenty-four chapters to discuss man's inability to earn salvation by his own means. Without grace, "good" works led solely to the praise of man, which was antithetical to the only requirement the Creator placed on the elect: the praise of God. Certainty of election, therefore, manifested itself in faith in Christ through Whom the Father is seen. Inner spirituality, reliance on the Bible, and one's love for his neighbor[48] were expressions of *laus Dei*. Similar expressions were also formulated by Linck.

Wenceslaus Linck, formerly prior of the Augustinian monastery in Wittenberg, a dean of the university's theological faculty, and a close associate of Staupitz, came to Nürnberg early in 1517. Here he remained as a preacher in the city's cloister until 1520, when he succeeded Staupitz as vicar general. Although he returned to the city a few years later and stayed until his death in 1547, his major significance for this essay was his relationship with Staupitz, Luther, and the Augustinians. As a preacher in Nürnberg, he rapidly became an influential member of the *sodalitas* and an acclaimed interpreter of Luther's views.[49]

When Luther passed through the city on his way to and from Augsburg in October 1518, he met many of the humanists. Linck, who had been associated with him in Wittenberg and who was also present at the Heidelberg Disputation earlier in April, accompanied the reformer to Augsburg. After Luther's hearing, when rumors spread about the reformer's imminent arrest, Linck began to preach on the Beatitudes in Nürnberg.[50] In these sermons, printed in 1519, Linck stressed one's inner spirituality, peaceful and righteous living expressed by doing good to one's fellow man, and sole reliance on God's word. While the content of these sermons was not theologically radical, it does exhibit characteristics associated with the *German Theology*, which Luther had edited in 1516 and again in 1518.[51] Of these characteristics, one of the most important was an emphasis on suffering: Linck concluded with "Above all, be in all things ready to suffer, for suffering is the way of salvation."[52]

These views expressed by Staupitz and Linck appear remarkably similar to if not coinciding with the religious orientation of Nürnberg's humanists. Certainly the stress on Christian ethics and inner spirituality echoed opinions elaborated by German humanists in general in the early sixteenth century and often referred to today as Erasmian humanism. Furthermore, insofar as these ideas were buttressed by late medieval mysticism,[53] with its emphasis on spiritual despair, contemplation, union with the will of God, and personal perfection, the religious attitudes were effectively conservative.[54] At this point, practical religion and practical political experiences reinforce each other: the potential anti-intellectual and anti-institutional aspects of mysticism appeal directly to solid middle-class burgher interests.[55]

Such ideas, discussed and disseminated by the humanists, reinforced a tendency already apparent in the city. In this light, it is not surprising that Wolfgang Volprecht, the humanist prior of the Augustinians, had one of Luther's sermons on indulgences printed after Nürnberg had received the Ninety-five Theses, and that Dürer gratuitously sent a few of his works to the reformer.[56]

While it is not possible to say that the views of the humanists were the same as those of the city council, evidence indicates a large measure of agreement, in addition to the high proportion of humanists forming the government. For example, Scheurl requested from Luther that he dedicate a "short Christian work" to the second in command in the council, Hieronymus Ebner. In August 1518, Luther responded by honoring the humanist councilor with his *Commentary on Psalm 110*.[57] Later, in September 1518, Elector Frederick wrote to both Anton Tucher and Scheurl requesting that the lawyer accompany Luther to Augsburg to meet Cajetan.[58] Since the council had commissioned its jurisconsult to go elsewhere on official business, however, he was unable to represent Luther. But when Scheurl returned to the city, he wrote Spalatin that Luther had favorably impressed the burghers when he had stopped in Nürnberg. He assured Spalatin that the city council would do everything possible to aid the monk, and he concluded by saying that he would keep Spalatin informed of the council's decisions with respect to Luther's affairs.[59]

This statement was a fairly firm commitment from one of the city's humanists to inform the Saxon official of the views of the city. It was fulfilled as Linck and others enlightened Spalatin and Luther of the machinations of the papal nuncio, Carl von Miltitz, who stayed in Nürnberg late in December 1518, while on his way to talk with Elector Frederick and Luther. Fearing for Luther's safety and attempting to ameliorate the impression of the monk's imminent doom derived from the Augsburg confrontation, the humanists counseled moderation and advised him not to let Miltitz depart from Altenburg with acrimony.[60]

Luther's popularity among the humanists was assured by his brief stay in Nürnberg in October. During this time, many of them had a chance to talk with him, and in one case in particular the conversations had an important effect on the subsequent reform in the city. Lazarus Spengler composed a tract in German entitled *Defense and Christian Answer of an Honorable Lover of God's Truth in Holy Scripture*, which was printed in 1519.[61] In it, Spengler made reference to his personal contact with Luther, and he defended the monk's teachings as an elucidation of Christian truth. Its publication, at first anonymously and presumably against the author's will, was in part responsible for the alienation of most of the humanists from the Roman Church, for Spengler, partially as a result of his authorship, was included in Luther's excommunication.

The council's inability to prohibit Nürnberg citizens from composing works that might be printed outside the city led to the second major cause solidifying the Nürnberg humanists. This was the anonymous publication of the *Eccius dedolatrus* in 1519-1520, a scathing attack on Johann Eck, Luther's opponent at the Leipzig Disputation.[62] The author of this work was assumed to be Willibald Pirckheimer who informed Eck, not too subtly, of his opinion regarding Eck's stance and abilities. Reminiscent of the most provocative literature brought forth during the Reuchlin affair, Pirckheimer incurred Eck's wrath, with the result that he, too, was named in Luther's excommunication.

One sees here a gradual alignment of the Nürnberg humanists with the Wittenburg monk. To what extent these Nürnbergers understood the depth of Luther's evangelical theology is not known, although Lazarus Spengler became the first important lay reader of the Lutheran Reformation. Yet, with only two or three exceptions, the members of the humanist circle stood in concert with the movement for church reform from 1517 to 1520, and in this accord they seemed to wield considerable power on the destiny of the city.

Perhaps the most obvious symbol of Nürnberg's inclination toward Reformation can be seen in its choice of representatives sent to the Diet of Worms in 1521. Three men were nominated: Leonhard Groland, Caspar Nützel, and Lazarus Spengler. The latter two were members of the humanist circle, and Nützel had been responsible for the translation of the Ninety-five Theses into German for publication. The symbol of Nürnberg's position, however, was Spengler's inclusion on the mission. Both Spengler and Pirckheimer had been named in the *Exsurge Domine* of June 1520, and neither one had yet been absolved from the threat of final excommunication; and, as a matter of record, both men were included in this final ban, *Decet Romanun Pontificum*, in January 1521. Thus, the stance of the Nürnberg government appears in favor of the Reformer.

There is little doubt that the Nürnberg humanists played a determinative role in the development of the city's Reformation. Although the members of the circle were not synonymous with the government, there was in fact a considerable overlap. But, because the humanists dealt with personal and scholarly affairs, they could be and were more spontaneous and impulsive than the government of the city could afford to be. This being so, it would not be incorrect to term these humanists the vanguard of the city's Reformation.

Although Moeller, Spitz, and Hillerbrand are wholly correct in general regarding humanist activity vis-à-vis reform activity, it seems that it would be difficult to imagine a more "establishment" oriented group of individuals than those found in Nürnberg. Perhaps the exception proves the point, though until more particular studies are made detailing age, education, and economic factors on members in local humanist enclaves, this remains only an unusual example.

APPENDIX

These notes on the Nürnberg humanists have been derived from the works listed in the footnotes to the text of this paper and from the *Allgemeine Deutsche Biographie* and the *Neue Deutsche Biographie*. They are simply notes and not biographical sketches.

Beheim, Georg (1448-1520) was a Nürnberger, but not from the patrician family of the same name; his brother was Lorenz Beheim, Pirckheimer's good friend. Educated at Leipzig, which he entered in 1482, he earned a B.A. in 1483, a M.A. in 1488/89; and promotion in 1490. A licentiate in theology, he taught theology at Mainz, where he was also a canon, and became provost of St. Lorenz in 1513, where he remained until his death.

Dürer, Albrecht (1471-1528), a Nürnberger, was apprenticed at early age to learn goldsmithing and became the closest of friends with Pirckheimer. Twice traveled to Italy, particularly to Venice, to study production of woodcuts and engravings connected to book publishing, he worked basically in Nürnberg, where he had many patrons, two of the most prominent being Elector Frederick and Emperor Maximilian. He also traveled to the Netherlands. He was concerned for Luther.

Ebner, Hieronymus (1477-1532), a Nürnberg patrician, studied law at Ingolstadt, traveled to France, entered the service of Maximilian, and then was called to the *Rat* in 1503. He became second *Losunger* in 1514, and first in 1524, upon the death of Anton Tucher. A number of works were dedicated to him, including Luther's *Commentary on Psalm 110*.

Fürer, Christoph (1479-1537), a Nürnberg patrician, entered the *Rat* in 1513 and remained until 1528. He was educated at the Latin school in city, then (1492) sent to Venice to learn business, where he stayed three years before returning to the family *Seigerhandelsgesellschaft*. He was not a scholar himself but had many interests, was against indulgences, and became member of humanist circle in 1512, along with his brother Sigmund. See Johann Kamann, "Der Nürnberger Patrizier Christoph Fürer der Ältere und seine Denkwürdigkeiten 1479-1537," *MVGN* 28(1928):209-311.

Fürer, Sigmund (?1478-1547), the older brother of Christoph, did not enter the *Rat* until 1518. He maintained a business in metals, was zealous toward new theology, and later works for the care of the poor in city. The two brothers worked together, and were named the founders and endowers of cloister Gnadenberg.

Hofmann, Wolfgang (?-1522/23), in Nürnberg around 1490 as agent of the Fuggers, loaned money to various princes, and had important connections, for example, Margrave Casimir.

Holzschuher, Hieronymus (?-1529), came from a very wealthy Nürnberg patrician family, which dated back to ca. 1240, traders in cloth and wool. He was member of the *Rat*; remembered, in part, because of Dürer's portrait.

Linck, Wenceslaus (1483-1547), born in Colditz near Leipzig; attended Leipzig (1498), where there was a humanist circle; received some classical learning; became an Augustinian; and earned a B.A. at Wittenberg in 1504 and a M.A. in 1506. He taught at university; in 1511 became director of theology; traveled with Staupitz, and became a preacher at an Augustinian monastery in Nürnberg early in 1517. He was an important link between the city and Wittenberg, accompanied Luther; left the city in the early 1520s but returned later.

Nützel, Caspar (1471-1529), was from one of the oldest patrician families in Nürnberg, destined for legal studies, entered the *Rat* in 1502, and became second *Losunger* in 1525, where he remained until his death. He was adviser to Swabain League (1509-1515); *Pfleger* for St. Clara's; translated Ninety-five Theses into German for publication; and represented Nürnberg at Diet of Worms. (Camerarius calls him one of the men most responsible for the introduction of the Reformation in the city.)

Pirckheimer, Willibald (1470-1530), was born at Eichstätt, where his father, Johann, was a legal adviser; his father later became *Ratskonsulent* of Nürnberg. With a formal education in law, basically at Italian universities (Pavia, Padua), he entered the *Rat* early, withdrew in 1502, returned in 1505, and remained until 1523. He occupied many positions, was good diplomat; very close with Dürer. Although a difficult man, probably the best known of the humanists, seen by his letters and works. He liked Luther and his reforms but did not care for the social consequences of these reforms. He had sisters and daughters in city's convents but was excommunicated with Luther.

Scheurl, Christoph (1481-1542), came from wealthy Nürnberg family, studied theology but moved toward law; attended Heidelberg then Italian universities; and graduated as doctor of both Roman and canon law from Bologna (1506). He taught law at Wittenberg (1507-1512), then accepted a legal post with the *Rat*, where he remained until his death. He left many letters and contacts and may be regarded as spokesman for city's humanists. Friends with both; he introduced Luther to Eck; he was involved with diplomatic activity and with Staupitz.

Spengler, Lazarus (1479-1534), came from prominent but non-patrician family; succeeded his father, Georg, as council secretary, and became an important diplomat and adviser to council. He attended Leipzig where studied law; wrote a number of Christian humanist works; and was the first important lay leader of Reformation. He was excommunicated with Luther.

Tucher, Andreas (1453-1531), was from one of most illustrious patrician families; educated in business, in Venice (?); entered the *Rat* in 1491; and remained there. He was general for the city during Landshut

War of Succession; won the battle; and eventually was knighted by the emperor, who became his patron. He was from the younger line of Tuchers. See Wilhelm Schwemmer, "Das Mäzenatentum der Nürnberger Patrizierfamilie Tucher vom 14. bis 18. Jahrhundert," *MVGN* 51(1962):18-59.

Tucher, Anton (1457-1524), was from the best patrician family and maintained many international trade relations with France, Italy, Spain, and so on. He spent a long time in Venice; studied law at Heidelberg, Pavia, Bologna; and entered the *Rat* in 1477, where he stayed from 1507 until his death. He was first *Losunger*. Tucher cultivated connections with the Elector Frederick; was patron to Scheurl, and many others. He was *Pfleger* of number of city's religious institutions and supported Stoss' work in St. Lorenz.

Tucher, Martin (1460-1528), cousin of Anton Tucher, was regarded as one of the richest men in the city. He spent most of his life in business in Geneva and Lyon, and did not enter the *Rat* until 1524. His important connections were through business.

Volprecht, Wolfgang (?-1528), became prior of the Augustinians in Nürnberg in 1516. He was inclined toward Luther, published one of Luther's sermons on indulgences so people would understand better the Ninety-five Theses, and in March 1524 performed the mass in German, giving cup to laity. He became preacher at Heilig-Geist Spital after Augustinians disbanded, where he remained until his death.

NOTES

1. Bernd Moeller, "The German Humanists and the Beginnings of the Reformation," in *Imperial Cities and the Reformation, Three Essays*, eds. and trans. H. C. Erik Midelfort and Mark U. Edwards (Philadelphia, 1972), 25-26. Moeller's essay appeared earlier as "Die deutschen Humanisten und die Anfänge der Reformation," *Zietschrift für Kirchengeschichte* 70(1959):46-61.

2. Ibid., 32. These issues had already been raised by Herbert Schöffler; see his *Die Reformation: Einführung in eine Geistesgeschichte der deutschen Neuzeit* (Bochum-Langendereer, 1936) and *Wirkungen der Reformation: Religionssoziologische Folgerungen für England und Deutschland* (Frankfurt am Main, 1960).

3. "The Third Generation of German Renaissance Humanists," in *The Reformation: Basic Interpretations*, 2d ed., ed. Lewis W. Spitz (Lexington, Mass., 1972), 44-59. Spitz's article was previously printed in *Aspects of the Renaissance, A Symposium*, ed. Archibald R. Lewis (Austin, Tex., 1967).

4. Ibid., 44-46.

5. *The World of the Reformation* (New York, 1973), 41.

6. Ibid., 38.

7. For example, Friedrich Roth, *Die Einführung der Reformation in Nürnberg, 1517-1528* (Würzburg, 1885); Max Hermann, *Die Reception des Humanismus in Nürnberg* (Berlin, 1898); Hans von Schubert, *Lazarus Spengler und die Reformation in Nürnberg*, Quellen und Forschungen zur Reformationsgeschichte, vol. 17, ed. Hajo Holborn (Leipzig, 1934) (hereafter Schubert, *Spengler*); Adolf Engelhardt, "Die Reformation in Nürnberg," *Mitteilungen des Vereins für Geschichte der Stadt Nürnberg* 33(1936):3-258 (hereafter journal is *MVGN*); Gerald Strauss, *Nuremberg in the Sixteenth Century* (New York, 1966); and the same author's "Protestant Dogma and City Government: The Case of Nuremberg," *Past and Present* no. 36(1967):38-58 (hereafter Strauss, "Protestant Dogma"); Franz Machilek, "Klosterhumanismus in Nürnberg um 1500," *MVGN*, 64(1977):10-45; and Harold J. Grimm, *Lazarus Spengler, A Lay Leader of the Reformation* (Columbus, Ohio, 1978). For humanism in general, see the fine contribution of James D. Tracy, "Humanism and the Reformation," in *Reformation Europe: A Guide to Research*, ed. Steven Ozment (St. Louis, 1982), 33-57.

8. Julie Meyer, "Die Entstehung des Patriziats in Nürnberg," *MVGN*, 27(1928):1-96; Ernst Pitz, *Die Entstehung der Ratsherrschaft in Nürnberg in 13. und 14. Jahrhundert*, Schriftenreihe zur bayerischen Landesgeschichte, vol. 55 (München, 1956); Strauss, "Protestant Dogma."

9. Cf. Heinz Dannenbauer, *Die Entstehung des Territoriums der Reichsstadt Nürnberg* (Stuttgart, 1928).

10. For some of the better accounts, see Theodor Kolde, "Uber das Kirchenwesen in Nürnberg im Jahre 1525," *Beiträge zur bayerischen Kirchengeschichte* 19(1913):57-74; Gerhard Pfeiffer, "Die Einführung der Reformation in Nürnberg als kirchenrechtliches und bekenntniskundliches Problem," *Blätter für deutsche Landesgeschichte* 89(1952):112-133; Gottfried Seebass, "Die Reformation in Nürnberg," *MVGN* 55(1967-1968):252-69, recently translated into English as "The Reformation in Nürnberg" in *The Social History of the Reformation*, ed. Lawrence P. Buck and Jonathan W. Zophy (Columbus, Ohio, 1972), 17-40 (hereafter collection is *Social History of Reformation*); Strauss, "Protestant Dogma"; Lawrence P. Buck, "Opposition to Tithes in the Peasants' Revolt: A Case Study of Nuremberg in 1524," *The Sixteenth Century Journal* 4(October 1973):11-22.

11. Roth, *Die Einführung*, 98-103, 108-10; Gottfried Seebass, *Das reformatorische Werk des Andreas Osiander*, Einzelarbeiten aus der Kirchengeschichte Bayerns, vol. 44; (Nürnberg, 1967); cf. Johann Christian Siebenkees, *Materialien zur nürnbergischen Geschichte* (Nürnberg, 1792-1795), vol. 2, 559-66.

12. Strauss, "Protestant Dogma," 55-56.

13. Joseph Pfanner, "Geisteswissenschaftlicher Humanismus," in *Nürnberg—Geschichte einer europäischen Stadt*, ed. Gerhard Pfeiffer (München, 1971), 127 (hereafter *Nürnberg—Geschichte*).

14. See the articles by Philippe Braunstein, "Wirtschaftliche Beziehungen Zwischen Nürnberg und Italien im Spätmittelalter"; Friedrich Lütge, "Der Handel Nürnbergs nach dem Osten im 15./16. Jahrhundert"; Gerhard Pfeiffer, "Die Bemühungen der oberdeutschen Kaufleute um die Privilegierung ihres Handels in Lyon"; and Hermann Kellenbenz, "Die Beziehungen Nürnbergs zur Iberischen Halbinsel, besonders im 15. und in der ersten Hälfte des 16. Jahrhunderts"—all in *Beiträge zur wirtschaftsgeschichte Nürnbergs* "Beiträge zur Geschichte und Kultur der Stadt Nürnberg," vol. 11, no. 1, ed. Stadtarchiv Nürnberg (Nürnberg, 1967) (hereafter *BWN*).

15. Pfanner, "Geisteswissenschaftlicher," 128-29; Lewis W. Spitz, *Conrad Celtis, the German Arch-Humanist* (Cambridge, Mass., 1957), 35-44.

16. Ludwig Keller, *Johann von Staupitz und die Anfänge der Reformation* (Leipzig, 1888), 28-29, and Gerhard Hummel, *Die humanistischen Sodalitäten und ihr Einfluss auf die Entwicklung des Bildungswesens der Reformationszeit* (Leipzig, 1940), 41-43, 93-95, passim.

17. Lewis W. Spitz, *The Religious Renaissance of the German Humanists* (Cambridge, Mass., 1963), 86.

18. Gustav Bauch, "Die Nürnberger Poetenschule 1496-1509," *MVGN* 14(1901):1-64; Jackson Spielvogel, "Willibald Pirckheimer's Domestic Activity for Nürnberg," *Moreana* no. 25(1970):22-24; Klaus Leder, "Nürnbergs Schulwesen an der Wende vom Mittelalter zur Neuzeit," in *Albrecht Dürers Umwelt. Festschrift zum 500. Geburtstag Albrecht Dürers am 21. Mai 1971*, Nürnberger Forschungen, vol. 14, ed. Verein für Geschichte der Stadt Nürnberg und Senatskommission für Humanismus-Forschung der Deutschen Forschungsgemeinschaft (Nürnberg, 1971), 33 (hereafter *Dürers Umwelt*).

19. *Epitome de generibus nominum declinationeque ipsorum. De preteritis item et supinis verborum.* See Josef Benzing, "Humanismus in Nürnberg 1500-1540: Eine Liste der Druckschriften," in *Dürers Umwelt*, 273, no. 140.

20. Pfanner, "Geisteswissenschaftlicher," 130; see also note 40.

21. See, for example, the correspondence between them in Josef Pfanner, ed., *Briefe von, an und über Caritas Pirckheimer (aus den Jahren 1498-1530)*, Caritas Pirckheimer—Quellensammlung, no. 3, ed. Caritas Pirckheimer—Forschung (Landshut: 1966).

22. Theodor Kolde, *Die deutsche Augustiner-Congregation und Johann von Staupitz* (Gotha, 1879); David Curtis Steinmetz, *Misericordia Dei: The Theology of Johannes von Staupitz in Its Late Medieval Setting*, Studies in Medieval and Reformation Thought, vol. 4 (Leiden, 1968), 5-9.

23. See Phillip N. Bebb "The Lawyers, Dr. Christoph Scheurl, and the Reformation in Nürnberg," in *Social History of Reformation*, 52-72.

24. Theodor Kolde, "Brüderschaftsbrief des Joh. von Staupitz für Christoph Scheurl der Älteren und seine Familie. 1511, 6 Oct.," *Zeitschrift für Kirchengeschichte* 6(1883-1884):296-98; Steinmetz, *Misericordia Dei*, 10-11.

25. See note 27.

26. Franz von Soden and J. K. F. Knaake, eds., *Christoph Scheurls Briefbuch. Ein Beitrag zur Geschichte der Reformation und ihrer Zeit* (Potsdam, 1867), Br. 114 (Hereafter cited as *Scheurls Br.*).

27. Notes were made on Staupitz's Lenten sermons and on conversations with him during mealtime. These are found in the Scheurl family archive in Fischbach über Nürnberg, Codex C. fols. 168r-174r. I wish to thank Hr. Siegfried Freiherr von Scheurl for making this material available to me. The notes are printed in J. K. F. Knaade, ed., *Johannis Staupitii, opera quae reperiri poterunt omnia: Deutsche Schriften*, vol. 1 (Potsdam, 1867), 13-49 (hereafter cited as *Johannis Staupitii*).

28. *Scheurls Br.* 159; see the appendix to this chapter.

29. Hofmann was involved in the purchase of properties for the Fuggers in the 1490s; see Götz von Pölnitz, "Die Fugger in Nürnberg," *BWN* 11, no. 1 (1967):226. Cf. Pölnitz's *Jakob Fugger, Quellen und Erläuterungen* (Tübingen, n.d. [1951]), vol 2, passim.

30. See Emil Reicke, ed., *Willibald Pirckheimers Briefwechsel*, 2 vols. (München, 1940-1956). Hostility may have been the reason that Scheurl excluded Pirckheimer's name from his list.

31. Emil Reicke, *Geschichte der Reichsstadt Nürnberg* (Nürnberg: 1896), 784 ff; Christa Schaper, "Lorenz und Georg Beheim, Freunde Willibald Pirckheimers," *MVGN* 50(1960):120-221.

32. *Scheurls Br.* 176.

33. There were forty-two councilors but eight of these were "commoners" virtually devoid of any power. For a description of Nürnberg's governmental structure written by Scheurl at the request of Staupitz, see "Christoph Scheurls Epistel über die Verfassung der Reichsstadt Nürnberg. 1516," *Die Chroniken der deutschen Städte* 11(Leipzig, 1874), 781-804.

34. In addition to the articles listed in note 14, see, for example, the collection by Eugene Vial, "Jean Cleberger," *Revue d'histoire de Lyon* 11(1912):81-102, 273-308, 321-40; and Reicke, ed., *Willibald Pirckheimers Briefwechsel*, passim.

35. Lore Sporhan-Krempel, *Nürnberg als Nachrichtenzentrum zwischen 1400 und 1700*, Nürnberger Forschungen: Einzelarbeiten zur Nürnberger Geschichte, vol. 10 (Nürnberg, 1968), 78.

36. *Scheurls Br.*, 150.

37. Erwin Panofsky, *The Life and Art of Albrecht Dürer*, 4th ed. (Princeton, 1971), 106.

38. Sporhan-Krempel, *Nürnberg als Nachnachrichtenzentrum*; see the notice in Tucher's account book, Wilhelm Loose, ed., *Anton*

Tuchers Haushaltbuch (1507 bis 1517), "Bibliothek des litterarischen Vereins in Stuttgart," vol. 134 (Tübingen, 1877), 16.

39. Franz von Soden, *Beiträge zur Geschichte der Reformation und die Sitten jener Zeit mit besonderem Hinblick auf Christoph Scheurl II* (Nürnberg, 1855), 505.

40. Irmgard Höss, *George Spalatin, 1484-1545* (Weimar, 1956), 6-9, passim; see also note 20.

41. Ernst Mummenhoff, "Anton Tucher," *Allgemeine Deutsche Biographie* 38:756-64.

42. Bebb, "The Lawyers," 60.

43. *Scheurls Br.*, 154-156.

44. *Scheurls Br.*, 160.

45. Schubert, *Spengler*, 163; Charles E. Daniel, "The Significance of the Sermons of Wenzeslaus Linck" (Ph.D. diss., Ohio State University, 1968), 70. Both of these accounts of the circle are based largely on Scheurl's letters.

46. The Latin original, *Libellus de executione aeterne predestinationis*, appeared in February 1517, a few weeks after Scheurl's translation, which is reproduced in Knaade, ed., *Johannis Staupitii* 136-184. Part of the treatise has been translated into English in Heiko A. Oberman, *Forerunners of the Reformation: The Shape of Late Medieval Thought* (New York: 1966), 175-203. Staupitz's theology is treated in Steinmetz, *Misericordia Dei,* and Arthur L. Henry, "Catholicity and Predestination in the Theologies of Johann Eck and Johannes von Staupitz, 1513-1517" (Th.D. diss., Graduate Theological Union, 1971).

47. Henry, ibid., 149.

48. Alfred Jeremias, *Johannes von Staupitz: Luthers Vater und Schüler* (Berlin, 1926), 161-71.

49. Wilhelm Reindell, *Doktor Wenzeslaus Linck aus Colditz, 1483-1547. Nach ungedruckten und gedruckten Quellen dargestellt. Erster Teil: Bis zur reformatorischen Thätigkeit in Altenburg. Mit Bildnis und einem Anhang enthaltend die zugehörigen Documenta Linckiana* 1485-1522 (Marburg, 1892), 49-131.

50. Wilhelm Reindell, ed., *Wenzel Lincks Werke. Erste Hälfte: Eigene Schriften bis zur zweiten Nürnberger Wirksamkeit* (Marburg, 1894), 11-112.

51. Steven E. Ozment, *Mysticism and Dissent: Religious Ideology and Social Protest in the Sixteenth Century* (New Haven, Conn.: 1973), especially 21-22; cf. Harold J. Grimm, ed., *Luther's Works. Career of the Reformer: I* (Philadelphia, 1957), 73-74.

52. Quoted in Strauss, *Nuremberg in the Sixteenth Century*, 162.

53. Harold J. Grimm, "Lazarus Spengler, the Nürnberg Council, and the Reformation," in *Luther for an Ecumenical Age*, ed. Carl S. Meyer (St. Louis, 1967), 111; Irmgard Höss, "Das religiöse Leben vor der Reformation," *Nürnberg—Geschichte*:137-46. Spitz explicitly

recognizes the role played by "German mysticism" in the Nürnberg humanist group; *Religious Renaissance*, 7.

54. See Strauss, "Protestant Dogma," 54-55, 56.

55. Ozment, *Mysticism and Dissent*, 11. In chapter seventeen of his treatise, for example, Staupitz wrote that the pursuit of philosophical studies resulted in a recognition of one's own ignorance: "Nement war, dits ist das endt aller kunst der Philosophen, memlich das wir erkennen unser unwissenheit." Knaade, ed. *Johannis Staupitii*, 164, no. 140; *cf.* Oberman, *Forerunners*, 138.

56. *D. Martin Luthers Werke.* Briefwechsel (Weimar: 1930-1948), vol. 1, 151-53 (hereafter *WA, Br.*). Roth, *Die Einführung der Reformation in Nürnberg*, 1517-1528, 61.

57. *D. Martin Luthers Werke.* Kritische Gesamtausgabe (Weimar, 1883-), vol. 1, 689-710.

58. *WA, Br.*, vol. 1, 211, n. 16.

59. *Scheurls Br.*, 172.

60. *Scheurls Br.*, 184; Reindell, *Doktor Wenzeslaus Linck aus Colditz*, 108-10.

61. *Schutzred und christenliche antwurt ains erbern liebhabers göttlicher warhait der hailigen geschrift.* See Schubert, *Spengler*, 189-95; Grimm, "Lazarus Spengler, the Nürnberg Council, and the Reformation," 112-13.

62. *WA, Br.*, vol. 2, 37, n. 6; 59-60, n. 3.

What Was Preached in German Cities in the Early Years of the Reformation? *Wildwuchs* Versus Lutheran Unity*

SUSAN C. KARANT-NUNN

D espite intensive research on the incipient Reformation by
generations of scholars, there is much that we still do not
know about it. Bernd Moeller's article in the 1984 issue of the
Archive for Reformation History, "Was wurde in der
Frühzeit der Reformation in den deutschen Städten gepredigt?" is
thought-provoking in both content and methodology.[1] Telling
Moeller much about the German Reformation is carrying coals to
Newcastle, yet his assertions do elicit a response. Moeller reacts
against Franz Lau's description of the early years of the German
Reformation as a time of *Wildwuchs*, literally of "wild growth."[2]
By this Lau means that, before the Reformation was adopted and
directed by urban, new ecclesiastical, or territorial authorities, it
was a matter of the individual heart and mind and that, in the
cities of the German Empire, numerous preachers conveyed to
the masses not only their enthusiasm for the teaching of Martin
Luther as they conceived it, but also their own doctrinal convictions. These convictions often resembled Luther's, but inevitably
contained elements of the preachers' invention. Having mentioned Billican, Bugenhagen, Menius, Johann Hess, Bucer, Brenz,
Hubmair, Schappler, and Capito, Lau advises his readers to take
into account that "that which was announced to be the Word of
God was in itself not entirely homogeneous but very strongly dif-
ferentiated. . . . Social or legal tones are much more audible than in

Luther (J. Strauss), and one will have to reckon with the more significant Reformation preachers having their own theology."[3] Lau summarizes his view as follows:

> The fact is that at first there were only differentiated Reformation sermons and in part a corresponding congregational life. . . . To view as Lutheran the many preachers and writers of the period before 1525 would be very rash. Naturally they all preached the 'Word of God' and felt themselves to be with little or no qualification in solidarity with Luther. For a time this was even the case with Müntzer and longer still with Zwingli. Even a man like Schwenkfeld . . . noticed only after some while (1525) that his path and Luther's had to diverge. The Reformation preachers of the period before 1525 were a many-faceted society; their sermons were as yet unshaped by new norms; that they all were, like Luther, pious toward those in authority could not be assumed. . . . For the period up to 1525 one can speak only with reservations and with careful commentary of a unified or even of a two- or three-pronged movement. Even the boundary between the classical Reformation and enthusiasm (Anabaptism and spiritualism, etc.) was not sharply drawn and was for many not yet visible at all.[4]

Moeller disagrees. Using 32 synopses, about 1500 printed pages in all, of sermons by 26 authors (preachers) from 27 cities of all types and geographical distribution throughout Germany,[5] Moeller concludes "that in the early years of the Reformation in the urban chancels of Germany from which adherents of the Reformation preached, a diffuse and frequently primitive 'Wildwuchs' did not predominate, but on the contrary, a theological teaching that in its basic features and main points was thoroughly unified and relatively self-contained, and which rested upon an underlying theological consensus."[6] These sermons were inspired by the printed teachings of Luther and did not significantly depart from them. Until 1525, they acknowledged Luther's leadership (*lutherische Engführung*) of the reform movement.[7] They concentrated chiefly on practical theology: justification, the church, Christian life, and the end of the world.[8]

To the small extent that they were socially critical, they dealt with the Catholic clergy and virtually never with world order.[9]

It would have been helpful to the reader if Moeller had identified his sources more fully. We are allowed to assume that the preachers mentioned in footnotes are those on whom the author bases his conclusions, but one of the striking features of the references is the preachers not included in them. The apparent problem of omission can be explained by looking at several preachers in Saxon and Thuringian cities whose sermons for one reason or another do not form part of Moeller's collection.

Let us begin with Zwickau, in 1518 the largest town in Ernestine domains. It is impossible to state that early Protestant sermons in this urban center were characterized by peaceableness and solidarity with Luther. Such Lutheran stalwarts as Friedrich Mykonius (briefly), Gaspar Güttel (very briefly), and Nicolaus Hausmann did indeed expound from city pulpits their interpretation of the Word of God, but this is by no means the whole picture. For example, Johann Sylvius (Wildenauer) Egranus was preacher in Saint Mary's Church until 1521, when he left for the new and burgeoning mining town of Joachimsthal, just across the Bohemian border. There, too, he preached his reform-minded, but never truly Lutheran, Catholic humanist beliefs.[10] So deviant did those who advised Pope Leo X find Egranus's attacks on the church that they succeeded in putting his name along with Luther's on the bull *Exsurge domine*.

The young Zwickau humanist Stephan Roth took notes on Egranus's sermons intermittently between 1519 and 1522, in both Zwickau and Joachimsthal. Egranus criticized the cult of Saint Anne and the exaggerated pomp and circumstance of Catholic ritual.[11] He opposed the pope's distortion of the historical place of Saint Peter.[12] He attacked indulgences.[13] He declared from the pulpit that Christ was the one true priest and men's only intercessor.[14] He affirmed only two sacraments, baptism and holy communion.[15] During Lent in Zwickau in 1519, he testified to his reliance upon Scripture: "The gospel of Christ is the light which ought to shine."[16] Roth noted this in Latin, but Egranus preached to the people in German.

How, then, may the career of this man be seen as part of a disorderly growth of the early Reformation? In addition to these teachings, which seem quite compatible with Luther's own although arrived at chiefly through his humanistic studies,

Egranus taught his congregations that even if communion had originally been distributed to the laity in both kinds, the church must have had good reasons for changing that practice six to seven hundred years earlier. Christian unity, he said, should not be destroyed over this technicality.[17] The common people should be spared the confusion that attends rapid change.[18] He stated that he had to believe that when the priest gave thanks over the bread, it was changed into Christ's flesh even though the manner of its transformation remained a mystery.[19] Not even the Bible ought to be used as ammunition here: "They should let the Gospel go and stay by the unity of the Church."[20] Someone must have criticized Egranus on this point, for he defended himself from the pulpit in Joachimsthal on the Thursday before Easter 1522:

> We should not be divided into sects so that we say, 'I am a Martinian, I am an Eckite, I am an Emserite, I am a Philippist, I am a Carlstadter, I am a Leipziger, I am a papist,' and whatever more sects there may be. I will follow Saint Paul and say that I am of Jesus Christ. I preach the gospel. . . . In sum, I am a follower of the Gospel and a Christian. Beyond that, I stand by the Church in its honest practices that are not in contradiction to the Gospel . . . one must not throw out all the good customs and rules of the Church.[21]

Another formally appointed preacher in Zwickau, and in regular conflict with Egranus between October 1520 and his dismissal in April 1521, was, of course, Thomas Müntzer. Even though we have no collection of this radical's sermons from his year there—we know much more about his preaching in Alstedt and Mühlhausen, also German cities—we dare not overlook his presence or his homiletic potency. In Zwickau, his incompatibility with Martin Luther first became apparent. The clues we possess from his sojourn in Zwickau permit us to say with fair certainty at least this much: Müntzer began to preach against the power of the magistrates, mocking Egranus and the city councilors for their mutual solicitude.[22] He raged against Egranus's reluctance to overturn the ecclesiastical status quo.[23] He sympathized with the economic plight of the ordinary woolweavers who packed Saint Catherine's Church to hear him. He highly praised the nonconformist weaver Niclas Storch as "raised above all priests as the one who best knew the Bible" and said that he was "highly perceptive (*erkannt*) in spirit."[24] He encouraged his listeners at Christmas to physically attack a rural Catholic pastor who dared to attend a sermon.[25] He taught that God could illuminate the individual Christian and that divine messages had a validity that rivaled Scripture's. This is not to deny the similarities between him and Luther that still existed. Luther himself, however, was not a man to cultivate a relationship with spiritual leaders whose views did not coincide with his on every point.[26] The break with Müntzer was not slow in coming.

Müntzer was a preacher in more than one German city, and he had a decisive effect upon his hearers. His popularity with many common people, even with two or three city councilors and one future councilor in Zwickau, cannot be overlooked. Müntzer confessed under torture in 1525 that he had entered into a conspiracy—to do what he did not say—with Zwickau's ever-rebellious woolweavers Hans and Heinrich Gebhart and their following.[27] We may be sure that this association did not aim to foster social and religious harmony in the city. The city fathers invited Luther in April 1522 and Caspar Güttel in June 1523 to preach in Zwickau, in large part to counter the lingering results of Müntzer's activities there.

We see at work in Zwickau, then, in addition to the teaching of Lutheranism by the pastor Nicolaus Hausmann and the guest Caspar Güttel, the biblical humanism of Egranus in Saint Mary's parish and the ever more radical antiauthoritarianism and spiritualism of Müntzer in Saint Mary's and Saint Catherine's churches. Egranus, as observed, continued on in Joachimsthal and Müntzer in Alstedt and Mühlhausen. Even in Zwickau after 1521, all was hardly the tranquil enunciation of Lutheran principles. It seems that Niclas Storch, in order to demonstrate his biblical erudition, must have engaged in something worthy of the label preaching even though he held no position in the church. Do we ignore his work because we have no summaries of his sermons?

Or what of the attacks, beginning about 1526, of the genuinely Lutheran preacher Paul Lindenau on burgomaster and councilor Hermann Mühlpfort? These do not appear in any summaries of sermons, but they were launched from the chancel nonetheless. In March 1527, Lindenau ranted against Mühlpfort before the congregation of Saint Mary's Church, who loved his insubordinate sermons better than Luther's:[28]

You whore, you lout, you proud wretch, you haughty boob, you highfalutin donkey. You let yourself think that no one is more clever than you. . . . You hold council against me, you brought me here and want to drive me out again because I won't condone your airs, misdeeds, knavery, shitting around, thievery, and whoring! Note well, your power hangs by a thread, and when it is broken, your power will well and soon come to an end.[29]

Was Zwickau exceptional in being the scene of widely varied and often polemical preaching during the early years of the Reformation? Let us consider the well-known case of Wittenberg itself. Certainly, Bugenhagen and Luther delivered sermons here, and like those of Güttel and Hausmann in Zwickau, they expounded the emerging orthodoxy. Were Carlstadt and Gabriel Zwilling merely spectacular exceptions to Moeller's rule?

Carlstadt's beliefs, like those of Müntzer in Alstedt and Mülhausen, are well known and require no detailed definition here.[30] What should be remembered is that Carlstadt took the city by storm, chiefly by means of the sermon. Not only was the people's enthusiasm great, but even the city council accepted as the new ecclesiastical order the dramatic changes introduced by Carlstadt, summarized in the "Ordnung der Stadt Wittenberg" of January 24, 1522.[31]

During the turmoil of the Wittenberg Movement, the Augustinian monk Gabriel Zwilling, an admirer but no slavish imitator of Carlstadt, preached his own beliefs to a packed monastery church and in many villages surrounding the city.[32] Zwilling and some of his fellow monks aroused even Carlstadt's concern because of the energy with which they urged upon their avid listeners the complete boycott of Catholic masses.[33] Zwilling declared that the Lord's Supper was not a sacrifice but only a ritual that Christ wished carried out in his memory.[34] Zwilling evidently denied the real presence. Frederick the Wise ordered Gregor Brück to investigate Zwilling.[35] Later that year the elector refused to allow Zwilling to take up the pastorate in Altenburg even though by then Luther was convinced of Zwilling's full submission and loyalty to himself.[36]

Carlstadt's influence was not confined to Wittenburg. We are familiar with his success in Orlamünde, the town to which he withdrew when remaining in Wittenberg became untenable.[37] Carlstadt preached there from the summer of 1523 until September 1524, when Luther succeeded in having him driven out. By this time, Carlstadt was very much a mystic and had come to reject infant baptism. His wife, who remained behind to bear their son, was sent packing when she declined to let the infant be christened.[38] In 1527, the first parish visitors had to order some babies baptised, evidence of Carlstadt's influence and not of the spread into Thuringia of Swiss or Austrian Anabaptism.[39]

Carlstadt left a considerable heritage behind him in Saxon and Thuringian cities, in the form of disciples who preached his and not Luther's religious perspectives. He was very popular in Joachimsthal, dedicated a number of treatises to leading citizens of this mining city, and evidently received gifts of money from them on several occasions.[40] Martin Reinhard, who had been with Carlstadt in Denmark, was driven out of his preaching post in Jena.[41]

To the territorial princes, the Albertine George and the Ernestine Frederick the Wise and his brother Johann, who jointly governed the silver-mining cities of the Erzgebirge, one of the most persistent and troublesome of Carlstadt's adherents was George Amandus, preacher in Schneeberg from December 1523 until August 1525.[42] I do not know whether Moeller missed Amandus's treatise, "Wye Eyn Geistlicher, Christlicher Ritter und Gottes Heldt in diser Welt streytten sall," published in Zwickau in 1524.[43] In this explication of his creed, Amandus reveals his affinity for the mystical *Gelassenheit* or self-abandonment that was central to Carlstadt's thinking. This physically lame cleric aroused both fervor and controversy within the mining population of Schneeberg by preaching the destruction of images. The annalist Christian Meltzer records disapprovingly, "The limping Amandus destroyed the images (*die Bilder gesturmet*) and even did away with the image of Christ on the cross." Following Amandus's example, a peasant from the village of Griessbach took a crucifix and used it to heat his house. George put the rustic in prison for this sacrilege.[44]

On Good Friday 1525, two of Schneeberg's patricians reported to Frederick the Wise—in reality to his brother Johann since Frederick lay dying in Lochau—that the common people were delighted by Amandus's homiletic assaults on authority; when the citizens heard rumors that the princes were going to fire their clergyman, they began conspiring to keep him.[45] Shortly thereafter, on April 25, 1525, a formal interrogation convened, presided over by officials of both branches of the Wettin house. They presented Amandus with a list of twenty controversial statements collected from his sermons over more than a year by high-ranking persons who were offended by his utterances. Amandus was alleged to have preached that the community ought to rule the city council and not the other way around, and even that a land should govern its prince.[46] The preacher insisted he had meant only that one should not deny the Holy Spirit and that no one could rule "the ground of our heart" (*den abrund unsers herzens*).[47] On Corpus Christi 1524, he said that the holiday had been thought up by the devil, and he denied the real presence of Christ's body and blood.[48] In replying, Amandus confirmed this accusation.[49] He was alleged to have criticized anyone who helped to build the new stone Saint Wolfgang Church, saying that the church was a devil's house and calling the pastor a fool and an ass.[50] Amandus answered that the Christian himself is the living temple of God and a church building should be thought of only if man was well provided for and there were extra resources. He admitted to criticizing the pastor as an opponent of Gospel order.[51] On March 25, 1525, he said that no office was so pious (*fromm*) that it was worth hanging anybody over, and that the *Amtmann*, an official of noble status, was a rascal.[52] Amandus could not recall saying this, but he thought anyone who used his office in the service of avarice should be punished.[53] He supposedly set a crucifix on fire in the city weighing office (*in der wag*) and broke up another.[54] Amandus did not deny the act; he said that Christians did not require images to remind them of their annointing (*salbung*); rather, the Holy Spirit reminded men "in their hearts."[55]

Elector Johann, who on May 5 succeeded Frederick the Wise, dismissed Amandus.[56] One miner had to spend two weeks in jail for his effrontery in offering to house Amandus himself, in order to evade the princely edict.[57] The authorities were well aware how attractive Amandus's opinions were and what a danger they posed at a moment when the peasants were in revolt and arousing great sympathy among the miners of the Erzgebirge. The advisors of Duke George and of Elector Johann investigated the unrest connected with Amandus's departure.[58] They forbade all future gatherings of the miners' brotherhood (*Knappschaft*) and of the community (*Gemeinde*).[59]

One more example may help to shed light on Moeller's generalizations as they relate to Saxony and Thuringia. Moeller refers to Jakob Strauss's "Ain trostliche verstendige leer."[60] It is not clear whether Moeller's compilation of sermons also includes the Eisenach preacher's controversial pamphlet, based on one or more sermons of 1523, "Das wucher zu nemen und geben unserm Christlichen glauben und brüderlicher lieb (als zu ewiger verdamnyss reichent) entgegen yst, unuberwintlich leer," or Strauss's fifty-one theses on usury "gepredigt zu Eysenach durch D. Jacob Straussen."[61] According to Joachim Rogge, Strauss developed his ideas independently of Luther; and, even when between 1522 and 1525 Strauss saw himself as a follower of Luther, his theology departed from that of the Wittenberg nightingale's on several points.[62] Luther and Duke Johann saw particular danger in Strauss's categorical repudiation of taking or paying interest. Luther himself had quickly repented of his own rigid stance in his first "Sermon von dem Wucher" of 1519 and the very next year directed his opposition only toward usury in commerce.[63] Two of Eisenach's officials were incensed by Strauss's words and reported to Johann in January 1524, "The preacher, Doctor Strauss, used these words and said several times in his sermons, 'Dear brothers in Christ, you are not obliged to pay the clergy the interest that derives from usury and *widerkauffen*.[64] For you sin mortally if you pay it. If somebody wants it and takes it from you by force, then give to that one who seizes your coat your cloak also.'"[65]

They accused him too of trying to persuade his hearers to take action (*euch bewegen lassenn*) against the council.[66] They quoted him as saying, "Your councilors are fools, blasphemers and murderers of God. They aren't worthy to govern a heap of pigs."[67] They asked Johann to initiate a hearing of both sides, and two such hearings took place: one in Weimar and one in Eisenach. Although these did not produce Strauss's condemnation, the preacher's views on usury brought over him a pall of suspicion that he wished to overthrow society's established order; these turned Luther against him[68] and placed Strauss, so far as Lutheran leaders were concerned, in the ranks of radicals like Müntzer and Carlstadt. Strauss abhorred the peasant's revolt.[69] But the fact remains that numerous individuals who had attended his fiery sermons took part in the uprising and believed themselves to act in accord with their preacher's will. So widespread was the belief in a tie between Strauss and Müntzer that under torture Müntzer was asked about him.[70] In the aftermath of the Peasants' War, Strauss was forced to leave Eisenach.

A basic precept of social historians today is that printed tracts alone may not convey a complete picture of the past. We cautious practitioners of the art of describing a foregone era try, at the very least, to see that when we use literature, one excellent source of information, we have before us a representative range of what is available. A lack of documentation from Saxon and Thuringian cities in the early years of the Reformation makes it questionable whether Moeller's collection of sermons is balanced. Assembling a truly representative group of sources is a formidable task.

If only through the presentation of examples—Egranus, Müntzer, Lindenau, Carlstadt, Zwilling, Amandus, and Strauss—I believe I have demonstrated that, at least in Saxony and Thuringia, what was preached in the first few years after 1518 was far more varied and unsettling than Moeller would have us believe. Not only did influential preachers like Müntzer and Carlstadt depart noticeably from Luther at an early date, they gathered adherents, some of whom in turn became preachers. Just when each of these men realized—indeed, just when Luther himself perceived—that they were not bearers of Luther's exact tidings is a highly individual matter, one not central to the theme under discussion. Nearly all felt Luther's inspiration, but they did not see themselves constrained to toe a line that could not yet be drawn in the unsettled dust of the German Reformation. Until 1525, only Luther's remarkable charisma and the bonds he forged with the Ernestine princes might have suggested that the future lay with him. The others were not visionaries. Their tongues were loosed, they were sure, by the same evangelic power that liberated his, and they spoke as earnestly as he.

A number of these men's sermons have come down to us, all ought to be taken into account. But what about sermons not in our possession, either because their deliverers did not put them into print or because no avid intellectual like Stephan Roth brought pen and paper to church and transcribed them? Some sermons were not printed because they departed too greatly from tolerated teaching. Both magistrates and princes controlled the output of presses where they could; though before the Peasants' War, the need was not as manifest to them as afterward. Too, a great many sermons were ordinary. Irrespective of their theological content, they were neither elocutionary models nor rousers of emotions. No doubt for this reason above all others, we lack evidence of the great majority of Reformation sermons given. Those sermons that did find their way into print were actually few and extraordinary. Finally, many sermons may have been printed that have not come down to us.

Does this mean that we cannot, that we should not, consider unprinted and non-surviving sermons in inquiring into the homiletic utterances of reform-minded men? On the contrary, if we fail to do so, we allow ourselves to see only a part of the available picture. Where we learn of sermons delivered but not recorded, we should bear their alleged content in mind and examine it in the light of ancillary sources. Reports *about* sermons are plentiful. In order to find these, scholars may have to read quantities of obscure material on subjects other than sermons and preachers. We have to rummage in city and other archives among unpublished minutiae. Above all, to inform ourselves on what was being said in the urban pulpits of Germany, we will have to become acquainted in detail with the milieu in each city and with the course of its Reformation. It is impossible to regard Güttel and even Hausmann as characteristic of Reformation preachers in Zwickau if one is aware of the complex, tension-laden course of events there. Whether this was also true of urban centers outside Saxony and Thuringia I must leave to colleagues with appropriate expertise. Johann Friedrich, nephew of Frederick the Wise and himself elector from 1532, described to Luther the situation in urban parishes in Ernestine lands in the middle of 1524:

> I lament to God that there are so many religious fanatics, which creates for us rulers a very great deal to do. I think, moreover, that they will not be stilled unless you take the time to travel from one city to another through the land (as Paul did) and see with what sort of preachers the cities of the faithful are provided. I believe that here in Thuringia you could do no more Christian deed. Whichever preachers you found unqualified, you could unseat with the help of the civil authority.[71]

Franz Lau grasped the early convolutedness of the religious landscape in German-speaking territories. He realistically saw that in the years before Luther's leadership became comparatively undisputed and his theology a touchstone and normative force for most evangelical sermons, preachers could not avoid enunciating individualistic views, even when they thought of themselves as Luther's disciples. One prominent by-product of the beginning Reformation was that it warmed hearts, stimulated minds, and opened mouths. Initially, an optimistic Luther himself urged everyone to read the Bible and let the power of the Word direct him. This every preacher believed himself to be doing, no matter that what issued forth sometimes turned out not to jibe with Luther's or even with any other major reformer's biblical perceptions. The wonder is that as many of Luther's ardent followers managed to agree with him as did, even before his faith was defined, its limits surveyed and staked out.

One of the strengths of Lau's work is that, despite his deep Lutheran faith, he could regard the events of the past dispassionately. Another is his impressive familiarity with many of the details of the religious flux of the early sixteenth century. Still a third is his common sense. In my judgment, all of these qualities compelled Lau to conclude that the early Reformation was a time of *Wildwuchs*, of the rapid and disorderly growth of the evangelical movement. If he were living today, it would be illuminating to discuss with him redefining the period of *Wildwuchs*: moving the opening date back, say, to 1518, when Luther's reputation began to grow, and ending with 1525, when, in Saxony and Thuringia, at any rate, magistrates and princes stepped in to direct religious belief. Lau is right; the early Reformation years *were* years of spontaneous religious individualism, years in which preaching posts were opportunities to display one's spiritual and worldly sensibilities. Among the early preachers were some of the most dynamic individuals of their cities, men whom those in authority thought they had to rein in.

If Lau remains a model to us, so certainly must Moeller. No book or article on the early modern German city fails to cite his essay, *Reichsstadt und Reformation*.[72] This study abounds with shrewd generalizations based on vast research, and it has had tremendous heuristic value to an entire generation. Another article of Moeller's has touched my own career as profoundly. I shall always remember as a graduate student in the late 1960s sitting in the reading room of the then British Museum with a copy of "Probleme der Reformationsgeschichtsforschung."[73] Moeller wrote, "In the last decades our research has been concentrated almost exclusively on Reformation *theology*. . . . Consequently, we have frequently lost sight of the Reformation as history, as an event of the distant past, and as a complex network of historical relationships."[74] I am convinced that just as we recall Lau today for the breadth of his knowledge and the accuracy of many of his conclusions about the spread of the Reformation, so must we honor Moeller for his keen and inspiring observations of the 1960s. I am also convinced that his assertions of 1984 bear the closest scrutiny.

NOTES

*Research for this article was financed by the International Research and Exchanges Board (IREX).

1. Jahrgang 75, 176-93.
2. Franz Lau and Ernst Bizer, "Reformationsgeschichte bis 1532," in *Reformationsgeschichte Deutschlands. Ein Handbuch* (Göttingen, 1964), 3-66.
3. Ibid., 19.
4. Ibid., 32-33.
5. Moeller, "Was wurde in der Frühzeit," 179, 181.
6. Ibid., 191.
7. Ibid., 193.
8. Ibid., 184.
9. Ibid., 192.
10. (Georg) Buchwald, "Die Lehre des Joh. Sylvius Wildnauer Egranus in ihrer Beziehung zur Reformation, dargestellt aus dessen Predigten," *Beiträge zur sächsischen Kirchengeschichte* 4(1888): 163-202.
11. Otto Clemen, "Eine merkwürdige Inschrift am Altar unserer Marienkirche," *Alt-Zwickau* 2(1929):8; Zwichau Stadtarchiv (hereafter ZSA), Ratsprotokolle (hereafter RP) 1519-1522, *1520*, fol. 12.
12. Buchwald, "Die Lehre des Joh. Sylvius," 170.
13. Ibid., 171-75.
14. Ibid., 178-79.
15. Ibid., 182.
16. Ibid., 195.
17. Ibid., 187.
18. Ibid., 189-90.
19. Ibid., 186.
20. Ibid., 199.
21. Ibid., 200-201. On Egranus's stay in Joachimsthal, see Heribert Sturm, *Skizzen zur Geschichte des Obererzgebirges im 16. Jahrhundert* (Stuttgart, 1965), 32.

22. J. K. Seidemann, *Thomas Müntzer* (Dresden and Leipzig, 1842), document 5c. For a fuller account of Müntzer's stay in Zwickau, see Susan C. Karant-Nunn, *Zwickau in Transition 1500-1547: The Reformation as an Agent of Change*, (Columbus, Ohio: 1987), chapter entitled "Humanist Oratory, Radical Revelation, Conciliar Resolve: The Coming of the Reformation."

23. On the relationship between Egranus and Müntzer, see Walter Elliger, *Thomas Müntzer, Leben und Werk*, 2d ed. (Göttingen, 1975), 132-66; and Steven E. Ozment, *Mysticism and Dissent: Religious Ideology and Social Protest in the Sixteenth Century* (New Haven, 1973), 61-68.

24. Paul Wappler, "Thomas Müntzer in Zwickau und die 'Zwickauer Propheten,'" *Wissenschaftliche Beilage zu dem Jahresberichte des Realgymnasiums mit Realschule zu Zwickau* (Zwickau, 1908), 12.

25. ZSA; RP 1519-1522, *1520*, fol 12.

26. Mark U. Edwards, Jr., *Luther and the False Brethren* (Stanford, 1975).

27. Dresden Staatsarchiv (hereafter DSA), Loc. 10327, "Wieder Täuffer zu Erfurth, Sachsenburg, Mülhausen, Der gefangenen Aussagen Dr. Johann Eck Schreiber, Thomas Muntzers Bekentnuss, Widerruff 1527 [sic]," fol. 15.

28. Weimar Staatsarchiv (hereafter WSA), Reg. Ii 245, fol. 32.

29. *D. Martin Luthers Werke* (Weimar, 1883-), *Briefwechsel 4*, 183. (Hereafter WA for Weimarer Ausgabe.)

30. Hermann Barge, *Andreas Bodenstein von Karlstadt*, vol. 1 (Leipzig, 1905).

31. Aemilius Ludwig Richter, *Die evangelischen Kirchenordnungen des sechszehnten Jahrhunderts*, 2 vols. (Weimar, 1871), 2, 484.

32. Barge, *Andreas Bodenstein*, vol. 1, 313-14, 362-64.

33. Ibid., 313.

34. Ibid., 313-14.

35. Ibid., 314.

36. WA, *Briefwechsel*, 2, no. 500, May 29, 1522.

37. Barge, *Andreas Bodenstein*, vol. 2, 95-143.

38. Ibid., vol. 2, 219.

39. WSA, Reg. Ii 198.

40. Sturm, *Skizzen*, 33; Barge, *Andreas Bodenstein*, vol 1, 197.

41. Barge, *Andreas Bodenstein*, vol. 2, 102, 139.

42. Otto Clemen, "Georg Amandus," *Beiträge zur sächsischen Kirchengeschichte* 14(1899):221-23; Felician Gess, "Die Anfänge der Reformation in Schneeberg," *Neues Archiv für sächsische Geschichte und Altertumskunde* 18(1897):esp. 37-49.

43. Zwickauer Ratsschulbibliothek XX. VII. 35[14], and XVII. XII. 4 [19].

44. *Historia Schneebergensis Renovata, Das ist: Erneuerte Stadt- und Berg-Chronica . . . Schneeberg* (Schneeberg, 1716), 298-99.

45. WSA, Reg. Ii 131, fol. 2; also WSA, Reg. N 35a, a report by Schneeberg's *Richter* of Amandus's utterances from the pulpit and of an early interview with the preacher.

46. Ibid., fol. 21. A complete list of the accusations leveled at Amandus along with his replies may be found in Felician Gess, ed., *Akten und Briefe zur Kirchenpolitik Herzog George von Sachsen*, vol. 2 (Leipzig, 1917), no. 868, 122-27, n. 1. Gess uses DSA, Loc. 4490, "Berghandlung quasimodogeniti auf den Ertz-Gebirgen ao. 1524-1533," fols. 79-94. An Ernestine copy of the questions without Amandus's replies is WSA, Reg. T 116, fols. 131-75.

47. WSA, Reg. Ii 131, fol. 27.

48. Ibid., fol. 21.

49. Ibid., fol. 27.

50. Ibid., fols. 21-22.

51. Ibid., fol. 28.

52. Ibid., fol. 22.

53. Ibid., fol. 30.

54. Ibid., fol. 24.

55. Ibid., fol. 30.

56. Ibid., fols. 5-6.

57. WSA, Reg. T 92, fols. 24-25; DSA, Loc. 4490, "Berghandlung . . . 1524-1532," fol. 120.

58. DSA, Loc. 4490, ibid.,; WSA, Reg. T 91, fol. 43.

59. DSA, Loc. 4490, ibid., fol. 104. Actually, assemblies were later allowed, as long as the city and mining officials gave prior permission and oversaw them.

60. Moeller, "Was wurde in der Frühzeit," 179, n. 9.

61. Joachim Rogge gives a careful summary of Strauss's life and writings in *Der Beitrag des Predigers Jakob Strauss zur frühen Reformationsgeschichte* (Berlin, 1957). On Strauss's writings, see especially 157-90. Rogge states categorically (29) that all the reformer's writings were based upon sermons he had given.

62. Ibid., 30.

63. WA 6, 1-9, 36-60. In 1540, Luther specifically supported paying interest to the reformed church for the use of its money (WA 51, 333).

64. A technical term referring to interest that was rendered to the church or others in perpetuity, that is, the debt was not paid off. Sometimes a church or city paid affluent individuals *widerkeuf* on money borrowed for ecclesiastical or civic purposes, but increasingly, both church and state preferred to take on debts that they would eventually reduce.

65. WSA, Reg. Ii 126, fol. 5.

66. Ibid., fol. 6.

67. Ibid.

68. WA, *Briefwechsel* 4, 116; WSA, Reg. N 821, fol. 30.

69. "Auffrur Zwitracht und Uneinigkeyt zwischen woren Evangelischen Christen für zu komen, kurtz auch unuberwindlich leer . . . 1525."

70. DSA, Loc. 10327, "Wider Täuffer zu Erfurth," fols. 13, 47.

71. WA, *Briefwechsel*, 3, 754.

72. Schriften des Vereins für Reformationsgeschichte, no. 180 (Gütersloh, 1962); translated as "Imperial Cities and the Reformation," in *Imperial Cities and the Reformation: Three Essays*, trans. H. C. Erik Midelfort and Mark U. Edwards, Jr. (Philadelphia, 1972).

73. *Zeitschrift für Kirchengeschichte*, ser. 4, 14(1965):246-57; translated as "Problems of Reformation Research," in *Imperial Cities and the Reformation*, ibid., 3-16.

74. From the English translation, ibid., 7.

Sebastian Castellio
and His Family

HANS R. GUGGISBERG

o the student of the sixteenth century, Sebastian Castellio is primarily known as Calvin's antagonist in the debate on the killing of heretics. This debate broke out, as everyone knows, after Michael Servetus had been burnt at the stake in Geneva on October 27, 1553. As editor and partial author of *De haereticis an sint persequendi* (published in March 1554), Castellio has become the first systematic advocate of religious toleration. He confirmed this reputation with a number of other writings, in which he repeated and elaborated his plea that men should never be put to death for religious reasons.

Castellio was also a humanist scholar of more than average importance. In his early years, he wrote Greek and Latin poems; later, he became an editor of numerous literary and historiographical works from Greek and Roman antiquity. Additionally, he wrote a school book for the combined instruction of Christian religion and classical Latin. Among the biblical scholars of his age he was unique in that he translated the Holy Scriptures not once but twice: first into humanist Latin, and then into the colloquial French of his Savoyard home country.

Through his many writings, Castellio became widely known, even in his lifetime. With some of them, however, he drew much hatred upon himself. Calvin, Beza, and other Reformed theologians attacked the former schoolmaster of Geneva repeatedly and relentlessly. His advocacy of toleration and his spiritualist thought appeared to them as a danger, and they considered him a traitor to their cause. In Basel, where he lived from the spring of 1545, he found some friends and influential protectors, but he nevertheless had to suffer discrimination there, too. The professorship of Greek at the university, to which he was appointed shortly before Servetus' death, released him from extreme poverty, but it did not bring peace to his life. He died at age forty-eight on December 29, 1563. Shortly before being stricken by his fatal illness, he had pondered the possibility of leaving Basel and emigrating to Poland.[1]

Although not all of his works are available in modern critical editions, it is relatively easy for the historian to familiarize himself with Castellio's thought and educational background. About his life and personality, on the other hand, we would like to know more. He is often mentioned by contemporaries, but many statements on him are distorted by hatred and prejudice. In the official documents relating to Basel's political and ecclesiastical history, he appears as one among many foreign refugee scholars who, although they enjoyed a certain amount of protection, were never really integrated into the urban community but always remained more or less on the fringes.

Of the domestic circumstances within which Castellio's daily life took place, we get only occasional glimpses. Neither in his writings nor in his personal letters does he say much about himself, except when he expounds his religious views.[2] One thing, however, emerges very clearly from these sources: his daily life was strongly influenced by the need to support a large family. Again and again, he appears to be very much attached not only to his wife and children but also to his brothers, sisters and kin. The scholar evidently took his domestic responsibilities very seriously.

What sort of family was the Chastillon, Castalio, or Castellio family? Where did it come from geographically and socially? How did it fare in Basel? What became of it after "Maystre Bastian's" death?[3]

Our knowledge is limited. Scattered information on the Castellio family can be found here and there in all kinds of sources, for example, in quite unexpected passages of Castellio's own works, in some of his letters, in letters of people who knew him, and in official documents. Ferdinand Buisson has brought forth many details, and in a more recent study Eugenie Droz added some interesting insights.[4] We shall present a few more facts, but our foremost aim is a different one: we would like to amalgamate the details into a more or less coherent picture and to find some systematic answers to the questions indicated earlier.

Our remarks will be divided into three parts. First, we shall deal with what is known about the origins of the Castellio family and about members of Sebastian's own generation. In the second part, we will take a look at the family's situation in Basel. Finally, we shall discuss the fate of some of Sebastian's children. The conclusion will contain a few general observations and an attempt to answer the question, Why do we know so little about the Castellio family?

Sebastian Castellio was born in 1515 in a small village, Saint-Martin-du-Fresne, situated in the territory of Bugey; that is, in the northwestern corner of the Duchy of Savoy, not far from the towns of Bourg-en-Bresse and Nantua. The only ancestor who emerges from anonymity is his father, a farmer of modest means whose name was probably Claude Chastillon.[5] In one of his later writings, Sebastian was to describe him very respectfully as an uneducated but honest and god-fearing man who loathed both larceny and mendacity.[6] Sebastian's mother, the farmer's wife, remains unknown. His parents had many children, some of whom can be identified, although their birthdates remain unknown. Sebastian had at least three sisters and three brothers. Whereas his parents never seem to have moved away from Saint-Martin-du-Fresne and probably remained faithful members of the Catholic church, most of the children left the village and sooner or later turned toward Protestantism. Sebastian seems to have been the only one to acquire a formal education. Between 1535 and 1540, he attended the "Collège de la Trinité" in Lyon. During these years, he also became acquainted with the ideas of the Reformation.[7] In 1540, he moved to Strasbourg and then to Geneva.

We observe that all of his three sisters appear in or near Geneva after 1540, too; they seem to have remained in touch with their brother. In 1542, Etiennette married one of Sebastian's "bacheliers" (subinstructors) at the Collège du Rive, Pierre Mossard (or Moussart), who came from La Charité-sur-Loire. He became a citizen of Geneva in 1553 and also taught school at Morges. Their daughter Anne was "Maystre Bastian's" godchild but died at age 19.[8] Sebastian's second sister, Jeannette, also seems to have settled in Geneva, although she may have arrived there considerably later. She was married to Evrard Vogiez (or Vouzie), a carpenter from Nantua who appears in the Geneva records as a "réfugié" after 1550.[9] They, too, had a daughter, Jeanne. Jeannette died in 1553 and her husband three years later. Jeanne was left an orphan at an early age, but we shall hear from her again.[10] The name of Sebastian's third sister was also Jeanne, and she must not be confused with Jeannette or her daughter. She was the wife of Matthieu Eyssautier (also Essautier or Yssotier), a preacher of anti-Calvinist inclinations who had been active in Provence and, in 1562, was a minister at Gex near Geneva. In the following year, he was rebuked by the Consistory for having read and distributed his brother-in-law's *Conseil à la France désolée*.[11] His wife had been summoned before the same body already in 1561 for having propagated another tract of Sebastian Castellio.[12] Matthieu and Jeanne Eyssautier had at least three children: Jean, Marc, and Marthe. Jean became a merchant in Geneva.[13]

The names of Sebastian's three known brothers were Pierre, Monet, and Michel. Of Pierre, we know very little except that he was the father of Michel Chastillon, who worked as a blacksmith in Geneva, was admitted to citizenship in 1562, and also became involved in the conflicts about the distribution of the *Conseil à la France désolée*.[14] It remains uncertain whether his father Pierre ever moved from Saint-Martin-du-Fresne. He may well have stayed there as a farmer.[15] Monet had become a citizen of Geneva by 1553. He is mentioned as "fils de feu Claude, de Saint-Martin-du-Fresne," and he also seems to have earned his living as a blacksmith.[16]

Michel is better known. In order not to confuse him with his nephew, Michel the blacksmith, we call him Michel the printer. He did not live in Geneva but in Lyon. Whether he was an independent printer we do not know.[17] We do know, however, that he was arrested and imprisoned in 1557 for having printed a tract by Sebastian Castellio on predestination and by having allegedly expressed his intention also to print a book of Servetus.[18] This is gloatingly reported by Beza in a letter to Guillaume Farel on August 2, 1557.[19] We also know that, after his release from prison, Michel the printer married a woman named Marie Françoise Roybet, the widow and heiress of another printer and keeper of a tavern. The marriage did not last long, however. Michel was very ill and died in December 1557, whereupon Marie Françoise married her third printer.[20] On January 25, 1558, she wrote a rather remarkable letter to Sebastian Castellio in Basel.

This letter is interesting for several reasons. First, it is an illustrative example of how an uneducated but intelligent and literate sixteenth-century Frenchwoman of the urban middle class expressed herself in writing. Then, it reveals the existence of relationships to friends who had been helpful to her during her second husband's illness. In addition, it enlightens us on Castellio's own contacts with relatives and friends in Lyon. Marie Françoise reports Michel's death, but she does not mention her third marriage. She mentions, on the other hand, that she and Michel had looked after Jeanne, the orphan (Jeannette's daughter), and that the girl is still living in her house. She sends greetings to Jean Bauhin, the French physician in Basel, who is an old friend of Sebastian and has often come to Lyon. Finally, she assures her former brother-in-law that she would like to see him again sometime and that she is willing to take care of everything he would like her to do on his behalf in Lyon.[21]

Eugenie Droz has shown that Marie Françoise Roybet stood at the center of a "petit monde fermé" of Lyon printers, other artisans, and occasional intellectuals. Many of these people came from the same region as the Castellio family. Some were related to the Basel professor, all of them shared his religious views and his anti-Calvinism. A few corresponded with him, such as Guillaume Constantin, who was the cousin of Sebastian's second wife, and "Maystre Jehan," whom Droz identifies as Jean de Tournes, the well-known printer.[22] Guillaume Constantin very clearly regarded the Basel professor as his spiritual leader.[23] He was the one to arrange for Jeanne, the orphan, to be brought to Basel so that she could grow up in her learned uncle's house and get a decent education under his supervision.[24]

The "petit monde fermé" was in fact a circle of "Castellionists" guided by a nucleus of Sebastian's relatives. The members of the group were all modest people without much formal education or wealth. It is perhaps no accident that Jean de Tournes defected after a relatively short time. Castellio himself seems to have been eager to keep up his contacts. He seems to have visited some of his Lyon disciples at least once. This must have been in 1557, but it is doubtful that he went to see them in the city of Lyon itself.[25]

We now turn to Sebastian Castellio's own ménage. He was married twice. His first wife, Huguine Paquelon was the daughter of Ami Paquelon, a tailor from the Dauphiné who had become a "bourgeois" of Geneva in 1521. The date of her marriage to "Maystre Bastian" is unknown, but it must have taken place in the early 1540s, when her husband was still teaching school in

Geneva. She moved to Basel with him in 1544 and died there in 1549.[26] They had three children: Susanna (b. 1544), Debora (b. 1547, d. 1549), and Nathanael (b. 1549). Only the first daughter was born in Geneva. Therefore, it would be incorrect to state that Castellio had a large family when he came to Basel; but, during the difficult years when he worked for the printer Oporinus and earned very little money, his family grew steadily. The months immediately following Huguine's death must have been particularly hard on him. Susanna became ill and lost her hair in February; in May, Debora died; and shortly afterwards Nathanael, whose birth brought on his mother's death, seemed to have reached the end of his own life, too. But, both Susanna and Nathanael eventually recovered. On June 20, 1549, Castellio wrote to his Spanish friend Francisco de Enzinas, "I thank God who, when he sends calamities, also sends the strength to endure them. Today I got married again. I pray that I may look forward to happier times." In quite characteristic fashion, he added, "I have just finished the Latin translation of the Bible. Now I shall start on the French translation."[27]

Of Castellio's second wife Maria, we only know the first name.[28] We do not know where she came from, except that she, too, had relatives in Lyon. She and Castellio had five more children: Anna (b. 1551), Barbara (b. 1552), Sara (b. 1554), Bonifacius (b. 1558), Thomas (b. 1559 or 1560), and Frederick (b. 1562, d. 1613). In 1558, Sebastian's niece Jeanne was taken into the family, which meant nine children to feed, clothe, and care for. In addition to this, Castellio often accommodated foreign students in his house. Most of these were paying guests, but they also demanded attention, care, and sometimes supervision.

On the whole, we know very little about the daily life of the family. Because Castellio was rarely away from Basel, there was no need for him to exchange letters with his wives. His children began to leave the house only after his death. When he died, his oldest daughter was just nineteen years old. There are a few testimonies to the fact that Castellio was a man of very strict moral standards who selected his lodgers very carefully. He demanded that they did not swear in his house, that they did not say anything in his absence they would not say in his presence, and that they did not look with "French eyes" at his wife and children. He was known as a very learned man who tended to lead a secluded life but did not disdain manual work. Moreover, Calvin's nonconformist critic had the reputation of being a very pious person, who imposed strict religious discipline upon his family. Thus, it was understandable that foreign visitors were sometimes reluctant to take lodgings in his house. Charles Utenhove, a Flemish student who later became a noted humanist scholar, protested that he did not want to live with Castellio: "The man is certainly learned and pious, but with so much piety we would hardly dare to live. And what would we become in the world if we had nothing but piety?[29]

It is not surprising to observe that Castellio was very much concerned about the education of his children. In his will, he expressed the wish that they should all learn German and French. He also provided that all of them should learn a craft in order to be able to support themselves with manual labor. In addition to this, he admonished his wife and children to abide in the faith, to observe God's commandments, and never to forget that He is the father of all widows and orphans.[30]

As far as we know, the Castellio family lived in two different Basel houses. In the 1550s, they occupied a house on the southern bank of the Rhine near the church of the former monastery of St. Alban, in the neighborhood of paper mills and other manufacturing establishments and not far from where the Birs river flows into the Rhine. The exact location of the house cannot be identified, and we have to assume that Castellio had rented it or at least part of it. He mentions it only once, in a well-known passage of his *Defensio ad authorem libri cui titulus est, Calumniae nebulonis*, a tract he wrote against Calvin in 1558. Here, he describes how, as a resident of the riverbank, he sometimes went out with others to collect driftwood when the Rhine threatened to overflow. He defends himself against the accusation of stealing wood, which the Geneva reformer had hurled at him.[31] It seems that, in the course of the years, the house in the St. Alban section became too small for the growing family. On February 14, 1559, Castellio bought a house in the Steinenvorstadt; here, he was to live until his death. The house no longer exists, but its location is clearly established.[32] The Steinenvorstadt was not one of Basel's more fashionable sections either; it was the street in which the weavers had their shops, and it belonged to the parish of St. Leonhard. Its inhabitants generally were not wealthy, and they were known to tend toward unrest and opposition against the authorities.[33]

In Basel, Castellio always remained a foreigner. He never sought to obtain citizenship, and he never seems to have acquired more than a fragmentary command of the German language.[34] We have seen that he wanted his children to be better integrated in the German-speaking urban community. He was also concerned that they should enjoy the protection of influential people in their later lives. This he sought to ensure by providing them with adequate godfathers and godmothers. Among them, we find the printer Jerome Froben, Thomas Platter, the theologians Siman Sulzer and Martin Borrhaus, and the eminent Bonifacius Amerbach. Some of these men had been closely associated with Erasmus of Rotterdam, who Castellio had never been able to meet. He also selected some foreigners as godfathers, such as Jean Bauhim, the Marchese d'Oria, and the Dutch Anabaptist Nicolas Blesdijk, who had been a disciple of David Joris. Among the women he asked to act as godmothers were Barbara Froben, Jerome's wife, and Agnes, the daughter of Celio Secondo Curione.[35]

Although the willingness to be godfather or godmother to a newborn child may often not have meant much more than a gesture of goodwill toward the parent, this list of names clearly show in which circles of Basel Castellio was known and respected. Among his best friends were refugees like himself, but he very evidently also sought the friendship of some of Basel's leading citizens.

Bonifacius Amerbach had been Castellio's benefactor all along. He had supported him financially on more than one occasion, and in 1546 or 1547, he had hired him as tutor of his son Basilius. On more than one occasion also, Castellio had expressed his gratitude to the elder Amerbach. The ties between the two families were to remain strong even after the Savoyard scholar's death.[36]

When he wrote his testament in 1560, Castellio designated Jean Bauhin and Johannes Brandmüller as "tuteurs," that is guardians, of his wife and children, ". . . asking them to take charge of my family because we are friends in Christ, and I hope that they will do it."[37]

Jean Bauhin (1511-1582), whom we have already mentioned, was probably the closest friend Castellio and his family had in Basel. He was not a very influential man, but he was a francophone, a neighbor or co-tenant in the house on the bank of the Rhine and as such always extremely helpful. He came from

Amiens, had left France as a Protestant in 1538 and since 1541 lived in Basel as a medical practitioner. In the 1540s he had also worked as a corrector for the printing firm of Froben and Episcopius, and in this capacity he had become acquainted with Castellio. In the history of medicine he is remembered mainly as the father of the two eminent physicians Jean II and Caspar Bauhin.[38]

Johannes Brandmüller (1533-1596) was much younger than Castellio. He had been born in the Swabian town of Biberach, had studied at Tübingen and Basel and eventually was to become a professor of Old Testament at the University of Basel. When he was associated with the Castellio family he still was a preacher at St. Theodor, a supervisor of students in the "lower college" and a lecturer of rhetoric.

While Bauhin's activities as a guardian of the Castellio family can be traced here and there, not much is known of Brandmüller in this respect. Both men, however, also seemed to have shared Castellio's religious views.[39]

The same can be assumed of Basilius Amerbach (1534-1591), Castellio's former pupil, who became a worthy successor of his father as a jurist and teacher of jurisprudence. In his testament Castellio had originally put down Basilius' name as a "tuteur" and then replaced it by that of Brandmüller. This may have happened because in 1560 Basilius Amerbach was away from Basel: he was finishing his studies and taking his doctoral degree at Bologna.[40] When he came back he resumed his close association with Castellio. Although not officially designated as such, in fact he became the most active guardian of his former teacher's children.

Quite obviously, the circle of those who were associated with the Castellio family was much wider than that of the more or less official protectors. It consisted of foreign students and scholars, but also of academic and non-academic townspeople. Many of those friends, colleagues and acquaintances can be identified. Among them were a considerable number of people who agreed with Castellio's religious and intellectual views, and particularly with his critical attitude toward doctrinal hairsplitting, dogmatic authority and intolerance. In addition to those already mentioned, there were the scholars, Curione, Felix Platter, Theodor Zwinger, and printers, Oporinus and Pietro Perna. Among the academic friends of Castellio and his family, there were quite a few who belonged to the younger generation, that is, to the generation born in the 1530s. But we must not forget that not everybody in Basel liked Castellio. He encountered suspicion especially among the Reformed ministers, and the discrimination which came from them very naturally also affected his family.[41]

His death brought the threat of poverty again upon his wife and children. But now his guardians and other friends at the university moved in efficiently. They were able to have Castellio's family freed from the customary fees which had to be paid by non-citizens on such occasions. A little later they also succeeded in convincing the city government to admit all the sons and daughters of the Savoyard scholar to citizenship.[42]

None of Castellio's children became as famous (or as notorious) as the father. We do not know the biographies of all of them, but in some cases we can catch at least a glimpse of what they did in their later lives. Here and there we can also observe how, and to what extent, they came up to their father's expectations.

Of his four sons, only two are known to have taken up university studies. Nathanael matriculated at the University of Basel in the academic year 1563/64, probably shortly before his father's death. He did not pay any fees "because of poverty" ("propter paupertatum").[43] After that, he almost immediately disappears from all records, and we do not know what became of him. One thing, however, is clearly established: at age fourteen or fifteen Nathanael Castellio was already a dexterous copyist of some of his father's letters and other texts which otherwise would not have been preserved.[44] He must have conducted his own correspondence at the same time. On August 19, 1564 his cousin Jean Eyssautier (the son of the pastor at Gex) sent him a belated and somewhat formal, but nevertheless quite moving letter of condolence for his father's death. Jean Eyssautier worked at that time for a merchant in Geneva. The letter is another testimony to the simple and straight-forward piety which prevailed among the relatives of Sebastian Castellio.[45]

Frederick (Fridericus) Castellio, Sebastian's youngest son, appears in the Basel university registers in the year 1580/81. He was then eighteen years old and had already spent some time at the University of Tübingen. He is the only one among Castellio's children whose career can be followed until his death. He passed the customary exams in the Basel arts faculty and eventually fulfilled pastoral duties in several villages around the city. In 1589 he was appointed to the chair of rhetoric at the university; six years later he was moved to the chair of eloquence, and from 1610 to his death in 1613 he served again as professor of rhetoric.[46] Frederick Castellio was not an original thinker and does not seem to have been strongly affected by the religious issues of his time (while he was active as a preacher and teacher, reformed orthodoxy gained its final victory in Basel),[47] Still, he was not entirely neutral. On a few occasions his sympathy for anti-Calvinist causes became visible.[48] In February, 1592, he was accused before the minister's convention of translating some of his father's writings. The validity of this charge has never been established with certainty. There is great probability, however, that he edited German translations of two works of the radical French refugee Antoine Lescaille who stirred up controversy in Basel at the same time.[49] On the whole, however, Frederick Castellio's scholarly achievements remained rather modest.[50] When he died, the name of his family vanished not only from the university but also from the city records. He does not seem to have any descendants. In only one respect did he surpass his father: he spoke and wrote fluent German.

Perhaps the most unusual insights into the "every day history" of the Castellio family after Sebastian's death can be gained from three letters of his youngest daughter Sara. These letters were written between 1578 and 1580 when Sara was 24-26 years old. They are unusual not only because they are by a young woman, but also because their author was at that time working in the rather lowly position of a maidservant far from home.

Together with her brother Bonifacius, Sara had been sent abroad at least as early as 1577. It is quite possible that the guardians of the Castellio family found places of work for them with people who had personal contacts with the city of Basel, and perhaps with Castellio himself. In 1577, Sara and Bonifacius were staying in or near Ghent. The Charles Utenhove who had been unwilling to live in Castellio's house as a student, but later had become an ardent admirer of the Savoyard scholar, mentions his teacher's children in a letter to Jean Bauhin of September 10, 1577. He points to the fact that Sara has just left for Basel and will inform Bauhin shortly about her work, while her brother is still living with a merchant in Ghent and learning a great deal.[51]

Later in the same year, the two young people seem to have moved to Duisburg on the Ruhr in the Duchy of Cleve, then the domicile of many radical Protestants, particularly of Anabaptists and adherents of the "Family of Love."[52] It is from there that we now hear from Sara herself. Her letters are written in fluent and correct if somewhat complicated German. They show that she had some careful basic instruction and that she had learned the language well while growing up in Basel. Her handwriting is regular and relatively easy to read.

The letter of March 3, 1578, is addressed to Basilius Amerbach whom Sara very respectfully calls "dear Mr. Guardian" ("Lieber herfockt"). She reports that she has recently returned from Basel to Duisburg and that the lady in whose house she works ("mein frauw") was glad to have her back. Unfortunately, we have not been able to identify this woman. Sara goes on to say that on her journey she stopped at Strasbourg where she wanted to visit her brother Thomas but could not find him: "and from my brother Thomas I did not hear anything; I looked for him everywhere in Strasbourg, but I could not find him." This is one of the very rare references to this otherwise totally unknown son of Sebastian Castellio who must have been an artisan's or merchant's apprentice at that time. Sara then expresses concern about her other brother Bonifacius. She does not mention his name here but doubtlessly refers to him who is with her in Duisburg. Bonifacius suffers from an inflammation in one eye, and she searched for a remedy during her recent visit to Basel. Now her Duisburg landlady has given her some advice, and she wishes to transmit it to Basilius Amerbach because she thinks that the treatment may be helpful to others. In the postscript she describes it in detail, but we do not have to follow her there. It mainly consists of compresses with a concoction of liquid white-of-egg and mother's milk.[53]

The second letter is not dated but must have been written at about the same time, or a little earlier. Here Sara speaks to her mother, "to the honored woman Maria, widow of the pious Sebastianus Castalionus." According to the address Castellio's widow no longer lived in the Steinenvorstadt, but in Dr. Bauhin's house. The letter is quite long and dominated by one theme: it is a testimony of a daughter's affection for her mother, of a feeling of close relationship in spite of separation, and of the consciousness of being united in the faith. As in other letters from the Castellio family and from the circle of friends surrounding it we find here again the expression of strong and simple piety, not elaborately and certainly not elegantly formulated, but put into honest and straight-forward words.

Sara speaks of her own good fortune and implies that she

likes her work in Duisburg. Nevertheless, she is not free from occasional pangs of homesickness. She would like to be with her
brothers and sisters in Basel, but above all she longs to see her
mother again. She reports that Bonifacius is well. He now works
in Duisburg as a tailor: "he is a tailor, and I hear nothing else about
him except that he works well and diligently." Sara makes it clear
that she and her brother get along well. Both of them would like
to visit their family, but if it cannot be they will accept God's will.
One thing worries Sara: she has not heard from her mother in a
long time. She therefore asks her to have someone write a short
letter on her behalf. This seems to imply that Castellio's widow
could not write herself, either because she could not write, or
because she was physically unable to do so. The letter closes with
greetings to the family and "to all the friends" in Basel.[54]

The third letter was written on July 15, 1580. Again the ad-
dressee is Basilius Amerbach, "beyder Rechten Doctor." He could
see that Sara did not really feel at home in Duisburg, although she
was not unhappy. Thus, Sara states, she has decided to leave
Duisburg at the time of the next Frankfurt fair, "because I do not
intend to stay in this country for my whole life, and because time
passes quickly." She plans to return to Basel permanently, and
asserts that Bonifacius also plans to return to Basel but that he may
not travel with her.[55]

This is the last we hear from Sara. We know she eventually
returned to Basel and married a printer named Georg Müssner in
1594.[56] From the glimpses her letters allow she was strongly attached to her family, and a caring and reliable person. In this she
clearly fulfilled the expectations her father had set down in his
testament.

We have surveyed three generations of the Castellio family:
that of his parents, his own and that of his children. To conclude,
we can assert that it was not a conspicuous family. Within three
generations it rose out of anonymity, became well known, largely
because of one single member, and then sank back into anonymity again. It was a family of peasants and artisans. The (partial) transition from rural to urban life can be clearly observed in the second generation. Academic education was and remained rare.
However, some of the family members who were not formally
educated, appear directly or indirectly to have been well informed people who traveled, spoke more than one language and
even wrote occasional letters.

The social position of the Castellio family in Basel was

modest. If it remained on the fringes of the urban community this was because it was foreign, non-conformist in religious matters, and not well-to-do. The fact that Sebastian's children spoke German and became citizens does not seem to have changed much in this respect, particularly because some of them were away from Basel for extended periods of time, or left the city altogether. The only one who attained a certain amount of local prestige was Frederick.

That Sebastian Castellio and his children enjoyed the protection of the members of Basel's social and political elite was certainly an essential precondition for their careers, but it did not basically alter the family's social status.

The members of the Castellio family held together firmly even if they lived far from each other. Communication between Basel, Geneva, Lyon, Savoy, Lower Germany and the Netherlands remained lively until about 1580. They were often animated by traveling friends and acquaintances who transmitted news or carried letters. By the end of the 16th century the surviving family members were scattered widely throughout Europe.[57] On the whole, the family did not show much social mobility in the vertical sense. Its mobility was rather horizontal.

To the question as to why we know relatively little about the daily life of the three generations of Castellio's family there is a very obvious answer: they were all humble people, unobtrusive, discreet and cautious. All of them knew what poverty, discrimination and persecution meant. Even those who knew something of the world did not write extensively. The few who did were exceptions. The greatest exception of them all, of course, was Sebastian Castellio himself. But even he did not write much about his own life and personal circumstances. Many of his ideas can, however, be better understood if one takes into account the kind of family from which he came.

NOTES

1. The most comprehensive biography of Sebastian Castellio is still that of Ferdinand Buisson, *Sébastien Castellion, sa vie et son oeuvre, 1515-1563*, 2 vols. (Paris, 1892: repr. Nieuwkoop, 1964), (hereafter Buisson I or II). For a brief survey of more recent literature on Castellio, see H. R. Guggisberg, "Castellio, Sebastian," *Theologische Realenzyklopädie* (TRE), 7 (Berlin, 1981), 663 ff., and *Basel in the Six-*

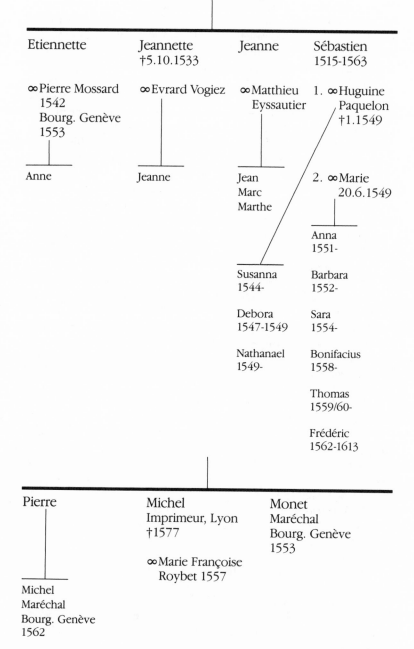

Claude Chastillon

Etiennette	Jeannette †5.10.1533	Jeanne	Sébastien 1515-1563
∞ Pierre Mossard 1542 Bourg. Genève 1553	∞ Evrard Vogiez	∞ Matthieu Eyssautier	1. ∞ Huguine Paquelon †1.1549
Anne	Jeanne	Jean Marc Marthe	2. ∞ Marie 20.6.1549

Anna
1551-

Susanna   Barbara
1544-   1552-

Debora   Sara
1547-1549   1554-

Nathanael   Bonifacius
1549-   1558-

Thomas
1559/60-

Frédéric
1562-1613

Pierre	Michel Imprimeur, Lyon †1577	Monet Maréchal Bourg. Genève 1553
Michel Maréchal Bourg. Genève 1562	∞ Marie Françoise Roybet 1557	

teenth Century: Aspects of the City Republic Before, During, and After the Reformation (St. Louis, 1982), 55 ff.

2. A considerable number of personal letters to and from Castellio were published in Buisson II, 381-476. Not much additional material has been discovered since. Unfortunately, however, Buisson often failed to present the complete texts. He also committed a number of errors. When quoting from Castellio's correspondence one still has to refer to the manuscripts themselves whenever possible.

3. The French form of the name was Chastillon or Chasteillon. As a young humanist scholar, Sebastian called himself Castalio, in memory of the well at Delphi. In Basel, while writing against the Geneva reformers, he changed his name to Castellio, but contemporaries kept calling him Castalio; his children also used this form of the name. He appears in some Geneva records as Maystre Bastian; cf. Buisson I, 181, 186 f.

4. Buisson I, 180 ff., 230 ff., 269 ff.; Eugenie Droz, "Castellioniana," *Chemins de l'hérésie*, II (Geneva, 1971), 325-432. In addition, see the brief note by Eugene Ritter, "Les parents de Castellion," *Bulletin de la société de l'histoire du protestantisme français* 46 (1897):187-89; 391-92.

5. See page 156.

6. "Nam hoc habuit meus pater boni, quamvis in magna religionis ignarantia, ut a furto, et mendacio in primis, et ipse abhorreret, et abhorrendum doceret. Itaque erat nobis vulgo me peruo, in ore hoc nostrate proverbium: *Ou prendre, ou rendre, ou les peines d'enfers attendre.*" Cf. "Defensio ad authorem libri, cui titulus est, Calumniae Nebulonis" (written in September, 1558), in *Sebastiani Castellionis Dialogi quatuor . . .* (Aresdorffii, per Theophil. Philadelph. [= Basel: Pietro Perna], 1578, 14 f).

7. L. Gerig, "Le Collège de la Trinite a Lyon avant 1540," *Revue de la Renaissance* 9 (1908): 73-94.

8. Buisson I, 181: *Le Livre des bourgeois de l'ancienne république de Genève*, ed. A. L. Covelle (Geneva, 1856), 239.

9. Buisson II, 273; *Livre des habitants de Genève*, ed. P. F. Geisendorf, vol. 1 (Geneva, 1957), 19.

10. See page 157.

11. Buisson II, 225 f.; *Registres de la Compagnie des pasteurs de Genève au temps de Calvin*, vol. 2, eds. R. M. Kingdon and J. F. Bergier (Geneva, 1962), 97 f.

12. Buisson II, 254.

13. Ritter, "Les parents," 188, also points out that Jeanne expressed pretensions of aristocratic descent and that in some records she appears as "noble." There seems to be no possibility, however, of linking the Chastillon family of Saint-Martin-du Fresne with the aristocratic Bugey family de Chastillon de Michaille. On Jean Eyssautier, cf. Buisson II, 274 f.

14. *Livre des bourgeois*, 274; Buisson II, 225.

15. Buisson II, 273, n. 1.

16. *Livre des bourgeois*, 239.

17. J. Baudrier, *Bibliographie lyonnaise*, I (Lyon, 1895), 92.

18. Buisson II, 108; Droz (see note 4), 355 ff.

19. *Correspondance de Théodore de Bèze*, II, eds. Hippolyte Aubert et al. (Geneva, 1962), 83.

20. Droz, "Castellioniana," 357.

21. Basel, Universitäts-Bibliothek (hereafter BUB), Ms. G2 I 23f, fol. 32. The letter is partly reproduced (with some errors of transcription) in Buisson II, 434 f. A much better and complete reproduction appears in Droz, "Castellioniana," 358 f.

22. Droz, ibid., 357 ff.; 397. On other Lyon printers who either went to Basel for religious reasons, or were in contact with Basel printers and scholars, see Natalie Z. Davis, "Holbein's Pictures of Death and the Reformation at Lyon," *Studies in the Renaissance* 3(1956):97-130, and "The Sacred and the Body Social in Sixteenth-Century Lyon," *Past and Present* 90(1981):40-70; see also Peter G. Bietenholz, *Basle and France in the Sixteenth Century* (Geneva, 1971), 218 ff.

23. BUB, Ms. G²I 23f, fol. 21; Buisson II, 430: here Constantin asked Castellio to send him a confession of faith. Castellio complied with this wish in a long letter that has been preserved in a manuscript copy by his son Nathanael: Rotterdam, Gemeentebibliotheek, Remonstrantse Kerk 505; Buisson II, 431 ff.

24. BUB, Ms. G²I 23f, 17, 18 (letters of August 7 and 17, 1588): Buisson II, 437 f.

25. See Constantin's letter mentioned in note 23; Droz, "Castellioniana," 378.

26. Buisson I, 181 f. Castellio's correspondence with Huguine's half-brother Jacques on the dowry is discussed there. Cf. BUB Ms. G²I 23f, fol. 25; Calvin to Pierre Viret, August 19, 1542, in: *Joanni Calvini Opera*, eds. G. Baum et al., vol. XI (Brunsvigae, 1873), 427 f.

27. Strasbourg, Archives et bibliotheques de la ville (Arch. de St. Thomas), F II, fol. 69; Buisson II, 411.

28. When, in 1559, Castellio bought a house in the Steinenvorstadt in Basel (see page 162), the contract stated that "Hans Scheltner un seine Frau Ellspetha, verkaufen an Sebastiano Castalione, Professor einer loblichen Universitat und jnwoner zu Basel, und seine Frau Maria Andre, das Haus und Hofstatt in Steinenvorstatt." This is the only instance in which Castellio's second wife is not simply called Maria. Whether Andre was her maiden name or a second Christian name remains unclear. Basel, Staats-Archiv (hereafter StAB), Historisches Grundbuch, Steinenvorstadt, alte Nr. 775, neue Nr. 26, Contract of February 14, 1559.

29. V. L. Saulnier, "Castellion, Jean Rouxel, et les oracles sibyllins,"

in *Autour de Michel Servet et de Sébastien Castellion*, ed. B. Becker (Haarlem, 1953), 225-243, esp. 226 f.; 230; Buisson II, 89.

30. "Le testament de Sebastian Chateillon" (signed December 4, 1569 and November 1, 1563), Rotterdam, Gemeentebibliotheek, Remonstrantse Kerk, ms. 506; Buisson II, 271 f.

31. "Defensio ad authorem libri," 12-13.

32. See note 28.

33. H. R. Guggisberg and H. Füglister, "Die Basler Weberzunft als Trägerin reformatorischer Propaganda," in *Stadt und Kirche im 16. Jahrhundert*, ed. B. Moeller (Gütersloh, 1978), 48-56.

34. Buisson II, 92.

35. The names of the godfathers and godmothers are listed in the baptismal registers of St. Martin, St. Alban, and St. Leonhard, StAB Kirchenarchiv W 12, 1, Fo. 65v (Debora), 72v (Nathanael); X8, 1, fols. 87v (Anna), 93r (Barbara), 99v (Sara), 119v (Bonifacius); BB 23, p. 277 (Frederick). A table is given in Buisson II, 276 ff., n. 3, but we do not need to reproduce it here. Only one point must be mentioned: the son Bonifacius was not given that name in honor of Bonifacius Amerbach but of Giovanni Bonifacio, Marchese d'Oria, the prominent Italian refugee who stayed in Basel for several months in 1557-1558 and during that time acted as godfather to Bonifacius Castellio.

36. On the relationship between Castellio and Bonifacius Amerbach, see the remarks of R. B. Jenny in *Die Amerbachkorrespondenz*, vol. 4 (Basel, 1967), 366-368. Amerbach had also helped Castellio purchase his house in 1559.

37. "les priant d'en prendre la charge e par l'amitie que nous nous portons en Christ, esperant qu'ils le feront," "Le testament."

38. *Die Matrikel der Universität Basel*, ed. H. G. Wackernagel, vol. 2 (Basel, 1956), 89 (hereafter Matr. Bas. II).

39. Ibid., 71.

40. Ibid., 61.

41. Buisson II, 103 ff., 243 ff.

42. Buisson II, 275 f.

43. Matr. Bas. II, 151.

44. Rotterdam, Gemeentebibliotheek, Remonstrantse Kerk, ms. 505. Several pieces of this fascicle are in Nathanael's handwriting. The testament (ms. 506), however, is preserved in Sebastian Castellio's own handwriting.

45. BUB, Ms. G2 I 23 f, fol. 24: Buisson II, 274 f.

46. Matr. Bas. II, 280. On his correspondence with Thomas Platter and Basilius Amerbach, cf. Buisson II, 281 ff.

47. Guggisberg, *Basel in the Sixteenth Century*, 47 f.

48. On October 24, 1589, he had been forced officially to declare his conformity with the Basel confession. StAB, Kirchenarchiv D I, 1 (Acta ecclesiastica, 1585-1601), 127.

49. StAB, Kirchenarchiv D 1, 1 (Acta ecclesiastica 1586-1601), 232,

anno 1592 conventus 153, 4 februarii: "Magister Frid. Castalio graviter admonitus de peccato, quod commisit vertendo scripta quedam Lescalii et partem Dialogorum patris de libero arbitrio, qui non sine consilio olim a Magistratu fuere suppressi." The titles of Lescaille's books that Frederick Castellio seems to have translated are: *Die alte Lehr von dem ersten, andern und dritten oder letzten Gericht* (s. 1. [Montbéliard, Strasbourg?], 1591); *Protestatio A. Lescallei wider die Kuetischen inquisition* (s. 1. [ibid.?], 1591). These writings were directed against Jaques Couet, the Calvinist pastor of the French church of Basel from 1588 to 1608. Probably as a punishment, Frederick Castellio also had to translate one of Couet's tracts: *Christliche und dieser Zeit notwendige Antwort* (Basel: Claude de Marne, Jean Aubry, 1599); Bietenholz, *Basel and France*, 98 ff., 279 (no. 329). Cf. StAB, Handel u. Gewerbe JJJ6, fols. r-v (December 4, 1603). I am grateful to Carlos Gilly for having drawn my attention to these documents and books.

50. A somewhat surprising literary activity was his collaboration in preparing a German translation of *Amadis de Gaula*, the famous Spanish romance of chivalry. This project was organized by Jacques Foillet, a French printer who had shops in Basel and Montbéliard. For him Frederick Castellio translated books 20 and 21 of *Amadis de Gaula* from French (not from the Spanish or Italian originals!) into German. They appeared in Montbeliard in 1593. Cf. Carlos Gilly, *Spanien und der Basler Buchdruck bis 1600* (Basel and Frankfurt am Main, 1985), 133 f; Hilkert Weddige, *Die "Historien vom Amadis Auss Frankreich." Dokumentarische Grundlegung zur Entstehung und Rezeption.* Beiträge zur Literatur des XV. bis XVII. Jahrhunderts 2 (Wiesbaden, 1975), 81 ff. On other translations Frederick Castellio did for Jacques Foillet, see also Bietenholz, *Basel and France*, 78.

51. BUB, Ms. Ki. Ar. 18a 3, fol. 402. For Bauhin's reply, cf. Buisson II, 278.

52. Buisson II, 280.

53. BUB, Ms. G II 29^1, fol. 56.

54. BUB, Ms. G II 33^1, fols. 27-28.

55. BUB, Ms. G II 29^1, fol. 57.

56. Felix Platter, *Beschreibung der Stadt Basel 1610 und Pestbericht*, ed. Valentin Lotscher (Basel, 1987), 428, no. 2158.

57. Ritter, 189, mentions a number of descendants of Jeanne Chastillon and Matthieu Eyssautier who can be identified even in the seventeenth and eighteenth centuries.

Samuel Usque's Jewish-Marrano Nicodemite-Christian Apology of Divine Vengeance.

JEROME FRIEDMAN

O f the different minorities populating the sixteenth-century religious landscape, surely the Marranos must be the most peculiar and the single group most defying simple definition or description.[1] Christian religious authorities were convinced Marranos were secret Jews, while rabbinic authorities were convinced they were sincere Christian converts. The Marranos themselves give many indications of being both, neither, or sometimes one or the other alternately under a Jewish or Christian Nicodemite guise. Because of their carefully nurtured exterior religious ambivalence, who the Marranos were, what role they played in Spanish life, and what their relationship was to both Christianity and Judaism are just several of the many questions that historians of early modern Europe have not been able to answer with confidence. This is hardly a minor issue since as many as 1 million people may have been involved and the most outstanding Spanish achievement of this age, the Spanish Inquisition, was created to deal with the Marrano problem.[2] Samuel Usque's intriguing volume, *Consolations for the Tribulations of Israel* enables the historian to better understand the problems surrounding the identification of this very strange group.[3]

Historically, the Jewish converts to Christianity known as Marranos were the creation of two separate factors: the religious fanaticism related to the reconquest of Spain from the Moors and alleged Jewish culpability for the plagues of the fourteenth century. The reconquest was completed in 1492 with the fall of Granada, but increasing Christian domination of the peninsula during the previous two centuries brought large numbers of Jews and Arabs into Christian society. The latter lived primarily in the south, were agrarian, and posed no threat to governing authorities once Moorish military might was broken. Jews, however, were urban, played a major role in international trade, and had provided the backbone of the administrative class in Moslem Spain. With the progress of the reconquest, Jewish talents were soon put to Christian use with many providing financial, technical and administrative services to their new Christian lords much as they had provided the same services to Moslem rulers previously. In both instances Jews played an administrative role in societies valuing military and feudal skills above executive ability.

As the reconquest progressed, however, a growing Christian religious fanaticism saw little reason to tolerate either Jews or Moors, and by the fourteenth century, both communities found themselves increasingly isolated. Because of their alleged culpability for the plagues, anti-Jewish sentiment increased. Widespread anti-Jewish rioting in 1391 led to massacres and the forced conversion of many Jews while others voluntarily chose baptism to avoid death. Massacres in 1415 again led many to save their lives through conversion, and again an equally large group of Jews determined voluntary conversion a prudent course of action. While some did return to the Jewish fold either in Spain or more usually outside of Spain, the majority of forced and voluntary converts remained within the church, even when crisis conditions passed. Estimates of the numbers involved vary. Some historians claim that, by 1492, a century after the first wave of mass conversions and the year all Jews were expelled from Spain, there were at least 600,000 *conversos* and possibly as many as 1 million when contemporary birthrates are considered.[4] Other historians have argued that these figures are too high, with a general consensus resting at approximately 250,000 Marranos and an equal number of Jews for the period ending in 1492. Either way, the numbers are great indeed.

These forced and voluntary conversions had curious and unanticipated results. As Christians, these former Jews found little to hamper any ambitious energies hitherto frustrated by repressive exclusionary legislation. Certainly, existing statutes limiting Jewish participation in many aspects of life and property ownership no longer applied. Indeed, it is likely that one reason so many Jews either voluntarily converted or remained Christian after having been forcibly converted may have been that only their formal identification as Jews kept them from greater wealth, position, and status. Whole new areas of achievement now lay open to converts, including the royal court and city government, membership in the land-owning *hidalgo* class, and of course, the church. As a result, in the century between 1391 and 1492, Marranos came to exert great influence in Spain's economic, institutional and cultural life and played a significant role in the urban *communero* movement. Indeed, in 1506, Vicenzo Quirini, the Venetian ambassador to Castile wrote home to a very interested audience that "it is estimated that in Castile and other Spanish provinces 1/3 consists of Marranos, that is, 1/3 of those who are burghers and merchants."[5] It was the Marranos' successful integration and assimilation into almost every aspect of Spanish cultural and economic life that made their Jewish identification by the Spanish Inquisition more political than religious, more cynical than spiritual.

Marranos often sought refuge in other parts of Christian Europe where they identified themselves as members of the "Portuguese Nation." In many northern cities, such as Hamburg, Antwerp, Amsterdam and Bordeaux, Marranos founded large communities. Existing charters from France, Italy, and England indicate great interest in Marrano skills with many "Portuguese" merchants gaining very favorable trading status. In France, for instance, Jewish residence was largely forbidden but Marranos began arriving in Bordeaux at the end of the fifteenth century. New Christians received patent letters from Henry II in 1550 authorizing "the merchants and other Portuguese called New Christians to reside in towns and localities of their choice."[6] Baptisms, marriages, burials and all other church services were performed by local Catholic priests "in accordance with the customary rites of the Portuguese Nation." Hence, in 1604 and in 1612, the Marechal d'Ornano, the lieutenant-general of Guienne issued an ordinance forbidding persons "to speak ill or do evil to the Portuguese merchants." Indeed, New Christian economic strength continued to grow so rapidly throughout the seventeenth century that, in 1683, the French government in Paris warned Bordeaux authorities to accommodate New Christian needs, for "if they are forced to leave Bordeaux, it would ruin the city's economy as the commerce is almost entirely in the hands of that sort of persons." Similarly, Marranos settled in Ireland, England, Brittany, India, the Caribbean, in the Low Countries and especially in Venice, indeed, wherever shipping and international trade were important.

Marranos were prominent in both the Dutch East and Dutch West Indies companies and founded the equivalent Portuguese corporations to compete with them. They were also involved in minting, armaments, shipbuilding, and other skills formerly practiced in Seville, where they still constituted a healthy presence in the gold monopoly. They were similarly active in the seventeenth-century slave trade and prominent in coral, sugar, and tobacco import. Many Marranos were educated, sophisticated, and skilled and represented an economic advantage to the communities accepting them. Peter Stuyvesant understood this when a shipload of Portuguese Christians appeared in New Amsterdam harbor in 1654; so did Queen Isabella much earlier, when the ships sent off to the New World with Columbus were filled with Marrano navigators, translators and others whose skills were needed. Nowhere more than in mercantile Venice and Amsterdam were New Christians so easily accepted into the business and social life of the times. Existing records present ample evidence that New Christians would not be harrassed by their new home if they did not disturb its social and religious peace.

Marranos also sought refuge outside of Christian Europe. Those wishing to reestablish their Jewish ties found welcome in the large Jewish communities of North Africa and the Turkish Mediterranean. Other Marranos wishing to remain Christians also found the more open intellectual, religious, and financial atmosphere of the Ottoman Empire conducive to settlement. Indeed, Marranos were made so welcome that one rose to position of Grand Visier to Suleiman the Magnificent, while others became dukes and lords of important Mediterranean trading areas. According to Ottoman records, Marranos constituted the single largest ethnic group in Salonika, though 20 thousand Jews resided in that city.

Marrano integration into the Spanish, European, and Islamic cultural worlds was such that they also contributed to the religious life of all their new homelands. Their fundamental importance to Alumbrado mysticism has been treated at some length, and in the area of more orthodox Christian letters, one need only mention a few such names as Luis de Leon, Luis Vives, Alphonso and Juan Valdez, St. Theresa of Avila and the Jesuit leader Diego Laynez all of whom were either themselves Jewish converts or of families recently converted to Christianity. Similarly, Marrano importance to the Reformation is only now becoming better understood. Much as Jews had been the primary translators of Arabic sources into Latin during the high Middle Ages, Protestant scripturalism stood tall upon the linguistic shoulders of *converso* flocking to northern European cultural centers and universities, where their skills were appreciated and rewarded. *Conversos* provided the skilled manpower for the Aldine press, and Daniel Bomberg's important Christian presses employed both Jews and *conversos* to the exclusion of Old Christians. Most important, Marranos such as Matthew Adrian served as Hebrew teachers at Protestant universities and schools of theology.[7]

As a Christian religious minority, Marranos possessed unique problems. Unlike other religious minorities of the age, such as English Catholics or French Huguenots or even the various radical gathered churches, Marranos were in the curious position of drawing upon two antithetical religious traditions. However much Protestantism and Catholicism might vary in their interpretation of a commonly held New Testament or in understanding their common historical tradition or common creeds, Marranos accepted Jewish and Christian ideas with a heritage of active opposition. Marranos were not simply caught between two stools but between stools in two different rooms. And, insofar as Marranos were Nicodemite and feigned loyalty to one or both groups, they often claimed ignorance of either stool or either room.

Despite Marranos' social utility, they represented a European problem of the first rank. They enjoyed access to the institutions in many societies that had only recently expelled Jews. Many countries that had expelled Jews several centuries earlier found growing numbers of Portuguese New Christians in their midst and were unsure how to deal with so peculiar a people. Many authorities accepted Marranos as legitimate Christians, but those convinced that Jews posed a grave social danger were even more positive that Marranos constituted a clever and deceptive Jewish strategem in a grand conspiracy clearly proving they were up to no good. Hence, at the moment when much of Europe was free of Jews and when so many countries sought some measure of religious uniformity in the seeming anarchy of Reformation Europe, Marranos increasingly found their way into these countries and into positions of commercial influence and religious significance. With Marranos playing a role in so many aspects of European life, fears of judaization were strong because there did seem to be "Jews" everywhere. Viewed as secret Jews, Marranos were perceived as a potential fifth column for Turkish interests, as pseudo-Christians, as a source of religious perversion, as Nicodemites, as the repository of all human vices. And yet, with fine tuned skills perfected during generations of service to Iberian Moorish and Christian governments, Marranos did seem able to multiply wealth in a most unusual, and beneficial, manner. Despite the certainty expressed by so many diverse religious authorities, were Marranos in fact Christians, Jews or some social hybrids discovering the value of being both and neither?

Samuel Usque's *Consolations for the Tribulations of Israel* was written about 1550 and represents an extraordinary example of Marrano cultural and religious eclecticism. Little is known about Usque's early life, but it is clear that he was educated in the manner of the wealthy and powerful. Though he had returned to the Jewish fold by the time he wrote this work, Usque's loyalty to Marranos motivated its publication. "My prime purpose," Usque explained, "is to serve our own Portuguese nation with this small branch bearing new fruit . . ." (p. 40). Usque dedicated his efforts to the veritable patron of Marranos in the Turkish world, "The Very Illustrious Lady, Dona Gracia Nasi." Likening Dona Gracia to Esther, he wrote about, "her inspiration [which] greatly encouraged . . . [those] in Portugal who were too poor and weak to leave the fire [of the Inquisition] and to undertake a lengthy journey. She generously provided money and other needs and comforts to the refugees who arrived destitute, sea-sick and stuporous in Flanders and elsewhere. She helped them overcome the rigors of the craggy Alps in Germany and other lands and she hastened to alleviate the miseries caused by the hardships and hazards of their long journey." (p.230)

There is much internal evidence in his volume that Usque was appealing to the educated and wealthy Marrano. His literary style, pattern of literary images, references, allusions and reasoning all seem carefully calculated to appeal to those who were culturally sophisticated.[8] In good Renaissance style, the volume opens with an appeal to Socrates for wisdom, and Usque entitles his chapters "Pastoral Life," "Hunt of Conies and Hares," "Hunt of Stags and Herons." He cites classical sources as Plutarch, Lucian, Ovid, and Augustine, as well as scriptural and patristic sources. In format, the work is a series of discussions between three shepherds watching over their flocks. One expresses what Usque understood as the Marrano's condition, while the other two participants provided the consolation and insight through which the Marrano might understand his position.

Beneath the fashionable exterior of a pastoral setting, Usque expresses bitterness and anger at Marrano ill treatment by both Jews and Christians. Yet, he feels frustrated to explain the Marrano's peculiar identity, which consists of a Nicodemite interpretation of Jewishness finding expression in a Christian life style. Usque tries to combine these many themes and elements into one composite that utilizes a Christian intellectual and conceptual framework to justify the role of the Marrano from a Jewish historical perspective. Further complicating matters, Usque argues that the Marrano, as Nicodemite Jew who must appear as a Christian, is the special hidden divine agent through whom God would redeem the world from evil. Even more, Usque concludes his discussion on an apocalyptic note and all this is understood from an Nicodemite vantage point, where it is necessary and desirable that things not appear as they truly are. In short, this is a very peculiar work expressing the intellectual vantage point of Europe's most eclectic and syncretistic religious group.

Perhaps because these themes are rather unusual, indeed complex and bizarre, Usque chose to put their presentation into the mouth of a symbolic prophetic spokesman for Marranos rather than argue their merits in his own name. Finding a credible spokesman for Marrano Nicodemism was difficult, however. Nicodemus himself might have been useful, especially since he was vindicated as one of Jesus' most faithful followers, but a Jewish argument might do better with an Old Testament personality. Many Marranos venerated Esther, the niece of Mordechai the Jew. According to the Book of Esther, she was able to save the Persian Jewish community from the machinations of the king's minister, Hamen the Evil, by concealing her non-Persian Jewish faith until after alluring and captivating King Ahasuerus with her beauty. King Ahasuerus, mad with desire, saves Esther's people, executes Hamen and makes Mordechai his advisor in Hamen's place. This positive portrayal of Nicodemite faith earned "St. Esther" the status of grand heroine among Marranos who created a series of holidays in her honor.[9]

Usque must have felt a still more powerful image was required, for he chose the patriarch Jacob to speak for the Marrano. Jacob, surely one of God's most steadfast servants, might seem an odd choice, but he, too, might be viewed as a Nicodemite. According to Scripture, when Isaac lay dying and wished to bless his first born Esau, Jacob fooled his nearly blind father by appearing in his older twin brother's garb. "You probably know, brothers," Usque has Jacob explain, "that I am that shepherd from days of yore who covered his neck and his hands with (Esau's) hair to deceive his father [Isaac] and succeed to the blessing" (p. 46). Like Esther, Jacob too succeeded through a justifiable Nicodemite deception.

The other two participants in the treatise are also Nicodemites of sorts. Though they present themselves as shepherds, they are in reality the prophets Nahum and Zachariah and only reveal their true identities at the very end of the volume. Their names mean "consolation" and "the Lord remembers" and they too were carefully chosen to serve a specific function within the volume.

In his discussions with the other two shepherds, Jacob has little difficulty identifying the Marrano. He explains that many wealthy Spanish Jews converted out of moral weakness, and "finding themselves [spiritually] naked, they could not resist their enemies' offer of further . . . great benefits if they converted and they consented to baptism" (p. 193). The rewards of conversion were great indeed, and Usque described how wealthy *conversos* "joined the ranks of Spain's grandees and noblest lords. They were therefore soon united in marriage with its leading families. They occupied posts of distinction and importance at court. They held the titles of count, marquis, bishop and obtained other high dignities which the material world bestows upon those who court it . . . [The result was that] as *conversos*, they were no longer recognized as Jews and their minds were at ease and their hearts secure since they were Christian." (p. 198)

The Marranos' successful courting of the world, like Adam and Eve's enjoyment of the senses, led to ruin, remorse, and sin. "I have become inured to my corrupting diet of sin" Jacob laments, "its need is now almost rooted in my nature like the need for poison [i.e., drugs] in those for whom poison is food" (p. 88). Like the intoxicating effect of some habituating drug, the sinner finds life without sin impossible. "The continual practice of sin now draws me like a wheel which is moved at first by a great force," Jacob explains, "and then continues to turn by its own momentum" (p. 88).

Despite the benefits of wealth and position, the Marranos' position soon becomes as difficult as the Jews' position had been before the expulsion in 1492. Jacob laments that "in my ignorance, while hidden in the garb of a Christian, I thought I could save my life, although it was just the reverse" (p. 207). Indeed, "though my children are parading their Christianity," Jacob declares, "it does not save their lives" (p. 199). Previously, Jews were hated because they were not Christians. Having converted, *conversos* are hated because they are wealthy and because their Christianity now keeps them from persecution. He explains how "preachers in the pulpits . . . began saying that any famine, pestilence or earthquake that came to the land came because these converts were not good Christians" (p. 205). Even so, Jacob continues, most Marranos "would have, no doubt, borne this patiently if calumnies and false reports [to the Inquisition] had not been raised up to destroy and uproot them from the world" (p. 205). Jacob makes abundantly clear that the Marrano is depressed and dejected but not whether this resulted from having abjured the true Jewish faith or the inability to convince Old Christians of his Christian religious sincerity.

The two prophets indicate to a sullen and depressed Jacob that God chose the Nicodemite Marrano to atone for the sins of the world. In order to prove that Marrano dissimulation is in fact part of a long-term divine plan for the world, they cite Micah 5:6, that "Degraded and crushed though you are, blessings come to the world because of you" (p. 234), and also "That the remnant of Jacob shall be in the midst of many peoples, as dew from the Lord, as rain upon the earth . . . your present condition as you move among the nations" (p. 234). For his part, Jacob has difficulty understanding of what value he might be to anyone since he can hardly defend himself. He describes himself as "lying unconscious on the ground, alone . . . deprived of all instincts including self preservation" (p. 16). And, adding moral corruption to personal weakness, Jacob asks, "And I, inured to so much evil, can I do good?" (p. 88).

The image of the Marrano as a latter-day Jesus whose degradation is his cross to bear in a second divine attempt to save the world runs through Marrano literature. Indeed, Jesus, too, might be understood as a Nicodemite Marrano of sorts. Much as Jesus was God in the visage of man, the Marrano is a Jew in the visage of a Christian. Like Jesus, who took on the form of a man to sum up all human experience within himself and save all mankind, the Marrano descends into the hell of human degradation, and is rejected by Jew and Christian alike, to suffer for all mankind. A seventeenth century Marrano mystic succinctly expressed this idea when he wrote, "It is ordained that the king Messiah don the garments of a Marrano and go unrecognized by his fellow Jews. In a word, it is ordained that he become a Marrano like me."[10] Similarly, Sabatai Sevi, the seventeenth-century false messiah, who may have claimed the loyalty of most Jews and certainly the faith and acceptance of almost all Jewish-oriented Marranos, converted to Islam in order to bring about his curious program of redemption of Israel from the Muslim world.[11] One finds this same image among other repressed radical groups, such as the sixteenth century Hutterite Anabaptists, who taught their own variants of the doctrine of the *descensus*, Christ's descent into hell to redeem humanity.[12] Their own persecution by contemporary orthodox Christianity, like Jesus' suffering, was their experience upon the cross of this world, without which none could be redeemed. Usque, too, draws upon his Christian background and has Nahum explain to Jacob that "sometimes the entire people sins and a general punishment from heaven is necessary. If there by any righteous person or persons . . . our merciful Lord accepts your ewe or your unblemished lamb as a sacrifice for all the people" (p. 125). This allusion to 1 Peter 1:19 places the Marrano as the lamb of God, as a latter day Jesus, through whose suffering all others would find atonement.

The agency through which this suffering would take place, the latter-day cross that the Marrano must bear and drag through the streets while being hooted and jeered, was the Spanish Inquisition. Usque called upon classical imagery to depict the Inquisition as a voracious beast consuming and destroying all in its path. It is clear that he was both horrified and intrigued by its awesome power.

126

The King [Ferdinand] and Queen [Isabella] sent to Rome for a wild monster of such strange form and horrible mien that all Europe trembles at the mere mention of its name. . . . Its body, an amalgam of hard iron and deadly poison, has an adamantine shell of steel and is covered with enormous scales. It rises in the air on a thousand wings with black poisonous pinions and it moves on the ground with a thousand pernicious and destructive feet. Its form is like both the awesome lion and frightful serpents in the deserts of Africa. Its enormous teeth equal those of the most powerful elephants. Its whistle or voice kills even more quickly than the venomous basilisk. Its eyes and mouth spew continual flames and blazes of consuming fire, and the food it eats is the fire in which human bodies burn. Its flight is swifter than the eagle's, but wherever it passes, its shadow spreads a pall of gloom over the brightest sun. Finally, in its wake it leaves a darkness . . . the green grass on which it treads or the luxurious trees on which it alights, dies, decays and withers and then is uprooted by the monster's devastating beak. It desolates the entire countryside with its poison until it is like the Syrian deserts and sands where no plant takes root and no grass grows (p. 198-199).

Like Jesus, Jacob fears that recent events indicate God's displeasure. Jacob says "I fear above all [else] that the Lord . . . has now rejected me" (p. 83-84) but is consoled when Nahum observes that "you have run the entire gauntlet of misfortunes and have reached the end of your tribulations" (p. 236). Elsewhere Jacob is again told, "in these punishments which you have received, you have begun to attain the final stage of your preparation for redemption" (p. 238).

After employing Christian concepts to explain the Marrano's Christlike role and classical imagery to describe the horrible beast of the Inquisition, Usque turns to traditional Jewish anti-Christian ideas to explain the nature of the evil for which the Marrano must atone. Ancient man, we are told, compounded disobedience to God in Eden with the belief that man himself was God. Usque explains that "the first god they worshipped was Ham, the son of Noah, the worst of the three sons . . . the wicked sorcerer" (p. 84). Because Ham was a magician, "these people took him for a god and as such they obeyed his laws and judgment . . . and they built cities and many temples in his honor" (p. 85). After Ham, others usurped God's position and Usque recounts how "they then worshipped Sabczius the Wizard, another mortal man" (p. 85). He explains that "through astrology he [i.e., Sabczius] was able to guess at events that would occur at the end of each epoch" (p. 85). Consequently, a new blasphemy was added to the rest, because "The people thought he had a relationship with heaven and the celestial bodies and at his death they said he had become one of them, the chief one" (p. 86). Like Ham's followers in earlier times, "all the people who came from this religion built altars and offered sacrifices and considered him their god" (p. 85). Other ancients, including the Persians, Chaldeans, Babylonians, Greeks, and Romans also believed much the same sort of blasphemy and also deified their mortal leaders whom, they believed, joined God at death. "Shall I show you the vanity of their foundation?" Usque observes about them all, "Like the Egyptians, they worshipped mortal men as Gods" (p. 85).

Incredibly, the condition of human belief degenerated even further from this already desperate situation. Usque laments that "the force of ancient error in worshipping mortal man went on to influence modern peoples," but he adds "and the rest I shall tell you in your ear" (p. 87) lest his words be overheard by the Inquisition. Christianity was the latest form of the ancient worship of mortal man but it also succeeded in reducing humanity to the level of totemism and animism. "They [Christians] are confused and have become [primitive] like brute animals," Usque explains, "they worship a piece of wood and an ornament made of silver . . . or what is made of refined gold, the work of a goldsmith's and artisan's hands." (p. 87) The world was slowly degenerating with "everything returning to its primeval chaos and corruption" (p. 66).

The world is not what is seems. Christianity is allegedly based upon the monotheistic Old Testament but is in fact an updated version of that evil worship of deified man finding its origin with Ham. The Marrano appears to be a Christian but is condemned as a Jew by Christians and as a Christian by Jews and is persecuted by both. This, too, is deceptive and Jacob is reminded that Marranos, "secure in their imitation of the Christian never exchanged the secret of their souls" (p. 206). While he is rejected by all, the Marrano is in fact a Christlike savior of the world. Though Jacob's suffering seems the result only of contemporary causes, the two prophets explain that is actually an important element in another, very old conflict between good and evil, the resolution of which will lead to the destruction of all evil.

Citing Malachi 1:2-3, Nahum reminds Jacob of his earlier conflict with his twin brother Esau. We are reminded that the two tumbled in the womb together for nine months, but that God loved Jacob and hated Esau, whom he promised he would destroy (p. 240). In rabbinic literature, Esau and the land of Edom are euphemisms for Christianity, with the conflict between the twins, Jacob and Esau, understood as a prophecy of the historical conflict between these two religions.[13] Hence, Esau's great physical strength is understood as Christianity's superior numbers and Jacob's inheritance of Esau's birthright is proof of God's love and Jacob's eventual victory over his brother. Nahum exploits this dichotomy when he explains "This is the manner of vengeance which the Lord shall perform for you by his hand. In order that you shall glory against those who have gloried and still glory in burning you and destroying you, and that they may pay by the measure which they meted out to you, the Lord says, "The House of Jacob shall be a fire . . . and the House of Edom shall be stubble . . . and there shall be nothing remaining from the House of Esau" (p. 240).

Trying to bolster a sullen Jacob, Nahum and Zachariah tell him that the Marrano's enemies will be destroyed, much as ancient Israel's enemies were all eventually destroyed. Nahum asks "What befell the empire of the Egyptians who plagued you in their lands? How did the monarchy of the Babylonians end? Who soaked you in blood? What has become of the memory of the Persians whose subjugation you suffered? . . . Their fate is notorious. A great number of Egyptians were drowned in the Red Sea and the rest were nearly destroyed by the Babylonians. The Babylonians were subjugated by the Persians and . . . the Persians' name was consumed by the Macedonians and the Macedonians were laid low by the early Romans" (p. 159).

The prophets indicate that throughout history God watched over those who did his service. For instance, the continual conflict among these many empires and peoples might have been very hurtful to the small and weak Hebrews, whose fate rose and sank like a cork on a wave. "You would long ago have perished from the wrath of only one of the peoples who had subjected you," Nahum explains. Similarly today, "if one kingdom rises up against you in Europe, another in Asia lets you live" (p. 227). Hence, "by scattering you among all the peoples, he made it impossible for the world to destroy you, for . . . if the Lord had not dispersed you, but instead . . . had isolated you in one corner of the earth . . . your life would be in jeopardy and the die for your destruction cast" (p. 227).

After listening in silence an ever sullen Jacob asks "Perchance, can you let me know when the misfortunes I presently suffer will have an end?" (p. 235). He understands that "All the nations that had mastery over me in past were speedily destroyed [and] their memory uprooted from the world and consumed because they followed erroneous belief and laws." But Jacob also notes that "those in whose captivity I now suffer do not meet a similar fate. In fact, their domination upon the earth has long continued" (p. 233). At this point Nahum and Zachariah introduce to Jacob an apocalyptic plan of divine vengeance. "Your hungry spirit will rest as soon as it imagines its vengeance," (p. 229) he is told, and "those who devour you . . . shall be devoured and . . . those who carry you off shall be carried off and those that spoil you, I shall make a spoil" (pp. 252, 229). God's plan involves more than mere violence and vengeance, however, and Jacob is told "reflect on the sweep of human history so that you can see more clearly how this message is fulfilled in your days" (p. 234).

Much as Jacob of old, appearing to the world in Esau's garb, victored over the Scriptural Esau, the Marrano, appearing to the world as a Christian, is the agent through whom God would destroy Esau-Christianity. Nahum explains that "Since throughout Christendom Christians have forced Jews to change their religion, it seems to be the divine retribution that the Jews [i.e., Marranos] should strike back with the weapons that were put into their hands to punish those who compelled them to change their faith" (p. 193.). As if addressing these same Christian rulers, the author writes "you should consider how much harm you bring upon yourself by compelling Jews to accept your faith" because "the end [i.e., the *converso*] becomes the means that undermine and destroy them [i.e., Christians]" (p. 193). Affirming Old Christian beliefs that Marranos are not true Christians at all, Nahum observes how "that generation of converts has spread over nearly the whole [Christian] realm and though a long time has elapsed, these converts still give an indication of their non-Catholic origin by the new Lutheran beliefs which are presently found among them for they are not comfortable in the religion which they received so unwillingly" (p. 185). Through this new heresy, the destruction of Christianity is already underway. In the process, the European powers that tore at Jewry now feed on each other. "We can say this of Spain," Usque observes, "that Italy is its grave; of France, that Spain is the means of its consumption; of Germany, that all its neighbors including the Turk, are its executioners" (p. 229).

The idea that Lutheranism was a Jewish strategem and constituted some divine retribution against a Catholicism that had persecuted the large Spanish Jewish community may seem peculiar from the distance of over four centuries. We must remember, however, that all sixteenth-century religions envisioned themselves in league with terrific cosmic powers. In the supercharged tension of Reformation age religious turmoil, every religious denomination saw God vindicating its position and it is therefore reasonable that Usque would find in the terrible violence and destruction of the Reformation a sign of God's anger with Christendom. Hence, if Christians could blame Jews for the Reformation and the division of Christendom,[14] Usque could take credit for such events and explain how this "Jewish" division of Christendom was a divine punishment for an evil Christianity maintaining the views of ancient paganism.

Usque's eclectic composite of so many varied ideas demonstrates the extent to which ideas moved from one group to another and the ease with which belief systems could be created to suit almost any occasion and satisfy almost any religious church, sect, or group. Protestant polemics against Catholicism and Catholic diatribes against Protestantism, as well as radical millenarian treatises against almost everyone, all wove skillful fabric from Scripture, tradition, and the apocalypse to suit their needs within the context of their times. Usque created a Marrano argument against Christianity, which actually used that religion's own concepts against itself in order to defend the Jewish integrity of those who, in fact, whether Usque accepted it or not, willingly left the Jewish religion. And if the Christian Inquisition might condemn the Marrano for being an inadequate Christian and really a secret Jew, Usque, the apologist for Marranism, would have the Marrano, as the Jew the Inquisition claimed the new Christian was, once again, save mankind from itself, because the Marrano was a secret universal Jesus once again in conflict with religious error.

It is clear Voltaire was quite wrong when he quipped that history is the trick the living play upon the dead. Perhaps, it might be more accurate to wonder if history is not the trick the living play upon themselves.

NOTES

1. The literature concerning the Jews in Spain and Portugal is vast. The most complete and recent bibliography is Robert Singerman, *The Jews in Spain and Portugal: A Bibliography* (New York and London, 1975). For general histories of Iberian Jewry see A. A. Neuman, *The Jews in Spain*, 2 vols. (Philadelphia, 1942); Y. Baer, *A History of the Jews in Christian Spain*, 2 vols. (Philadelphia, 1961, 1966). Also very helpful, with excellent footnote-essays is vol. 13 of Salo W. Baron, *A Social and Religious History of the Jews* (New York, 1969). Concerning Jewish life in Moslem Spain, the reader might consult Eliyahu Ashtor, *The Jews of Moslem Spain* (Philadelphia, 1973). Though many general histories present some information on Marranos, the best studies are the following: Cecil Roth, *A History of the Marranos* (Philadelphia, 1932); B. Netanyahu, *The Marranos of Spain*, (New York, 1966) and *Don Isaac Abravanel, Statesman and Philosopher* (Philadelphia, 1953); A. D. Ortiz, *Los Judeoconversos en Espanya y America* (Madrid, 1971); I. S. Revah, "Les Marranes," *Revue des éudes juives* vol. 118. A new and excellent treatment of the Marrano problem in Italy is Brian Pullan, *The Jews of Europe and the Inquisition of Venice, 1550-1670* (Totowa, N. J., 1983). Also see Emile van der Vekené, *Bibliographie der Inquisition: Ein Versuch* (Hildesheim, 1963); H. J. Zimmels, *Die Marranen in der rabbinischen Literatur* (Berlin, 1932). A more popular treatment is Joachim Prinz, *The Secret Jews* (New York, 1973). More books are cited in note 6.

2. The literature concerning the Inquisition in Europe, the New World, Asia and India is extremely extensive. The best bibliography is Vekené. The standard secondary source on the subject is H. Lea, *A History of the Spanish Inquisition* 4 vols. (New York, 1906-1907). More general treatments include, from a general perspective, H. Kamen, *The Spanish Inquisition* (New York, 1965) and from a Jewish perspective, Cecil Roth, *The Spanish Inquisition* (London, 1937); Also, Antonio J. Saraiva, *Inquisic«ao e crit«aos-Novos* (Porto, 1969). The books in note 1 also present extensive discussions of the Spanish Inquisition. Concerning the relationship between Marranos, the Inquisition, the pure blood laws and antisemitism, see Jerome Friedman, "Jewish Conversion, the Spanish Pure Blood Laws and the Reformation; A Revisionist View of Racial Antisemitism," *Sixteenth Century Journal*, Vol. 18, no. 1, (Spring, 1987) p. 3-29.

3. Samuel Usque, *Consolacam as Tribulaçoens de Israel*, trans. Martin A. Cohen (Philadelphia, 1977). Rather than separately noting each of the more than fifty citations from this work appearing in the paper, each citation will be immediately followed with its page reference.

4. Netanyahu, *The Marranos of Spain*, see especially p. 235-245 concerning the number of Marranos.

5. Eugenio Alberi, ed. *Relazioni degli ambasciatori veneti al Sanato*, first series (Firenze, 1839) Vol. 1., 28f.

6. *Encyclopedia Judaica* (Jerusalem, 1971), vol. 4, 1244, for the next few citations as well. Concerning New Christians in Bordeaux, the reader might consult Georges E. A. Cirot, *Recherches sur les Juifs espagnois et portugais a Bordeaux* (Bordeaux, 1908), and *Les Juifs de Bordeaux* (Bordeaux, 1920); Theophile Malvezin, *Histoire des Juifs a Bordeaux* (Bordeaux, 1875) repr. Marseilles in 1976. The economic life of Marranos has been studied by a great number of historians, who often include them within more general discussions of Jewish participation in the economic life of early modern Europe. The following discuss New Christians as separate from their more general Jewish discussion. H. I. Bloom, *The Economic Activity of the Amsterdam Jews*, (Williamsport, Pa., 1937); M. Grünwald, *Juden als Reeder und Seefahrer* (1902); Werner Sombart, *Die Juden und das Wirtschaftsleben* (Munich, 1928); *Encyclopedia Judaica*, vol. 15, p. 1307. A new and very good book is James C. Boyajian, *Portuguese Bankers at the Court of Spain, 1626-1650* (New Brunswick, N. J., 1983) which deals with more than the title indicates. Also see Zosa Szajkowski, "Trade Relations of Marranos in France with the Iberian Peninsula in the 16th and 17th centuries," *Jewish Quarterly Review*, Vol. 50 (1959-1960) p. 69-78. Sombart is still seminal for the social implications he discusses.

7. For a short portrait of Adrian, see Harry S. May, *The Tragedy of Erasmus* (St. Charles, No., 1975) 115-116. Adrian was courted by Luther who attempted to bring him to the University of Wittenburg. On this, see Jerome Friedman, *The Most Ancient Testimony: Sixteenth Century Christian-Hebraica in the Age of Renaissance Nostalgia* (Athens, Ohio, 1983).

8. See Martin Cohen's discussion of Usque's sources in Usque, *Consolaçam*, Appendix B, "The Sources of the Consolaçam" 269-287.

9. Cecil Roth's influential study *History of the Marranos*, describes Esther's importance. See 186-188.

10. See Jerome Friedman, "Sixteenth Century European Jewry: Theologies of Crisis in Crisis," *Social Groups and Religious Ideas in the Sixteenth Century*, ed. Miriam U. Chrisman and Otto Grünler, (Kalamazoo, Mich., 1978) 102-112, note 31 where Abraham Cardozo is discussed. This citation comes from *Sefer Inyanei Shabtai Tzvi*, (in Hebrew) ed. J. Yeser (Berlin, 1913), 88.

11. Concerning this very important man, see Gershom Sholem's excellent, *Sabbatai Sevi, The Mystical Messiah*, trans. R. J. Zvi Werbloswsky (Princeton, 1973).

12. Concerning these radical interpretations of Christ's descent into hell, see Jerome Friedman, "Christ's Descent into Hell and Redemption Through Evil. A Radical Reformation Perspective," *Archiv für Reformationsgeschichte.* 76 (1965); 217-230. For more orthodox interpretations of the *decensus*, see Dewey D. Wallace, Jr. "Puritan and Anglican: The Interpretation of Christ's Descent Into Hell in Elizabethan Theology," *Archiv für Reformationsgeschichte.* 69(1978): 248-287.

13. On the rabbinic identification of Esau and the kingdom of Edom with Christ, Christianity and the papacy, see G. D. Gordon, "Esau as Symbol in Early Medieval Thought," in *Jewish Medieval and Renaissance Studies*, ed. A. Altman (Cambridge, Mass., 1964).

14. Jews were held responsible for the Reformation and for Huss' dissension from the church as well. The logic seems to have been that only Jews would cause such terrible events that divided Christendom. See Jerome Friedman, *The Most Ancient Testimony*, p. 190.

Printing, Censorship, and Antisemitism in Reformation Germany

R. PO-CHIA HSIA

For Luther, printing was a wonderful invention, a great gift of God, which would further the spread of true religion in all languages to every corner of the world.[1] This marvelous technological innovation was the harbinger of a new age or moral rejuvenation, ecclesiastical reform, and imperial restoration. Surely, the advent of the moveable type must have been to the Wittenberger, and to many others, a sign of the millennium. Luther's enormous and rapid success is unthinkable without the aid of the printing press. The great evangelical tracts of 1520, written in Germany and intended for "the Common Man," went through numerous editions.[2] In fact, the decade of the 1520s witnessed a remarkable explosion of printed literature, mostly pamphlets and flysheets, prior to a leveling off after the initial fervor of the evangelical movement.[3]

In the euphoria of the early Reformation years, when everything seemed possible, when God's wonders were ubiquitously manifest, Luther appealed to the Jews to heed the evangelical message and be reunited with the Christians under the one true Messiah. *Dass Jesus Christus ein geborner Jude sei* (1523), a moving condemnation of the oppression of Jews and a courageous testimony to the exhilarating idealism of the early evangelical movement, went through nine German and two Latin editions.[4] In the tract, millenarian expectations fueled missionary fervor. Appended to Justus Jonas's Latin translation of the work is a letter by Luther to the converted Jew Bernhard, which expresses the hope that the effort to convert Jews would proceed at the rapid pace of the evangelical movement.[5] The reformer's high hopes were dashed on the rock of Jewish steadfastness, obstinacy as Luther would call it, and the early enthusiasm gave way to a mature anger in the antisemitic writings of 1543. *Vom Schem Hamphoras und vom Geschlecht Christi* and *Von den Juden und ihren Lügen* both appeared in that year. The first work went through seven German editions in two years,[6] the second, two German and one Latin edition in the sixteenth century, and a 1613 German edition in Frankfurt, just before the Fettmilch Uprising.[7] In addition, these two polemical works were included of course in the many editions of Luther's collected works.

How did the "common man" of Reformation Germany receive the vitriolic, hateful antisemitic polemics of the old Luther? It seems that the history of books and printing is more feasible than the history of reading; and, for assessing Luther's influence on the transmission of antisemitic ideas, the reception of his 1543 antisemitic writings needs to be studied. A contemporary of Luther, Josel of Rosheim, leader and spokesman of the Jewish communities in the Holy Roman Empire, who had corresponded with the reformer and was personally acquainted with him,[8] remembered in his memoirs that the appearance of Luther's *Von Schem Hamphoras* in 1543 prompted Elector Johann Friedrich of Saxony to revoke all concessions to Saxon Jews and also unleashed mob violence against Jews in many Protestant areas, especially in Brunswick and Saxony.[9] Fortunately for the Jews of Alsace, Josel's appeal to the tolerant Strasbourg magistrates succeeded in preventing a local printing of *Von den Juden und ihren Lügen*.[10] Luther's earlier pamphlet, *Dass Jesus Christus ein geborner Jude sei*, which condemned the persecution of Jews and called for their conversion, was the only one of his writings on the Jews to be published in Strasbourg.[11] It was clear that the transmission of antisemitic ideas in print was very much dependent on the attitude of the local authorities.

A censorship case in 1595 offers a clue toward a tentative answer to the question of the transmission and reception of antisemitic ideas.[12] Arnd Westhoff, a printer in the imperial city of Dortmund in Westphalia, published a booklet, mostly probably in early 1595, with the title: *Christian Instruction of Doctor Martin Luther / On Jewish Lies concerning the Person of Our Lord*

*Jesus Christ / his beloved Mother Mary / and most necessary for
all Christians to read From which every Christian can easily
conclude / whether one should properly tolerate Jews or not.*[13]

The booklet, in octavo, forty-one pages, without illustrations, is an inexpensive "pocket book" printed on cheap paper. It
summarizes thematically Luther's antisemitic writings, primarily
from *Von den Juden und ihren Lügen*, excluding most of the
reformer's theological references while retaining the hateful content: a stripped down version, one may say, of the essence of
Lutheran antisemitism. The four parts of the booklet are a summary of the "crimes" of the Jews; what one should do with them;
admonition to the authorities and pastors; Luther's last sermon in
Eisleben against the Jews.

The contents sound similar enough. The Jews are accused of
cursing Jesus and Mary in their daily prayers, and the charge of
ritual murder, prohibited by repeated imperial mandates, was
again raised in public. Proscribed actions against Jews in the empire repeat Luther's recommendations in *Von den Juden und
ihren Lügen*: one should burn their synagogues, destroy their
houses, confiscate their prayer books, forbid rabbis to teach, and
ban travel and usury.[14] Other stereotypes that form the stuff of
Protestant antisemitism are repeated. The Jews of the Holy
Roman Empire were racially and in their "character" different
from Mosaic Jews: the ancient Israelites obeyed God's laws
whereas the imperial Jews were talmudic; one people lived in
their own country, in the holy land, but the other crucified Christ
and were consequently dispersed by the Roman emperors. The
imperial Jews in Germany, argues the tract, should be forced to
do hard labor and not allowed to "suck the blood of Christians."[15]

Arnd Westhof was a minor printer with a local market, publishing sixteen works in Dortmund between 1575 and 1603.[16] He
had close connections with the Gymnasium and produced
several school texts for its students.[17] The humanist texts in his
booklist include an anthology of Latin poems edited by the
Münsteraner humanist of the early sixteenth century, Johannes
Murmellius, distichs by Cato, an anthology of Greek poems, and
distichs by the Lutheran schoolteacher in pre-Anabaptist Münster
Johannes Glandorp. In catechismic and devotional literature, his
list included a devotional handbook by Spangénburg, Luther's
small catechism, and two devotional works for the young by the
Dortmund schoolmaster Arnold Quiting. Funeral orations and a

chronicle of the ducal house of Jülich-Cleve make up the remainder of the booklist.[18]

In order to understand the circumstances surrounding the publication of the antisemitic booklet by Westhoff, the context of its reception and attempts at censorship, we must first look at the confessional situation and the position of Jews in the Westphalian imperial city. In the 1520s, an evangelical movement began in Dortmund, just as it swept across all of Germany, but the citizens who clamored for reform failed to pressure the magistrates to declare for the new faith.[19] While city after city openly professed the Augsburg Confession of Faith, the city council in Dortmund refused to endorse the reform movement because of familial ties between the patrician-dominated magistracy and the personnel of the ecclesiastical establishment. In the 1530s, the evangelical movement steadily gained strength, carrying with it the vast majority of the citizenry, especially the guildsmen, a part of the clergy, and some magistrates. But with the specter of religious revolution in nearby Anabaptist Münster in 1534-1535 and the defeat of the Schmalkaldic League in 1547, the Catholic establishment in city hall and the parish churches remained entrenched.

In the middle decades of the sixteenth century, under the leadership of the schoolmasters at the Gymnasium and magistrates who wanted to find a *via media* out of the morass of confessional confrontation, limited reforms were carried out. Evangelical services were introduced in 1552; and in 1562, the city council allowed citizens to choose either the Lutheran or the Catholic rite of communion. Schilling argues that civic humanism provided a possibility for a nonconfessional reform movement to articulate some of the voices of religious renewal without severing entirely the continuity with the old church. Politically, it allowed the magistrates to balance the conflicting claims of foreign and domestic politics, with the city council caught in between obedience to the emperor as its direct lord and the terms of the 1548 Interim and an agitated, influential guild community calling for total reform.

But the generation of the mid-century that was inspired by the irenic ideals and the pragmatic solutions of Erasmian humanism yielded to a new generation that matured with firm confessional identities. By 1570, a new group of magistrates committed to the Reformation declared officially for the Augsburg Confession. Just when the Reformation seemed triumphant, the Counter-

Reformation attacked. A small group of politically important patrician families in Dortmund not only held on to the old faith, but furnished a new generation of fervent supporters for the Catholic renewal. In 1572, the small Catholic minority helped to bring in the Jesuits, and throughout the 1580s, attempts were made to guarantee the parity of Lutheranism and Catholicism. The city was embroiled in lawsuits at the *Reichshofrat*, brought against it by Catholics outside Dortmund to try to enforce the provisions of the Interim.[20] In the 1590s, when the Spanish Army of Flanders took up winter quarters in Westphalia, the imperial city came under the constant threat of recatholicization by Hapsburg arms. In 1604, Emperor Rudolf II ordered the city to turn over to the Catholics all the parish churches, chapels, schools, and hospitals. This extreme tactic worked and the magistrates conceded the right of Catholics to worship in the three cloisters in the city much against the will of the populace.

It is thus crucial to understand the sense of persecution and threat felt by the Lutherans in Dortmund in the 1590s. The very integrity and identity of a Christian and civic community was in danger, not only from the emperor and the Jesuits, but also from the Jews, who enjoyed the privileged protection of the emperor as his direct subjects.

The Jewish community in Dortmund dated back to at least the fourteenth century, when in the wake of the Black Death it was expelled from the city, a fate shared by practically all the Jewish communities of the cities in the Holy Roman Empire. After being readmitted to Dortmund in 1384, the Jews came under the protection of the emperors, the archbishops of Cologne, and the counts of Mark at various times. The small community made its living mainly from moneylending and pawnbroking.[21] Hostility grew toward the end of the fifteenth century. In 1486, when the Jew Michael cut keys to break into other people's houses and tried to cut his own cloth, he was arrested, convicted, and hung together with two dogs.[22] The Jews were expelled once more before 1500. In 1543, the city council allowed Jews to settle, to sell meat, and to lend money at a fixed interest rate of 3 pfennig on the daler per week, in return for an annual protection fee of 18 dalers.[23] But the Jews were soon involved in many lawsuits with citizens over the payment of interests and loans; and, in addition to the constant popular antisemitism, zealous pastors added their sermons calling for expulsion. Finally, the magistrates wavered and in 1596 denied residence permits to the few Jewish families in the imperial city.[24] The antisemitic tract *Christian Instruction of D. Martin Luther* in all likelihood was published in 1595, on the eve of the expulsion of Jews; its appearance represented the use of the printing press to mobilize public opinion to exert pressure on city hall. In excoriating the Jews, by declaring them enemies of the "true Christian religion," the Lutherans were also asserting their identity against Catholic counterattack. After all, as Luther exclaims in *Von den Juden und ihren Lügen*, both Jews and papists embodied the old, degenerate religion of dead law, which must yield to the new, vigorous religion of the living spirit.[25] For the evangelical burghers of Dortmund, the expulsion of Jews was an act of defiance against a Catholic emperor, who was after all their protector, and a defense of a Christian civic community against an alien and polluting marginal social group.

What might have been just another conflict in the potentially explosive German Northwest—a region dotted with points of confessional tensions and bordering on the war-torn Nether-lands—became a test case for the contestation of imperial law and authority. Although the Dortmund Jews were too few to defend their interests, there was a flourishing community in Frankfurt, where the booklet published by Westhoff probably appeared as one of the numerous titles exhibited at the 1595 international Book Fair. Thoroughly alarmed, especially by the charge of ritual murder in the booklet, the Frankfurt Jews drew up a petition addressed to Emperor Rudolf II in Prague, sending along a copy of the offensive print.[26]

The letter of petition, signed by a Wendel, who represented the Frankfurt *Judischait*, the community of Jews, complains that the libelous booklet

> was not only contrary to the general reason of God's Word and commandments, but also utterly against the praiseworthy laws, especially injurious of Divinity and Your Imperial Majesty, also against communal law, the much beloved peace and unanimity; and especially on account of communal agitation should neither [be allowed] in private or in public to be furthered by speech or by writing, let alone in open print.[27]

Wendel goes on to summarize the contents of the booklet; that Jews were accused of lying, murdering, robbing, and scheming to kill Christians, that they prayed daily for their deliverance from Christian captivity; that they were "thirsty bloodhounds and murderers of all Christians"; that they stole and killed Christian children. Defamation of this sort was clearly in violation of imperial constitution. Wendel cites the *Reichstagsabschied* of Augsburg 1530 against breaking peace, an injunction that was repeated in the 1541 Regensburg Diet, the 1548 Augsburg Imperial Police Ordinance, and the 1570 Speyer Diet. The Jews feared that the booklet would incite "the Common Man" (*der Germainer Mann*) against them. After giving a precis of the recommended measures in the booklet against Jews, Wendel reminds the emperor in the petition that he was their beloved lord and protector and that any evil which might befall Jews would harm imperial interests as well. Above all, the petitioner feared that "the libelous booklet would come into the hands of the Common Man in the land and in towns" and would lead to violence against all Jews.[28] To conclude, Wendel beseeches Rudolf II to order the arrest of the printer Westhoff and the instigation of an inquest leading to the punishment of the anonymous author, the confiscation and destruction of all copies of the book, and the issuance of an imperial mandate explicitly prohibiting any future defamation of Jews.

Having read Wendel's petition with sympathy, Rudolf II ordered his chancery to compose a mandate of interdict. Two imperial mandates were issued on July 10, 1595, one directed to the city council of Frankfurt and the other to Dortmund. The first mandate to Frankfurt condemns the tract *Christian Instruction of D. Martin Luther* as

> a libelous booklet, in which shameless, blasphemous, and abominable things were strewn out, and many things can be found which advocate the destruction and annihilation of all Jews, and are also against our Christian, Catholic religion, God the Almighty himself and his holy angels; [they are] explicitly contrary to Our Imperial Religious Peace and other highly punishable laws; and in effect [they] seek no other fruit other than unrest, bloodshed, and the division of peace. . . .[29]

Rudolf II informs the Frankfurt magistrates that he has ordered the Dortmund city council to confiscate and destroy all copies of the booklet and similar defamatory publications and to punish the culpable. Likewise, the emperor admonishes the Frankfurt councilors that he, as head of the empire, must enforce the police ordinance and has ordered all authorities in the Holy Roman Empire:

> wherever prominent printers and booksellers might be, to insure that similar libelous books and writings should not be printed openly or in secret, or be transported around, and when they do turn up, not be [allowed] to spread, but stopped right away, and as many as possible might be confiscated and destroyed; the lawbreakers should be, according to the Law, the opportunity, and the particular situation, diligently punished. Thus we want to earnestly admonish and order you, as a prominent Imperial and commercial city . . . on account of your authority and office, to search diligently by this order for the annoying, shameless, libelous book, in all the printing shops and bookstores, without respect or forewarning to anyone, to confiscate and do away with all the copies which come into your hands, to hold in seeming punishment, all those who own the worktools and the merchandise, as well as the buyers and other possessors of such books, by whom they might be found, each according to the shape of things and circumstances.[30]

The second mandate, addressed to the magistrates of Dortmund, repeats the injunction against the printing and distribution of the booklet "on pain of limb and fine" (*bei straff leibs und geits*).[31] It echoes the fear, first expressed in the petition of the Frankfurt Jews, that such inflammatory and demagogic works would incite the "Common Man" and the rabble (*Pöbel*) to violence against the persons and properties of Jews. The condemned work was found to be offensive against imperial peace and the Catholic religion. Rudolf worried lest tumults and bloodshed may follow; such propaganda must be suppressed at once.

The 1595 imperial edicts were based on a well-developed law of censorship in the empire.[32] In the late fifteenth century, ecclesiastical authorities were the first to perceive the potential disruption of the new technological innovation of printing. The first censorship ordinance came from the Archbishop of Cologne in 1478, followed in 1482 by one promulgated in the diocese of Würzburg, and in 1486 by another in the archdiocese of Mainz.[33] The first imperial, as opposed to territorial censorial ordinance, was the appointment of a general superintendent of books for Germany by Maximilian I in 1496. In 1512, the same emperor also issued the first edict of censorship against the humanist, lawyer, and enemy of Pfefferkorn, Johannes Reuchlin, who defended talmudic learning and Hebrew books against the Cologne Dominicans and the Jewish convert.[34]

Religion, printing, and censorship continued to form an uneasy triad throughout the sixteenth century. With innumerable books, pamphlets, and broadsheets spreading the message of reform, the 1521 Worms censorship ordinance against Lutheran tracts remained essentially a dead letter. The confessional division in the empire implied that censorship laws could only be enforced by territorial authorities, who would exercise their judgments as to what constituted dangerous material. The inability of imperial authority to enforce religious censorship was tacitly recognized in the *Reichstagsabschied* of Speyer (1529) and Augsburg (1530), which entrusted local authorities with the actual responsibility of censorship. In 1570, an imperial ordinance was declared that aimed at confining printers to imperial cities, university towns, and cities with princely residences in order to facilitate control.[35]

Arnd Westhoff in Dortmund continued his printing business after 1595, showing the ineffectiveness of imperial authority in the face of the refusal of the local authorities in enforcing the censorship mandate because of confessional and political differences. In 1609, a Johann Westhoff succeeded Arnd in the business, and the Westhoff Press continued to specialize in Lutheran polemics, including two massive works, each over nine hundred pages, defending Lutheran orthodoxy against Catholic attacks.[36] For the evangelical burghers of Dortmund, the printing press was indeed God's instrument to defend their faith.

This brief incident in 1595 throws light on some of the larger forces at work behind censorship, antisemitism, and confessional conflicts. There are three hypotheses one can formulate. First, antijudaism seemed to have been an essential component of

Lutheran identity in the late sixteenth and early seventeenth centuries, when the Lutheran Reformation was under threat, not only from the competition by Calvinists but directly from a militant Catholicism. Antisemitism reinforced a sense of corporate consciousness in that it sharpened the image of the outsider; in the case of Dortmund, the assertion of an evangelical, corporate, communal identity was inextricably linked to heightened hostility toward Jews and Catholics. Second, constitutionalism in the empire was potentially a real and growing source of political stability. In addition to the 1555 Religious Peace of Augsburg, which was designed to ensure peace between Catholics and Lutherans, the legal rights of Jews were also more clearly defined by various imperial diets and imperial ordinances. The fact that Rudolf II reacted favorably to the petition of the Frankfurt Jews was a case in point. The crucial question then became one of whether the territorial and local authorities would want to enforce these laws. The growing confessional identities represented the element of instability, undermining the workings of the imperial constitution. Finally, a general fear of violence and uprising was reflected in the language of the petition and the imperial mandates. The "Common Man" was referred to interchangeably as the rabble and the common scoundrel; he was particularly susceptible to religious violence, directed either against the Jews or against Catholic, imperial authority. The countermeasure was strong and swift and asserted the unquestioned right of *Obrigkeit* over subjects. The fate of the German Jews would vacillate between two struggles in the Holy Roman Empire: between the confessional conflicts and between the contest of two views of authority, the communal and the hierarchical.

APPENDIX

Imperial Edict of Censorship to the City Council of Frankfurt, July 10, 1595 (From Stadtarchiv Frankfurt Ugb E 46 ad J1; punctuations have been added)

Rudolff der Ander von Gottes genaden Erwelten Römischer Kaiser zu allen Zeitten Mehrer des Reichs:

Ersame liebe getreuen, was wir an unser unnd des heiligen Reichs Statt Dorttmundt, auf Clag unnd anruffen gemainer judenschafft im Reich, von wegen aines daselbst in druekh aussgegangenen zur erwurgung unnd vertilgung aller Juden verfassten Schmächbuchlins, in welchem auch wider unsere Christliche Catholische Religion, dazur Gott den allmechtigen selbst unnd seine heiliger Engel, schamlose lasterliche unnd abscheuliche ding aussgeschüttet seind unnd vil sachen zufund, so aussdruekhlichen unsern unnd des heiligen Reichs Religionfriden und andern hochverpeenten Sazungen gestraekhs zuwider, unnd damit in effectu khein ander Intent oder frucht gesucht wird dann unruhe blutvergiessen unnd zertrennung fridlichen wesens, wohlbedächtig unnd nottwerdig, schreiben, verordnen und beuehlen thuen. Habt Ir aus neben verwahrter abschrifft [fo.1ᵛ] wie auch vorgedachter Juden supplication unnd ubergebenem Exemplan desselben Buchs nach lengs zuvernehmen. Wiewol wir unns nun hir unnd von ermaltem Rath zur Dorttmundt, khaines andern dann der gebur nach schuldigen gehorsambs versehen, derweil aber doch in dergleichen fällen unsere unnd das heiligen Reichs publicierte offters widerholete unnd gescherffte Policeij unnd andere ordnungen, mit allen ernst gebieten unnd wollen, das alle und yede Obrigkheiten, unns unnd dem heiligen Reich, Unterworff bevorab, wo fürneme Truekherrijen und Buchhandlung seyen, anfachtung unnd fursehens haben sollen, das dergleichen schmächeliche Bücher unnd schrifften bey Ihnen nit weder haimblich noch offenlich gedruekht, oder frylgetragen, unnd do sy am Tag khomen, nit aussgebraitt, sondern von stund an aufgehebt, und sovil Innern muglich cassirt und vertilgt, die verbrecher aber, vermög der Recht, unnd Ihr nach gelegenhait oder gestalt der sachen, unnachlessig gestrafft werden sollen. So haben wir euch als eine furneme Reichs unnd handels Statt, dessen auch in disem fall heimit zuerinnern ein notturfft geachtet, darauf euch grundig unnd ernstlich ermahnendt, und bevehlendt, wollet, von Obrigkheit unnd amptswegen, obbeueltem ergerlichem Schamlosen Schmachbuch, in allen Truekhereij nnd Buchläden, bey Euch ohne jemandt Respect oder Verwarnung mit Vleiss nach forschen, die Exemplaria so Ir zu handen bringet, confiscirn, hinweg thuen, unnd sowol die werkhauffer unnd feil haben, als Kauffer unnd andere Innhaber solcher Bücher, so damit betritten unnd bey denen sy gefunden, gestalten sachen unnd umbstunden nach, in geburliche straff nehmen. Auch damit hirfuro solch Buch khains weegs erneirert, noch etirs grösser weitterung dadurch erweekht solt, dasselb nyrgendts zu druekhen, sovil zutragen, oder sonsten zubehalten unnd zu haben, durch scharffe hochverpeente Edicta gebieten unnd verschaffen, das beschicht zu gebur unnd billighait, unnd Ir erstattet daran unsern gefelligen endlichen willen und meinung denen wir mit kaiserlichen [fo.2ʳ] genaden genaigt seind. Geben auf unsernn künigelichen Schloss zu Prag den Zehenten tag Julij anno im funfundneunzigsten, unserer Reiche des Römischen im Zwainzigsten des hungerischen im dreyundzwanzigsten, und des Behemischen auch im Zwanzigsten,

Rudolf

145

NOTES

1. *D. Martin Luthers Werke, Kritische Gesamtausgabe* (Weimar, 1883-), *Tischreden* 1, no. 1038: "Typographia postremum est donum et idem maximum, per eam enim Deus toti terrarum orbi voluit negotium verae religionis in fine mundi innotescere ac in omnes linguas transfundi. Ultima sane flamma mundi inextinguibilis." (Hereafter cited as *WA*.) See also Otto Clemen, *Luthers Lob der Buchdruckerkunst* (Zwickau, 1939).

2. For the indispensable role played by the printing press in disseminating reform ideas and for the different editions of Lutheran pamphlets, see Otto Clemen, *Die lutherische Reformation und der Buchdruck* (Leipzig, 1939); Josef Benzing, *Lutherbibliographie, Verzeichnis der gedruckter Schriften Martin Luthers bis zu dessen Tod* (Baden-Baden, 1966); and Helmut Claus and Michael A. Pegg, *Ergänzungen zur Bibliographie der zeitgenössischen Lutherdrucke* (Gotha, 1982).

3. See Miriam Usher Chrisman, *Lay Culture, Learned Culture: Books and Social Change in Strasbourg, 1480-1599* (New Haven, 1982), 156 ff. and Robert W. Scribner, *For the Sake of Simple Folk: Popular Propaganda for the German Reformation* (Cambridge, 1981).

4. *WA*, vol. 2, 308-10.

5. Ibid., 310: "Utinam vero hoc negotium cum Iudaeis tam procedat feliciter, quam alias per tam celerum cursum verbi intra iam breve tempus miram mutationem et magnifica opera dei vidimus."

6. *WA*, vol 53, 575-77.

7. Ibid., 415-16.

8. *WA Briefwechsel* vol. 8, no. 3157; *Tischreden*, vol. 1, nos. 369, 741, 3912; vol. 3, no. 3597.

9. See Selma Stern, *Josel of Rosheim, Commander of Jewry in the Holy Roman Empire of the German Nation*, trans. Gertrude Hirschler (Philadelphia, 1965), 196.

10. *Ibid.*, 192-93.

11. It appeared in Johann Lonicer's Latin translation, published in 1525 by J. Knobloch. See Miriam Usher Chrisman, *Bibliography of Strasbourg Imprints, 1480-1599* (New Haven, 1982), 286 (P1.1.20).

12. The documents arising out of this censorship case are found in Stadtarchiv Frankfurt (hereafter StdA F) Ugb E46 ad J1.

13. *Christlicher Unterricht D. Mart. Lutheri / von den Jüden Lügen wider die Person unsers Herren Jesu Christi / seiner Lieben Mutter Maria / und aller Christen / hochnötig zu lesen. Dar aus ein jeder Christ liechtlich schliessen kan / ob man die Jüden billich bey sich leiden solle doer nicht.* A copy of the booklet is bound with other folios in StdA F Ugb E46 ad J1, fols. 13-54.

14. Ibid., sig. B^{4v-6v}.

15. Ibid., sig. B^{7r}-C^1.

16. On Arnd Westhoff, see Josef Benzing, *Die Buchdrucker des 16 und 17 Jahrhunderts im deutschen Sprachgebiet* (Wiesbaden, 1963), 82.

17. For a brief history of the gymnasium, see August Döring, *Die Geschichte des Gymnasiums zu Dortmund* (Dortmund, 1874).

18. On Westhoff's press list, see Klemens Löffler, "Der Dortmunder Buchdruck des 16. Jahrhunderts" in *Beiträge zur Geschichte Dortmunds und der Grafschaft Mark* 13(1905):27-78: 16(1908):1-10; 23(1914):428-33; and Karl Wülfrath, *Bibliotheca Marchia, Die Literatur der westfälischen Mark, Teil I: Von den Frühdrucken bis 1666* (Münster, 1936), nos. 623, 624, 840, 1224, 1250. The antisemitic booklet bears no date of publication. Wülfrath arbitrarily and incorrectly assigns the year of publication to be 1575.

19. The best analysis of the Reformation in Dortmund is Heinz Schilling's "Dortmund im 16. und 17. Jahrhundert—Reichsstädtische Gesellschaft, Reformation und Konfessionalisierung," in *Dortmund, 1100 Jahre Stadtgeschichte,* eds. G. Luntowski and N. Reimann (Dortmund, 1982), 153-202. See also Luise von Winterfeld, *Geschichte der Freien Reichsund Hansestadt Dortmund,* 4th ed. (Dortmund, 1963). The following summary of the Reformation is based on these accounts.

20. In Strasbourg, the alliance between the city council and the populace rendered the Interim utterly unworkable; see Erdmann Weyrauch, *Konfessionelle Krise und Soziale Stabilität. Das Interim in Strassburg, 1548-1562* (Stuttgart, 1978).

21. See Karl Maser, *Die Juden der Frei- und Reichsstadt Dortmund und der Graftschaft Mark.* Ph.D. diss., Münster, (1912), Chapter 1.

22. See the chronicle of Dietrich Westhoff, in *Die Chroniken der westfälischen und niederrheinischen Städte. I. Bd. Dortmund. Neuss. (= Die Chroniken der deutschen Städte vom 14. bis ins 16. Jahrhundert, Bd. 20),* ed. Historische Kommission bei der Bayerischen Königlichen Akademie der Wissenschaften (Leipzig, 1887), 349.

23. Ibid., 447-48.

24. Maser, *Die Juden,* 44-46.

25. *WA* 53, 542-44.

26. StdA F Ugb E 46 ad J1.

27. StdA F Ugb E 46 ad J1, f. 2^r: "welche nicht allein allgemeinner vernunft, Gottes wordt unndt Gebothenn, ja allen löblichen Rechten gennzlich zurwider sonndernlich absque lasione divina ac Casaraeae Vestrae Majestatis auch gemeinnes hochbeliebten friedenns Einigkeit unnd sonnderlichen Gemainnem Ergenuss weder haimblich noch öffentlich nicht phödern, geredt oder geschribenn, viel wenninger in offeren Truckg publicirt werden."

28. StdA F Ugb E 46 ad J1, f. 4r: "sonnderlichenn die weill dess schenndtbuchleinn alberaith auf die lannlieln auch dem Gemainnen Man der Orther zur hanndtenn khommen."

29. See the appendix to this paper.

30. See the appendix to this paper.

31. StdA F Ugb E 46 ad J1.

32. For censorship in the Old Reich, see Ulrich Eisenhardt, *Die kaiserliche Aufsicht über Buchdruck, Buchhandel und Presse im Heiligen Römischen Reich Deutscher Nation (1496-1806). Ein Beitrag zur Geschichte der Bücherund Pressezensur* (Karlsruhe, 1970); Dieter Breuer, *Die Geschichte der literarischen Zensur in Deutschland* (Heidelberg, 1982); and Helmut Neuman, *Staatliche Bücherzensur und -aufsicht in Bayern von der Reformation bis zum Ausgang des 17. Jahrhunderts* (Karlsruhe, 1977).

33. Cf. Eisenhardt, ibid., 4-5.

34. Ibid., 5.

35. Ibid., 6-7.

36. Cf. Wülrath, *Bibliotheca Marchia*, nos. 497, 501.

Statistics on
Sixteenth-Century Printing

MARK U. EDWARDS, JR.

N ot many years ago, if you mentioned computers and statistics to intellectual historians, at best they would grudgingly concede that such tools might have a place in social or economic history but offer little or nothing to their own specialty. That view has changed remarkably in the last decade, and Miriam Usher Chrisman is one of the pioneers who brought about this change. Chrisman was one of the first historians of the sixteenth century to realize that a quantitative analysis of publication statistics could shed significant light on the intellectual world not only of the scholar but also of the wider lay readership.

In her *Lay Culture, Learned Culture: Books and Social Change in Strasbourg, 1480-1599*, Chrisman demonstrates the insights a statistical analysis of the Strasbourg printing industry can produce about sixteenth-century intellectual life, insights available through no other method or source. Or course, she goes beyond quantitative data to analyze content and authors in the style of more traditional intellectual history. Nevertheless, the statistics provide the backbone of her analysis and point to her central thesis, summarized in the title of the book, that there were two literate cultures in Strasbourg, lay and learned, and that for a brief but crucial period the interests of the two converged and assisted the birth of the Protestant Reformation.[1]

Given her pioneering status in this line of research, it seemed not inappropriate to honor her in this *Festchrift* with a discussion of other recent work on publishing and the Reformation. In what follows, I shall compare the results of three studies of printing and the Reformation: Richard A Crofts' "Printing, Reform, and the Catholic Reformation in Germany (1521-1545),"[2] my "Catholic Controversial Literature, 1518-1555," and the statistical analysis in my *Luther's Last Battles: Politics and Polemics in the German Reformation, 1531-46.*[3] Although drawn from different sources, Croft's data and my own correlate highly with each other, which, after some preliminary observations, allows the focus more on issues of interpretation than on statistics per se. But, we must begin with the data and their source.[4]

Any study of sixteenth-century publications must necessarily deal with incomplete data. War, fire, and time have taken their

Table 1. Catholic Controversial Literature

Date	Latin & German (Edwards)	Latin & German (Crofts)	German (Edwards)	German (Crofts)
1521	25	15	12	8
1522	36	13	20	6
1523	53	22	24	12
1524	93	25	51	16
1525	68	33	27	12
1526	76	18	35	10
1527	80	22	35	7
1528	87	23	62	17
1529	71	17	29	7
1530	54	14	23	8
1531	48	5	20	2
1532	47	7	21	1
1533	37	9	24	6
1534	61	20	22	8
1535	51	15	24	8
1536	53	11	21	7
1537	48	8	20	3
1538	49	8	15	3
1539	35	6	14	2
1540	21	1	8	0
1541	31	7	7	2
1542	42	3	12	0
1543	26	7	3	2
1544	25	12	4	0
1545	37	15	14	4
Totals	1254	336	547	151
German as Percent of Total	43.6	44.9		

toll on the printed works of that period. We can only offer samples from a universe that no longer exists. Crofts drew his sample from the collection housed in the British Library and catalogued in the *Short-Title Catalogue of Books Printed in the German-Speaking Countries*.[5] For my study of Catholic publications, I used Wilbirgis Klaiber, *Katholische Kontroverstheologen und Reformer des 16. Jahrhunderts: Ein Werkverzeichnis*; Martin Spahn, *Johannes Cochläus: Ein Lebensbild*; and J. Metzler, "Verzeichnis der Schriften Ecks," in *Tres orationes funebres*.[6] For Luther's publications, I used Kurt Aland, *Hilfsbuch zum Lutherstudium*; and Joseph Benzing, *Lutherbibliographie: Verzeichnis der gedruckten Schriften Martin Luthers bis zu dessen Tod*.[7]

How do these samples compare with each other? To begin with, Crofts examines more categories than do I but with a smaller sample. Whereas I studied Catholic controversial theologians and Martin Luther, Crofts also examined nonpolemical Catholic publications and publications by Protestant writers other than Luther. Although involving fewer categories, my data sets are substantially larger than Crofts and, in the case of data on Luther's publications, approach the "universe." Tables 1 and 2 show my sample of Catholic controversial literature and printings of Luther, which contains about three times the number of entries as Crofts.[8] But this disparity in absolute numbers in no way invalidates the trends that Crofts uncovered. As figures 1-4 indicate, our data follow each other very closely. In the case of printing and reprinting Luther's works, what is obvious from visual inspection is borne out by statistical testing: the correlation over time between the two samples is well above .9.[9] There is more "noise" in the two Catholic samples, but these samples are still highly correlated.[10] Since the two samples are so highly correlated and since my samples come about as close as we can at this point to recreating the total printings of the period (the "universe" of the samples), I think that Crofts is fully justified in placing confidence in his sample. So with fairly high confidence in the data, let us turn to the far more interesting issue of their interpretation.

Crofts reaches several conclusions from his data concerning the relative use of the press by Catholics and Reformers. He observes that although the number of Catholic publications in both Latin and German after 1525 was "surprisingly high" and nearly matched the total of the Reformers, on the whole, Catholics "either failed to recognize the value of publishing in

151

Table 2. Publications of Luther (printings)

Date	First Editions (Edwards)	Total (Edwards)	Total (Crofts)	Polemics Against Catholics (Edwards)	German First Editions (Edwards)	German (Edwards)	German (Crofts)	Polemics Against Catholics (Edwards)	% German (Edwards)	% German (Crofts)	Ratio of Reprints to Firsts (Totals)	Ratio of Reprints to Firsts (German)
1516	1	1		0	1	1		0	100.0		0.00	0.60
1517	3	6		4	1	2		0	33.3		1.00	1.00
1518	17	87		38	6	41		9	47.1		4.12	5.83
1519	25	170		68	14	107		28	62.9		5.80	6.64
1520	27	275		116	15	235		93	85.5		9.19	14.67
1521	26	174	86	114	20	136	73	90	78.2	84.9	5.69	5.89
1522	45	248	125	96	39	235	111	88	94.8	88.8	4.51	5.03
1523	55	390	159	187	45	346	152	159	88.7	95.6	6.09	6.69
1524	34	232	91	89	30	210	82	77	90.5	90.1	5.82	6.00
1525	32	237	71	48	28	211	61	41	89.0	85.9	6.41	6.54
1526	26	141	30	44	25	121	26	31	85.8	86.7	4.42	3.84
1527	16	110	33	40	15	98	24	37	89.1	72.7	5.88	5.53
1528	15	64	12	34	13	60	12	30	93.8	100.0	3.27	3.62
1529	12	76	10	25	12	70	10	24	92.1	100.0	5.33	4.93
1530	26	138	47	84	23	126	44	78	91.3	93.6	4.31	4.48
1531	17	94	23	49	16	86	22	47	91.5	95.7	4.53	4.28
1532	12	46	18	8	7	33	17	5	71.7	94.4	2.83	3.71
1533	16	59	16	23	16	53	15	21	89.8	93.8	2.69	2.31

continued ▲

Table 2. Publications of Luther (printings) *CONTINUED*

Date	First Editions (Edwards)	Total (Edwards)	Total (Crofts)	Polemics Against Catholics (Edwards)	German First Editions (Edwards)	German (Edwards)	German (Crofts)	Polemics Against Catholics (Edwards)	% German (Edwards)	% German (Crofts)	Ratio of Reprints to Firsts (Totals)	Ratio of Reprints to Firsts (German)
1534	10	35	13	11	5	28	11	8	80.0	84.6	2.50	4.60
1535	19	68	15	29	14	58	13	24	85.3	86.7	2.58	3.14
1536	10	40	8	7	5	25	7	4	62.5	87.5	3.00	4.00
1537	16	47	12	35	9	34	10	29	72.3	83.3	1.94	2.78
1538	18	62	18	33	10	40	12	24	64.5	66.7	2.44	3.00
1539	12	56	14	24	9	43	11	21	76.8	78.6	3.67	3.78
1540	5	26	8	10	2	20	7	9	76.9	87.5	4.20	9.00
1541	7	34	13	25	5	30	10	22	88.2	76.9	3.86	5.00
1542	9	49	9	21	7	42	9	20	85.7	100.0	4.44	5.00
1543	11	58	13	11	6	39	11	5	67.2	84.6	4.27	5.50
1544	7	38	12	8	4	24	10	4	63.2	83.3	4.43	5.00
1545	12	74	22	40	9	56	17	30	75.7	77.3	5.17	5.22
1546	3	48		30	3	35		23	72.7		15.00	10.67
1521-1545 Totals	544	2596	878	1095	414	2224	777	928	85.7	88.5		
1516-1546 Totals		3183		1351		2645		1081			4.85	5.39

Figure 1. Total Printings of Luther's Publications

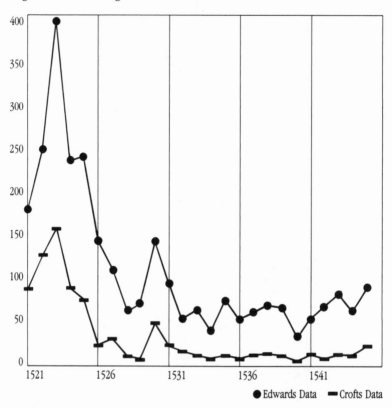

● Edwards Data ▬ Crofts Data

German or were unwilling to do so." No Catholic author matched the literary talents or popular appeal of Martin Luther. And Crofts speculates that had the Catholics such a similarly talented, popular author, perhaps the course of the Reformation would have been different, noting that "if Luther's works are excluded from the reformers' total, the Catholics outpublished their opponents."[11]

But to compare meaningfully Catholic and Protestant use of the press in their controversy with each other, we must distinguish between overall publications and polemical (or controversial) literature, a subcategory of the whole. The use of the press to further or hinder the spread of the Reformation is more meaningfully gauged by the latter than the former. That an author is Catholic or Protestant is largely irrelevant if the treatise has little or nothing to do with the issues dividing the parties. In this regard both our statistics are less complete than we might wish. Crofts gives figures for overall Catholic publications and for Catholic controversial literature: Catholic controversial literature makes up about 34 percent of the total Catholic publications in Latin and German and about 44 percent of all Catholic publications in German. He does not offer a similar breakdown for Protestant literature, however. In my data, I lack a figure for overall Catholic and Protestant publications, although I can offer a breakdown for Luther's works: about 42 percent of the overall printings of Luther's works in Latin and German were polemics against Catholics (see Table 2).

Where, then, does that leave us? By Crofts' data, if we compare Catholic printings with Protestant printings over the period 1521-1545, including, of course, both polemical and nonpolemical literature, we find that for every four Catholic treatises printed, there were seven Protestant printings. If we restrict our attention to German-language publications, which presumably were targeted at a larger, more popular audience, the ratio increases to four Protestant treatises for every one Catholic treatise. These figures, especially for German-language printings, show a substantially greater use of the press by Protestants but not necessarily for polemical purposes. To isolate the category of "polemics", we need a breakdown of the Reformers' publications into controversial and noncontroversial writings. Lacking this breakdown in Crofts' data, we must make do with my narrower but more complete statistics for Catholic controversialists and Luther (see Tables 1 and 2). If we compare Luther's controversial writings against Catholics with Catholic controversial writings against Protestants, we find that nearly as many anti-Catholic treatises by Luther were printed as anti-Protestant treatises by all the Catholic controversialists (actually, about four treatises by Luther for every five treatises by Catholics). If we restrict ourselves to German-language publications, the comparison becomes even more dramatic: for every four anti-Protestant printings in German you can find seven anti-Catholic printings of works by Luther.[12]

It has long been recognized, and these statistics confirm, that Luther's works were printed and reprinted in astonishing numbers. No Catholic author came close to his productivity. The two most prolific Catholic writers in the period 1521-1545,

Johann Cochlaeus and Georg Witzel, saw just 170 and 111 printings, respectively (for Cochlaeus, there were 100 Latin printings
and 70 German printings; for Witzel, 47 Latin printings and 64
German). Witzel, it should be added, made his contribution largely after mid-1530. For the same period, some 2596 printings of
Luther's works appeared.

Had the Catholics, as Crofts speculates, found a writer as talented and prolific as Luther, perhaps the course of the Reformation would have been different; but, of course, this argument is
counter to reality and problematic in other ways as well. The publication statistics suggest that after the initial four or five years of
the Reformation movement (that is, by 1526), Luther had become
a considerably less popular and more regional author. Over the
course of Luther's career as a publicist, 49 percent of his publications and 57 percent of the printings and reprintings of these
publications appeared by the end of 1525; 265 different publications of a total of 544, excluding editions of the partial or full
Bible, and 1820 printings of a total of 3183 printings, once again

Figure 2. Total Publications (Printings) of Catholic Controversial Literature in German

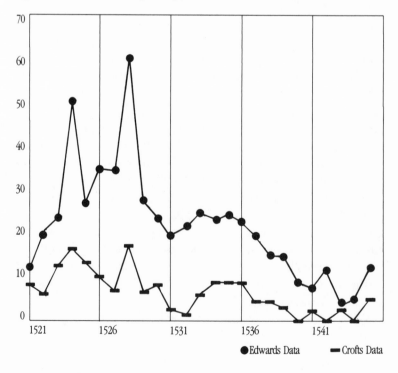

156

Figure 3. Total German Printings of Luther

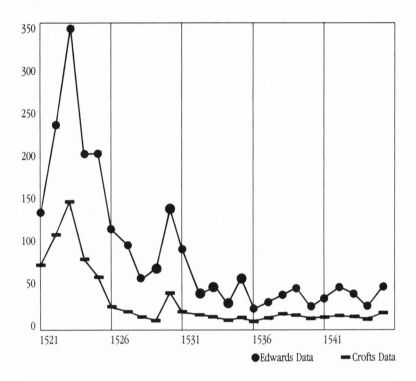

● Edwards Data ▬ Crofts Data

excluding full and partial Bibles. The ratio of reprints to first editions declined dramatically over this same period, suggesting a waning interest for his works among the public. For the period 1516-1525, almost six reprints appeared for every first edition (5.94 to 1). For the period 1526-1546, there are only a bit over three reprints (3.36 to 1). If we single out those publications with at least a moderately anti-Catholic controversial tone, the decline is still clear: from 5.55 to 1 in the period 1516-1525 to 3.38 to 1 in the period after 1525. Moreover, if we examine the geography of the printing and reprinting of his works, we note that after 1525 his works increasingly were published largely in staunchly Lutheran cities in central and northern Germany.[13] Although printing declined overall during these years, there is also a change in authorship in southern Germany, with local Protestant authors replacing Luther in the local presses. These changes suggest that, had Luther died, say, in the Peasants' War, others could have filled the vacuum created by his passing.

More problematic still is Crofts' observation that if Luther's works are excluded from the Reformers' total, Catholics outpublished their opponents. By Crofts' statistics, if we exclude Luther's German and Latin works from the total of the Reformers' German and Latin works, then Catholics outpublish Protestants only slightly (829 Protestant printings versus 992 Catholic printings) and the difference could be due as much to sampling error as to any real difference. If we restrict ourselves to German-language publications, which presumably reached a wider audience, the slight Catholic advantage turns to an unquestionable Protestant domination: 596 Protestant printings versus 345 Catholic printings.

In any case, we should be comparing the printing of controversial works, not total output. For this, however, we lack relevant information. If we assume, for lack of a better estimate, that controversial works made up the same percent of the total for all Reformers as they did for Luther (42 percent), then the Reformers produced an estimated 348 controversial works to the Catholics' actual 336 works. For German controversial works, the figures would be an estimated 250 Protestant printings to an actual 151 Catholic printings. Of course, there is no compelling reason to accept Luther's percentage as applicable to all Protestant printings, but the conclusion to be drawn nevertheless should be clear. Luther undoubtedly dominates the publication statistics for the period 1520-1545. But even if his contribution is discounted, Protestant printings matched or exceeded Catholic printings, especially in the vernacular language. And, since Luther's contribution cannot in fact be excluded, the challenge to the historian is to explain why the Protestants, including Luther, so outproduced their opponent.[14]

Another statistic also is quite revealing: the location where works were printed and reprinted. I have also tabulated the places where Luther's publications and the publications of the Catholic controversialists were published. To begin, the shipment of books and treatises was one of the most expensive aspects of book production in the sixteenth century and could add substantially to the price of a book. In fact, it was often cheaper, especially for more popular, vernacular treatises, to reprint a work in a distant town than to send a large shipment from the place of original publication. Therefore, statistics on the place where a work is printed, and especially reprinted, can be used to gauge the range of influence of an author or a publication.

This reasoning underlies my argument earlier in this essay,

and in more detail in my *Luther's Last Battles*, that Luther became a more regional author in the years after 1525.[15] A similar analysis of the Catholic data revealed a striking concentration of Catholic controversial publication in two centers: one in west-central Germany (Cologne and Mainz), the other in east-central Germany (Leipzig and Dresden). Dresden and Leipzig of Ducal Saxony account for more than 50 percent of the vernacular Catholic controversial publications of the 1530s! This striking geographical concentration raises a number of new questions in the understanding and analysis of the Catholic polemical effort.[16] In his article, Crofts does not analyze the publication data beyond the date

Figure 4. Catholic Controversial Literature in Latin and German

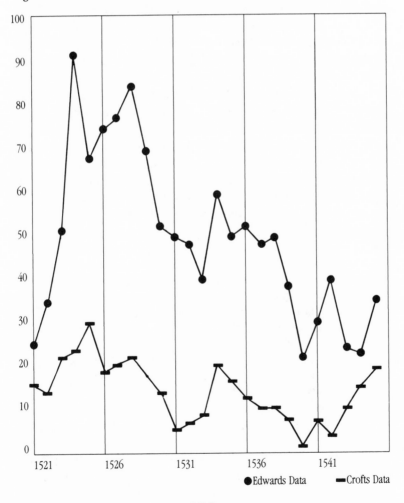

159

of publication. If Crofts were to break out his data according to place of publication, I strongly suspect that he would find a much wider distribution in the printing of noncontroversial Catholic literature than in the printing of controversial Catholic literature and, furthermore, that Protestant literature of both a controversial and noncontroversial nature would be more widely published than its Catholic counterpart. If proven correct, this surmise will provide dramatic evidence for the Protestant dominance of the polemical area during the first decades of the Reformation.

Karl Schottenloher has suggested that local ordinances favored Lutheran publication.[17] Printing presses were to be found mainly in cities, and as numerous studies have shown, the Reformation was especially well received by urban polities.[18] It is hardly surprising, therefore, that printing helped turn cities Protestant, and once Protestant, cities restricted publication of Catholic works. But this does not take us very far. There is undoubtedly an interaction between the printing shops and their market. Printers helped create a market for Protestant works, especially in the early years of the Reformation movement, but it would be naive to assume that ideology was the major driving force behind their publication of Protestant writers. Printers were in business and if their works did not sell, they did not stay in business very long. Printers, it seems reasonable to conclude, published Protestant works because people would buy them. When the city council of Leipzig petitioned the staunchly Catholic Duke Georg of Saxony on behalf of the city's printers on April 7, 1524, the conflict between ideology and economics was starkly presented.

> The printers have often and bitterly complained to us now and in the past that they are completely losing their livelihood and that if it should continue in the same fashion they will lose house, home, and all their livelihood because they are not allowed to print or sell anything new that is made in Wittenberg or elsewhere. For that which one would gladly sell and for which there is demand, they are not allowed to have or sell. But what they have in overabundance [Catholic treatises] is desired by no one and cannot even be given away.[19]

Ordinances can cut both ways. Ordinances may eventually have favored the Protestants, but Catholic rulers such as Duke Georg

160

could enforce ordinances against the publication of Protestant writings—and apparently injure the printing industry in the process.

The numbers of printings and reprintings, the geographic distribution of these printings, and the market demand for these works must ultimately allow us to conclude some things about the interests—and yes, even the convictions—of the literate readership in sixteenth-century Germany. Natalie Davis warns that we cannot confidently infer from the contents of a book its readers' outlook, and that the relatively low rate of literacy lessens the significance of printing.[20] Robert Scribner makes much the same point in *For the Sake of Simple Folk*.[21] While such admonitions are salutary, they should not be exaggerated. The sheer mass of the printing effort and its wide geographic distribution— and the amount of trade that this production and distribution represents— allows us to draw with some assurance inferences about the popularity of certain beliefs and convictions. If we assume conservatively that each printing of a work by Luther numbered from two hundred to one thousand copies, we are talking about an output for Luther alone of 620,000 to 3,100,000 copies during the period 1516-1546! And this total does not include the numerous whole and partial editions of Luther's Bible translation. To sell this many treatises and pamphlets, significant numbers of people had to be spending significant sums of money to read Martin Luther. And he is only one author. In light of publication statistics such as these, it seems far more plausible to assume a certain meeting of minds between author and audience than to deny it. Catholicism may well have recovered the propaganda initiative in the second half of the century,[22] but the years between 1520 and 1550 belong to the Protestants and to their ideas.

Much remains to be done. The data I have drawn from the Klaiber bibliography, supplemented by a variety of other bibliographies, give us reasonably good statistics on Catholic controversialists. But we need to undertake a similar survey for Protestant controversialists. In the meanwhile, perhaps Crofts will take his data on publications by the Reformers and break out those works that are controversial in nature. But both our surveys deal largely with major contributors. We need to get a better idea of the vast numbers of pamphlets and treatises published anonymously or by minor figures. Perhaps the extensive resources of the Tübingen *Flugschriften* project will allow us to understand better this important aspect of the problem. Miriam Chrisman has shown with one city the type of thorough research in both statistics and in content analysis that needs to be done for all the publishing centers of Germany. Now we must follow her example.

NOTES

1. Miriam Usher Chrisman, *Lay Culture, Learned Culture: Books and Social Change in Strasbourg, 1480-1599* (New Haven, 1982), and Miriam Usher Chrisman, ed. *Bibliography of Strasbourg Imprints, 1480-1599* (New Haven, 1982).

2. Richard A. Crofts, "Printing, Reform, and the Catholic Reformation in Germany (1521-1545)," *Sixteenth Century Journal* 16(1985): 369-81. In an earlier article, Crofts dealt with the period 1510-1520 ("Books, Reform and the Reformation," *Archive for Reformation History* 71[1980]:21-36).

3. Mark U. Edwards, Jr., "Catholic Controversial Literature, 1518-1555: Some Statistics," *Archive for Reformation History* (forthcoming: 1988). My article was accepted for publication before the appearance of Crofts' piece. Rather than rewrite substantial portions of the article to include Crofts' findings, I thought it better to compare the two pieces in this *Festschrift*.

4. The richest repository for a statistical study of German publications for the period 1500-1530 can be found in the computers of Tübingen University and the *Flugschriften* project headed by Hans-Joachim Köhler. In addition to the yearly microfiche of German pamphlets produced by the project, the scholars at Tübingen have built up an extensive, descriptive data base covering both the pamphlets published in the microfiche series and a wide selection of additional pamphlets. The significance of this data base for a better understanding of printing and intellectual life in the first third of the sixteenth century can scarcely be underestimated. Unfortunately, the project is scheduled to be discontinued before its task is completed.

5. *Short-title Catalogue of Books Printed in the German-Speaking Countries* (London, 1962).

6. Wilbirgis Klaiber, ed., *Katholische Kontroverstheologen und Reformer des 16. Jahrhunderts: Ein Werkverzeichnis*, Reformationsgeschichtliche Studien und Texte, vol. 116 (Munster, 1978). For a critical evaluation of this bibliography, see Jean-François Gilmont, "La bibliographie de la controverse catholique au 16e siècle; quelques suggestions méthodologiques," *Revue d'histoire ecclesiastique* 74(1979): 362-71. Martin Spahn, *Johannes Cochläus: Ein Lebensbild* (Berlin,

1898); J. Metzler, ed., Verzeichnis der Schriften Ecks, in *Tres oriationes funebres*, Corpus Catholicorum, 16 (Münster, 1930), lxxii-cxxxii.

7. Kurt Aland, *Hilfsbuch zum Lutherstudium*, 3d ed. (Witten, 1970); Joseph Benzing, *Lutherbibliographie: Verzeichnis der gedruckten Schriften Martin Luthers bis zu dessen Tod* (Baden-Baden, 1966). For a discussion of my methodology and additional statistical analysis, see Mark U. Edwards, *Luther's Last Battles: Politics and Polemics, 1531-46* (Ithaca, N.Y., 1983).

8. The absolute figures for Crofts' data, in some cases, have been reconstructed from the percentage figures given in his article.

9. For total numbers of printings and for total numbers of German works, the Pearson correlation coefficient is .96 with $n=25$, $T=17$, and $p=<10^{-6}$

10. The Pearson correlation coefficient for total number of Catholic controversial works is .71 with $n=25$, $T=4.96$, and $p=5.0 \times 10^{-5}$, and the Pearson correlation coefficient for such works in German is .84 with $n=25$, $T=7.57$, and $p=<10^{-6}$.

11. Crofts, "Printing, Reform, and the Catholic Reformation," 381.

12. I offer some possible explanations for these dramatic differences in Edwards, "Catholic Controversial Literature."

13. See Edwards, *Luther's Last Battles*, 20-23.

14. See Edwards, "Catholic Controversial Literature."

15. See Edwards, *Luther's Last Battles*.

16. See Edwards, "Catholic Controversial Literature."

17. Karl Schottenloher, "Buchdrucker und Buchführer im Dienste der Reformation," in *Realencyclopedie für Protestant Theologie und Kirche*, ed. Johann Jakob Herzog (Leipzig, 1913), Vol. 23, 272. Cited by Crofts, "Printing, Reform, and the Catholic Reformation," 369, n. 4.

18. For an overview of the literature, see Thomas A. Brady, Jr., "Social History," in *Reformation Europe: A Guide to Research*, ed. Steven Ozment (St. Louis, 1982).

19. Felician Gess, ed. *Akten und Briefe zur Kirchenpolitik Herzog Georgs von Sachsen* (Leipzig, 1905), vol. 1, 641.

20. Natalie Z. Davis, *Society and Culture in Early Modern France* (Stanford, Calif., 1975), 190-91. Cited by Crofts, "Printing, Reform, and the Catholic Reformation," 370.

21. Robert W. Scribner, *For the Sake of Simple Folk: Popular Propaganda for the German Reformation* (Cambridge, 1981), 1-7.

22. This is only an impression that I have. Actual statistical research on this point remains to be done.

The Lower Orders
In Early Modern Augsburg

ELLIS L. KNOX

T raditional analyses of social structure in early modern German cities use two main sources: tax books and city constitutions. The only thorough examination of Augsburg's middle class, for example, is an essay by Friedrich Blendinger, in which he ranks the guilds of the city according to taxed wealth.[1] Although his approach is traditional in that he bases his analysis on tax records, Blendinger recognizes one important fact about early modern German society: the middle class must be analyzed according to occupation, as represented by the guilds. Blendinger fails, however, to take advantage of the other sources available in Augsburg relevant to the guilds; namely, the *Handwerker-Akten* that exist in such abundance.[2] These sources supplement the tax records nicely to permit a close look inside Augsberg's middle class.

Such a supplement is necessary because tax records alone are simply not a reliable measure of social class. The tax books are not difficult to read; most entries are routine, and Claus Peter Clasen has written an excellent guide to their interpretation.[3] The difficulty lies in deciding what we mean by rich and poor. Since capital goods and property were the principal objects of taxation, the best modern term that would apply is gross worth, or the total value of a person's assets without deducting outstanding debts. The worth of a person could be all in cash and other liquid assets or wholly in fixed assets such as property and equipment. It would have been entirely possible for one artisan to owe a fairly high tax, yet have very little cash and be saddled with heavy debts, while another artisan, paying the same tax, had a high income and few debts. The first we would call poor, the second rich. There is no way to distinguish between the two for individual cases using the tax books alone.

Differences in wealth as represented by the tax paid, therefore, cannot be taken at face value, nor does the fact that two people paid the same tax necessarily mean that they were equally wealthy. This point should be stressed, for most of the guildsmen of Augsburg were at or near the level of *habnits* (literally, "have nots"), those who had so little that they paid only the base tax of thirty-six *pfennige*. Simply because most artisans paid the same tax, however, does not permit the conclusion that most belonged to the same social class. These considerations tend to vitiate the utility of tax books in developing a realistic analysis of class and make all the more attractive an approach based on status, which is the approach taken here, wherein the guild is treated as the fundamental unit of analysis. The principal questions are concerned with discovering what factors determined social status within the middle class, and what factors affected social mobility.

The term middle class can be fairly clearly defined: it encompassed the nonnoble citizen and his dependents, what was called in contemporary sources the common man.[4] In Augsburg, this meant the so-called incorporated people.[5] These were the guildsmen of the city, from wealthy and powerful members of the Merchants Guild to the humble craftsmen making belts or needles. Above this group was the upper class: the patriciate, the urban nobility whose families by tradition held the reins of power within the city. Below the middle class was the lower class, which consisted of two groups: those who would one day join the ranks of the middle class, respectable but junior members of legitimate society such as journeymen and apprentices, and the disenfranchised, such as the poor, the disreputable, the criminal, the insane.

The middle class itself was not homogeneous.[6] Within it were several social groups, each of which recognized in the others its social superiors or inferiors. The highest-ranking guilds in Augsburg were the mercantile trades: merchants (*Kaufleute*), retailers (*Krämer*), and the salt and wine dealers (*Salzfertiger*). These not only were among the wealthiest citizens, they also held many of the important civil offices.[7] Next came the so-called artistic crafts, the painters, goldsmiths, porcelain makers, and others, who made objects of great beauty and value. These were normally ranked above the general run of craftsmen, both legally and socially. Below them came the common artisans. At the top of these were prestigious trades such as brewer and baker; at the bottom were the poor crafts, like shoemaker or carpenter.[8] All were respectable trades replete with privileges and a protected, if modest, social station. Below the common artisan was a group referred to as the lowly trades, the *verfemte Berufe*, so considered because of some social stigma associated with them. Here were the fishers, millers, bathhouse keepers, barbers, and other such guilds.[9] These craftsmen were on the very edge of respectability, even though some of them made more money than other craftsmen more highly regarded. Certain occupations ranked even below the lowly trades. These were so socially unacceptable that they were not allowed the honor of incorporation as a guild. Among these were executioner, grave-digger, and night watchman. These were counted not in the middle class but among the lower classes and were denied the privileges of guild membership and citizenship.[10]

Traditionally, tax records have provided the principal source of information for analyses of the middle class, but the structure and dynamics of the internal hierarchy just presented cannot be explained by tax records alone. Few historians have bothered to look very far inside the middle class, preferring to treat it as a single, homogeneous group. Others have examined the great merchants in exhaustive detail but refer to them as the middle class, as if the merchants alone composed the entire class. Those who have pried into the inner structure have found it difficult to produce a clear hierarchy, largely because they have used wealth as the only criterion for such a classification.

In studying the guilds of Augsburg, I have found that three factors were crucial in determining social status within the middle class: cultural prejudice toward certain occupations, the economic conditions that obtained in a given craft, and individual circumstances such as personal reputation and wealth. Each factor had its place and its consequences.

Cultural prejudice could elevate a trade or malign it. Certain crafts were highly regarded simply because of the beauty and value of their finished products. These were the *Kunsthandwerke*, the artistic crafts.[11] Since the craft was respected, so was the craftsman. Moreover, it should be noted that the primary consumers of beautiful objects were the urban elite and the frequent contact with the upper classes helped raise the status of a gold-smith or a painter. This observation is reinforced by a passage from sumptuary legislation issued in Augsburg in 1735.[12] This act divided the city into five classes, with most guildsmen belonging to Class Four (Class Five was the lowest). In Class Three, however, were not only the *Kunsthandwerker*, but "all those who are famous in their craft." In other words, all those whose skill had brought them fame among the upper classes, for no other sort of fame mattered.

At the other end of the spectrum, cultural prejudice played an equally significant role, serving as a dividing line between the middle class and the lower classes. That line was named respecta-bility.[13] Any trade that operated under servitude or serfdom, the term used was *Leibeigenschaft*, was not a respectable craft and could not gain guild status.[14] Here were those who served feudal lords or who were under the authority of such a lord; for exam-ple, the huntsman, the forester or warden, and the tax official. Very often, this meant that citizenship, too, was denied.[15] Personal freedom was a prized attribute of the burgher; it set him apart from the countryside. No true burgher could, as the medieval phrase went, "be the man of another man." Even a history of former servile status was sufficient to lower a craft's prestige.[16] Both millers and fishers in Augsburg had once been the servants of feudal lords, the former of the imperial governor (the *Stadt-vogt*) and the latter of the bishop, As a result, their status was lower than it might have been otherwise. Even though that condition had ended with the Middle Ages, still the "stain" (*Makel*) of servi-tude lingered.[17]

Respectability entered into the picture another way, too. Certain trades were suspect because immoral practices were tradi-tionally associated with either the craft or the workplace. The best example of this is the public baths. Musicians loitered and worked at the bathhouse.[18] Prostitutes solicited there. Sexual liaisons were held there, not to mention generally loose and improper behavior.[19] Journeymen, who were notoriously immoral because of their youth and their vagabond way of life, also frequented the baths.[20] By the sixteenth century, moreover, the bathhouses were recognized as breeders of disease.[21] All of these attitudes, coupled with the denunciations ringing down from reformist pulpits, served to keep the bathhouse keeper forever at the fringe of re-spectable society. This helps explain why the barbers of Augsburg, long a part of the Barbers and Bathhouse Keepers Guild, split away in 1638 to form their own guild.[22] Barbering did not share the bawdy history of the bathhouse. By the seventeenth century, barbering had laid down its servile past, and was achieving a respectable standing.[23] Continued association with the bathhouse keepers was no longer desirable.

Cultural prejudices could further affect social mobility, as can be seen in the case of the journeyman shoemakers. A number of these journeymen were Catholic, probably immigrants from the Catholic countryside that surrounded Augsburg. The city's artisans, however, were predominantly Protestant, and the Shoemakers Guild was no exception.[24] A Catholic journeyman found it nearly impossible to find a wife in the city, for as soon as his religion became known, the courtship was cut short by the woman's family. Without a wife, a journeyman could not become a master; without mastership, the journeyman could not become a citizen; and without these two vital privileges, the journeyman was forever consigned to the ranks of the lower classes. Naturally, the journeymen complained bitterly over what they viewed as an injustice, but they received no help from the city government, and the Shoemakers Guild itself stubbornly refused to alter its rules of admission.[25] Perhaps the guild was deliberately trying to keep Catholics out. It is equally possible that it was trying to close out immigrant rural shoemakers. Both groups would have been unacceptable to the urban, Protestant, master shoemakers of Augsburg.

Economic forces were as significant as cultural forces. The basic division here concerned the size of the market for a particular craft. Generally speaking, those guilds that engaged in trade had a higher status than those that did not, while those that traded beyond the city walls ranked higher than those that dealt locally.[26] The contrast between shoemakers and weavers will illustrate some of the consequences of this division.

Weaving was the dominant industry of Augsburg.[27] On the eve of the Thirty Years' War, over 2000 master weavers lived in the city, as compared to 150 or so masters in the next largest guild.[28] Augsburg cloth was exported throughout Germany and the Low Countries, and the fortunes of many of Augsburg's leading families had been founded on the cloth trade.[29] Although technically members of the Weavers Guild, some masters were not weavers at all but were cloth merchants who found it expedient to remain in the guild rather than join the Merchants Guild. Most weavers, however, were impoverished, dependent upon a merchant for their very livelihood. The merchant supplied the wool, bought the finished product, and loaned money during hard times or for new equipment. In all but name, such a weaver was the merchant's employee. This dependency, as much as their actual poverty, served to place master weavers low in the middle class hierarchy.[30]

By contrast, shoemakers, equally as impoverished, were at least members of respectable society, because the shoemaker worked in entirely different circumstances. The shoemaker not only made shoes, he sold them, either in a city market or out of his shop window.[31] Members of the Shoemakers Guild made only new shoes, and the poor people of the city came not to them but rather to the cobbler for shoes.[32] Shoemakers, therefore, dealt with the middle and upper classes. Weavers, on the other hand, rarely dealt with the public at all, but dealt instead with a merchant. True, the shoemaker bought leather from the butcher and tanner, but he sold his finished goods to the general public; and butchers and tanners did not control shoemaking in the way that merchants controlled weaving. Though poor, shoemakers were at least independent, fulfilling the traditional social ideal of self-sufficiency (*Selbstständigkeit*).[33] These factors, based on market conditions, were behind the difference in social status.

Economic factors could affect social position in more indirect ways as well. Milling in a city was fundamentally different than it was in the countryside, for in a city almost no one owned an oven. City dwellers bought bread from the man who had an oven, the baker. The urban miller, therefore, did not mill for the average citizen, but rather for the bakers, confectioners and brewers. The effect of this was that urban millers came into contact with a mere handful of customers. Unlike most craftsmen, who dealt with many citizens, the miller was comparatively isolated. This was in contrast, too, with the rural miller, who had the entire village as his customers. This may help explain why most popular images of the millers are of the country miller, the most famous being the Miller in Chaucer's *Canterbury Tales*. His urban counterpart, isolated by the conditions of his craft, was simply less often in the public eye and so was less evident in the popular imagination. One practical consequence of this social obscurity is that, during bread crises, the bakers of the city, not its millers, were attacked by angry mobs.[34]

The third factor affecting social status was personal reputation. Belonging to a specific guild was no guarantee of social stability. On the contrary, the maintenance and improvement of one's standing was a lifetime's work, and the scales could tip either way. Individual social mobility was limited and conditioned not only by the circumstances of one's craft but also by personal merit and luck.

The case of Martin Baur illustrates how an individual could slip a rung on the social ladder. In January 1611, Baur first appeared before the city council with a petition for mastership, which had been denied him on the grounds that his training took place in a village, where standards may have been more lax than in Augsburg. Baur argued that although he had apprenticed in a nearby village, it had been with his own father, who had been a citizen master in Augsburg. Thus, while he had been apprenticed in a foreign place, he had not apprenticed with a foreigner. Moreover, Baur had spent seven years' journeymanship in the city. The guild stated flatly that foreign was foreign and Baur's petition was denied.[35] He repeated his request the following month and was again denied.[36] Two years later, Baur asked to be allowed to make a masterpiece and to marry the widow for whom he had been working for the last few years.[37] He was again denied, whereupon the widow herself wrote a petition in support of Baur, stating with a simple persuasiveness that Baur was "a pious and respectable man, who has worked for three impoverished masters in this city and has done all that he was asked."[38] Baur was once more turned down, yet he returned in April 1614, "even though my request has been denied in the past." Baur this time tried a new approach, speaking not of his rights but of the widow's welfare. "I will not be establishing a new shop," he assured the city council, "but rather will take over an existing one that is now operated by a widow and her three fatherless children." He asked permission to make a masterpiece and to marry the widow, becoming father to the children, "that I might provide for their welfare."[39] Baur's request was refused, after which we hear from him no more.

It may seem strange that Baur persisted for so long in an apparently hopeless cause, but that is just the point. His situation, so long as he was denied mastership, was genuinely hopeless. Without guild status and a respectable marriage, Martin Baur would slip out of the ranks of the middle class into the lower class. He would become a cobbler or be forced to return to the countryside. Either way, the social position, the *Stand* held by his father would be lost.

Another path downward was crime. Georg Hötsch was a master joiner. His son, Hans, committed a crime, the exact nature of which is not known, but it was some type of assault.[40] For his crime, he was banished from the city for a time. He was later reconciled and allowed to return, but only by the city council. The guild refused to allow Hans to make a masterpiece and join the guild, because of his crime. His father repeatedly begged the city to intercede with the guild overseer on his son's behalf, arguing that Hans had paid for his folly (*mentschlichen blödigkeit*) but to no avail.[41] The guild simply would not accept someone with such a reputation. The son thus slipped from the ranks of the middle class. The father's status also slipped. In his final petition, Georg added another reason why he wanted the city to force the guild to accept his son: it was proving impossible for Georg to find journeymen who would work for him. The son's reputation was affecting that of the father.[42]

Upward mobility, too, was conditioned by these factors. For example, joinery was the craft of wood construction using wood joints and glue (no nails). Joiners made armoires, chests, beds, stairs, ornamental ceilings and other such products.[43] Although wood crafts traditionally ranked low in the middle class, joiners stood above because of the skill and beauty of their craft. A significant portion of their work was made to order, by contract, creating some piece of furniture or architecture for a wealthy burgher or for a public building. This arrangement often meant close contact with the urban elite, raising the joiner's status. It would be quite natural for a rich merchant to favor the master craftsman with whom he had been consulting by bringing the joiner's son on as an apprentice clerk or perhaps by financing the lad's education. A shoemaker's son, on the other hand, was not likely to receive such patronage. Even though rich merchants bought shoes, the contact between merchant and customer was simply not intimate enough and the social gap between them was too wide.

The examples presented here give some indication of how occupation and social structure were intertwined. Three points need to be emphasized in regard to the social structure of the urban middle class in general.

First, the lower reaches of Augsburg's middle class composed a significant social group in their own right and deserve more attention than they have received. These artisans were vital elements in the social fabric, for they were the foundation on which the power elite of the city, the rich merchants and the patricians, rested and thrived. The common man paid the bulk of the taxes, made up the bulk of the citizen militia, and filled the scores of lower civic offices. The common man produced most of the city's necessities, most of its goods for export, and was the city's principal consumer. The common man was the guardian and perpetuator of Augsburg's urban values, a world-view that was as unique to the city as was its dialect, which differed even from the surrounding Swabian countryside.[44] Moreover, the ordinary artisans of Augsburg are not lost to us. Even if the common people were relatively inarticulate, leaving few diaries or similar documents, we are not limited to perusing tax books; abundant records remain regarding their activities. In Augsburg, for example, there are thousands upon thousands of petitions to the city council, written by ordinary guildsmen and touching upon virtually every facet of guild life, from the sixteenth century well into the nineteenth century. The examples of Georg Hötsch and Martin Baur were drawn from these sources. New citizen lists, muster books, tax books, and numerous other archival sources provide enough information to paint a picture of the common man far more detailed than any that has yet appeared.

The second point is that the traditional sources for social history are not adequate. Neither legal status nor taxed wealth are satisfactory measures of social position. Historians have long recognized the limitations of legal sources in indicating social class. The social fabric was more complex and more dynamic than the broad categories of citizen and foreigner, patrician and commoner.

As already discussed, taxed wealth likewise is not a sufficient measure of social position. Although some historians have recognized the problems with using wealth as a yardstick, many others use it without qualification or comment.[45] They simply compile the numbers, then divide the middle class, if at all, into the "upper middle class," the "lower middle class," and inevitably, the "middle middle class." Both approaches are wrong-headed.

Wealth as a measure of social position ought not be used at all. Dividing society by the tax books does not yield a picture of class, it yields a picture of the distribution of wealth. It is not accurate to say that members of a given tax bracket were of comparable social status. Wealth was not equivalent to class. The point that seems to be missed by others is that wealth pertains to individuals, not to groups. The tax records can certainly be used to abstract hierarchies of wealth, which can then be analyzed, but each category so created necessarily includes individuals who don't "belong" there; that is, the individual will have made more or less money than he was "supposed" to; had a level of wealth inappropriate to his class. Using wealth to define social groups is simply incorrect, however carefully or cautiously done. Tax records can shed light on the distribution of wealth, but they can only mislead and confuse in regard to social stratification.

The third point follows from the second: the social history of German cities needs to be reexamined in terms of occupation, because the guild was the fundamental social unit beyond the family. A man's status was established by the status of his guild. He could raise or lower this status by his behavior and the behavior of his family. He could even change guilds, which could entail a change in social position. In some guilds, the range of potential social mobility was very great; in others it was very restricted. The limits were set by the influence of cultural prejudice and the economic conditions of the craft.

NOTES

1. Friedrich Blendinger, "Versuch einer Bestimmung der Mittelschicht in der Reichsstadt Augsburg vom Ende des 14. bis zum Anfang des 18. Jahrhunderts," in *Stadtische Mittelschichten*, eds. Erich Maschke and Jürgen Sydow (Stuttgart, 1972).

2. These sources have been microfilmed and are available to scholars in this country at the Genealogical Society Library in Salt Lake City, Utah. The size of the collection is almost overwhelming: the *Handwerker-Akten* alone, which run from the sixteenth through the eighteenth centuries, comprise over 100 rolls of film.

3. Claus Peter Clasen, *Die Augsburg Steuerbücher* (Augsburg, 1976).

4. Robert Lutz, *Wer war der Gemeine Mann? Der dritte Stand in der Krise des Spätmittelalters* (Munich, 1978), 119.

5. The phrase used was *einverleibt Löbl*. See Roland Bettger, *Das Handwerk in Augsburg, beim Übergang der Stadt an das Königreich Bayern (1788-1818)* (Augsburg, 1979), 33.

6. Blendinger, "Versuch einer Bestimmung," 63.

7. Erich Maschke, "Verfassung und soziale Kräfte in der deutschen Stadt des späten Mittelalters, vornehmlich in Oberdeutschland," *Vierteljahrschrift für Sozial- und Wirtschaftsgeschichte* 46 (1959): 289-349, 433-476.

8. Erich Maschke, "Mittelschichten in der mittelalterlichen Zeit," in *Stadtische Mittelschichten*, Maschke and Sydow, eds. 16-18.

9. Werner Danckert, *Unehrliche Leute. Die verfemte Berufe* (Bern, 1963), discusses these at length.

10. Rudolf Wissell, *Des alten Handwerks Recht und Gewohnheit*, 2 vols. (Berlin, 1929), 67.

11. The muster lists for 1611 and 1619 reflect this hierarchy clearly, placing the artistic crafts immediately after the mercantile guilds; for a survey of the *Kunsthandwerke* in Augsburg, see Paul von Stetten, *Kunst-Gewerbe-und Handwerks Geschichte der Reichs-Stadt Augsburg*, 2 vols., (Augsburg, 1779 and 1788).

12. See the *Kleiderordnung* of 1735, cited in Bettger, *Das Handwerk in Augsburg*, 33-35.

13. E. Mummenhoff, *Der Handwerker in der deutschen Vergangenheit*, 2nd ed. (Jena, 1924), 85.

14. Wissell, *Des alten Handwerks Recht*, vol. 1, 117.

15. Mack Walker, *German Home Towns: Community, State and General Estate, 1648-1871* (Ithaca, N.Y., 1971), 49.

16. Wissell, *Des alten Handwerks Recht*, vol. 1, 144.

17. Ibid., 67.

18. Danckert, *Unehrliche Leute*, 103.

19. Ibid., 105.

20. Mummenhoff, *Der Handwerker in der deutschen Vergangenheit*, 34.

21. *Handwerker-Akten, Verordnete Bericht*, ca. 1550. Genealogical Society Library Microfilm (GSLM) 581,004.

22. *Handwerker Akten, Decretum in senatu*, June 8, 1638, GSLM 581,006, reports the resolution to split the guilds; the separate *Ordnungen* were issued September 9, 1638. These documents are also in the Stadtarchiv and are microfilmed on GSLM 581,006.

23. A. Martin, *Deutsches Badewesen in vergangenen Tagen* (Jena, 1906), 93.

24. See the statistics compiled in Ellis Knox, "The Guilds of Early Modern Augsburg, A Study in Urban Institutions," diss., University of Massachusetts, 1984, Table 33, 239.

25. *Handwerker Akten, Schuhmacher*, Sebastian Seüdel, *Supplication*, March 2, 1610; Georg Erhardt, *Supplication*, September 3, 1615; Michael Secklmair, *Supplication*, May 9, 1617. All documents are found on GSLM 548,059. These are merely samples; there were many more petitions on this subject.

26. Blendinger, "Versuch einer Bestimmung," 313.

27. Claus Peter Clasen, *Die Augsburger Weber. Leistungen und*

Krisen des Textilgewerbes um 1600 (Augsburg, 1981), is the most complete work on the weaving industry of Augsburg.

28. Clasen, *Augsburger Weber*, 22.

29. Wolfgang Zorn, *Augsburg, Geschichte einer Stadt* (Augsburg, 1972), 153; Jakob Strieder, *Jacob Fugger the Rich; Merchant and Banker of Augsburg, 1459-1525,* trans. Mildred L. Hartsough, ed. N. S. B. Gras (Hamden, Conn., 1931).

30. Christopher R. Friedrichs, *Urban Society in an Age of War; Nördlingen, 1580-1720* (Princeton, 1979), touches on how merchants could subjugate poor weavers; see also Friedrichs, "Capitalism, Mobility and Class Formation in the Early Modern German City," *Past and Present* 69 (1975): 24-49.

31. Hermann A. Berlepsch, *Chronik der Gewerke*, 9 vols. (St. Gall, 1850-1853), vol. 3, 59.

32. *Handwerker Akten, Schuhmacher*, Peter Jorgen, *Supplication*, ca. 1550, GSLM 469,945.

33. Wissell, *Des alten Handwerks Recht*, 134-135.

34. George Rudé, "The Outbreak of the French Revolution," in *The New Cambridge Modern History*, vol. 7, *The American and French Revolutions 1763-93*, ed. A. Goodwin (Cambridge, 1965), 677, discusses how Paris mobs attacked merchants and bakers in July 1793, even though no grain shortage existed but rather a drought had made it impossible for the waterwheels to turn at the mills. The bottleneck was at the mill, yet it was the merchant and baker who suffered the public's wrath.

35. *Handwerker Akten, Schuhmacher*, Martin Baur, January 27, 1611, GSLM 548,059.

36. *Handwerker Akten, Schuhmacher*, Martin Baur, February 26, 1611, GSLM 548,059.

37. *Handwerker Akten, Schuhmacher*, Martin Baur, October 10, 1613, GSLM 549,059.

38. *Handwerker Akten, Schuhmacher*, Apolonia Gerbstin, ca. 1613, GSLM 548,059.

39. *Handwerker Akten, Schuhmacher*, Martin Baur, April 26, 1614, GSLM 548,059.

40. *Handwerker Akten, Kistler*, George Hötsch, *Supplication*, October 31, 1615, GSLM 534,607.

41. *Handwerker Akten, Kistler*, George Hötsch, *Supplication*, May 26, 1618, GSLM 534,607.

42. *Handwerker Akten, Kistler*, George Hötsch, *Supplication*, June 11, 1618, GSLM 534,607.

43. François Lévy-Coblentz, *L'art du Meuble*, vol. 1, *Du gothique au baroque 1480-1698* (Strassbourg, 1975), 11.

44. Mack Walker, *German Home Towns*, demonstrates how the uniqueness of each German city served to protect it from potentially hostile influences.

45. Maschke equates wealth with class; Blendinger says there is no better source; and Clasen apparently does not consider it an issue. These are but three examples of a whole body of literature wherein wealth and class are seemingly interchangeable terms.

Paternalism in Practice:
The Control of Servants
and Prostitutes in
Early Modern German Cities

MERRY E. WIESNER

T hroughout the Middle Ages, city governments attempted to oversee and prescribe everything that went on in their town down to the smallest detail, from the length of men's doublets to the ingredients in bread. These moves were always justified as contributing to the "public good," by promoting economic growth, improving the town's physical security, assuring consumers of fair weights and measures, or protecting the residents' health. They demonstrate clearly the paternalistic nature of city governments, the sentiment on the part of authorities that they could best identify and implement what served the good of the community as a whole.

During the early modern period, city governments became increasingly concerned with maintaining morality and order along with economic and physical security. This concern, evident in Catholic, Lutheran, and Reformed cities, led to two trends in municipal legislation. The first was the extension of regulation into the household, and the second, the exclusion of certain groups from considerations of the "public good." The first development may be traced by an examination of the regulations regarding domestic servants, and the second, by the ordinances restricting and eventually closing the public brothels. Such prescriptive sources do not reveal much about the actual experience of domestic servants or prostitutes and nothing about their thoughts and desires. They do reveal the ideals and attitudes of urban political leaders and describe their strategies for putting these ideals into practice. They are thus useful in assessing how far a political elite was willing to carry considerations of the communal good, and how it determined where the margins of the "community" would be set.

DOMESTIC SERVICE

City governments first regulated the public aspects of domestic service. They set up systems of employment agents, to whom girls or boys coming in from the countryside could go if they had no relatives or personal contacts in the city. The earliest mention of such agents is in Nuremberg in 1421, when both men and women are listed; but, by the sixteenth century, domestic service was strictly a female occupation. The wording of the appointment of employment agents in the Nuremberg city council minutes is exactly the same as that for a master craftsman or minor city official. They first received a comprehensive ordinance in Nuremberg in 1521, in Strasbourg in 1557, and in Munich in 1580, although it is clear in all of these cities that the system was already in operation before the ordinance was drafted. The ordinances were usually issued to clear up disagreements and solve problems that the city councils saw in the agents' handling of servants. They are all somewhat different in that they respond to particular problems in each city, but many of the clauses are the same in all of them.[1]

The number of official employment agents was limited: to eight in Nuremberg and Munich, and to five in Strasbourg. All were to hang out signs in front of their houses so that people coming in from the countryside would know where to locate them. Servants were to be sent out to all households, rich and poor, without favoritism, unless the agent knew the employer had a history of mistreating servants.

City councils felt that servants were changing positions much too frequently and so ordered the agents to refuse to find a new position for anyone who had not worked at least six months. Indeed, any servant who left a household without just cause, like the death of an employer, was suspect and was to be investigated before being sent to a new position. In Munich and

Strasbourg, two special days, six months apart, were set as the only times during which servants could change jobs; in Nuremberg, servants were to change positions only once a year.[2] Ann Kussmaul, in a recent study of servants in husbandry in early modern England, notes that specific dates for changing positions was necessary in rural areas, where households were far apart; hiring fairs where servants and employers could find each other were organized on these days in many counties.[3] The urban practice may be partly a continuation of this rural pattern, but it was also motivated by a desire to limit mobility among domestic servants. Individuals in cities did not have to travel the long distances to find prospective employers that they did in rural areas and could easily have changed positions frequently had the law allowed it.

The agents were paid for placements both by the employer and the servant, with the employer paying about twice as much as the servant. The amount a servant paid varied according to his or her rank, with cooks and other higher level servants paying two to three times that paid by a children's maid or stable boy. The rates that the agents could charge were set in the ordinances, although they could charge an extra fee for extra work, for "much running back and forth." They were always forbidden to accept any presents, with a stiff fine and possible loss of office if they did.

Employment agents were not to keep the trunks or goods of any servants, first because this would enable the servants to leave a place of employment more easily, and second because the trunk could contain stolen goods. In fact, Strasbourg specifically ordered its employment agents not to be a part of any stealing ring or accept any goods they felt might have been stolen "because they as the holder give the stealer the opportunity and cause to do such a deed."[4]

These early ordinances reflect many of the same aims as other municipal market regulations—control of wages and prices, limitation of the numbers of individuals in any occupation, public transaction of all exchanges, prevention of theft, and orderly transfer of goods, which in this case happened to be people. Clauses that were added later have a different tone and do not stem from economic considerations. Employment agents were to reinforce the distinction between master and servant, not praising or denigrating any master in front of any servant. They were not to offer new jobs to any servants, "because no one can

181

keep servants these days—who would otherwise gladly stay—as the agents run after them with promises of a better position."[5] Most importantly, they were not to house any servants and to report anyone who was housing servants, for, the city governments asserted, this allowed servants to "walk up and down freely whenever they want to, and is a source of great annoyance."[6] Thus, along with facilitating the hiring of servants, employment agents were expected to assist city authorities in enforcing standards of conduct among the servants they had placed.

The emphasis on order and decorum led many city governments to begin regulating the activities of servants themselves. In 1499 in Nuremberg, maids were not allowed into any dances at the city hall without their mistresses; they were always to be seated behind their mistresses if they did attend, for the council felt the maids' conduct did not always show the proper deference. Later, an attempt was made to forbid them attendance altogether, but enough wealthy women complained and the maids were again allowed to accompany their mistresses, however, they had to stay in a separate locked room until they were needed. If a woman wanted her maid, she could send for her.[7] The conduct of maids at dances was also seen as a problem in Frankfurt, where the city council discussed canceling all dances "because maids seduce other servants, and cause them not only to do questionable acts, but also to stay away from their work longer than is proper."[8]

During the middle of the sixteenth century, a number of city councils passed ordinances for servants, mainly because they felt that wages were too high. Strasbourg limited the wages a normal servant could be paid to six gulden a year, "although one may certainly pay less"; employers were not responsible to pay servants anything if they found them unsuitable or if the servants left without cause. The following year, a second, sterner notice was issued because the council heard that servants were even demanding gifts of their employers and were, in general, behaving in a "disobedient, contrary, untrue, and otherwise inappropriate manner."[9] In addition to their regular salary, only servants who had served "obediently, truly, and industriously" for a long time were to be rewarded with anything extra, and this was to be done only once. Servants who did not own at least one hundred gulden worth of property themselves were not allowed to wear silk or satin, a property limit which probably excluded all servants. The council stated that this was to prevent extravagant expenditure on the part of servants. But, as this restriction even applied to clothing they had inherited or been given by a generous employer, it is clear the council was also attempting to maintain social distinctions.[10]

An ordinance passed at the same time in the Duchy of Württemberg was even stricter than that in Strasbourg. Servants were specifically charged with causing the general inflation, as they demanded a salary along with their room and board, so that salary was to be strictly limited.[11] No one was to be taken on as a servant without proof of her or his conduct and honorable dismissal from the last position.

The Munich ordinance from 1580 sees a great amount of distrust between employer and servant. Servants were not to leave the house for any reason without the knowledge of their employers. They were to take no food out of the house at any time and had to open their chests and trunks if their employers suspected them of having taken anything. If they pretended to be ill to get out of work, the servants were to be banished. If they really were ill and the employer didn't want them around, they could go to some unspecified "honorable place" until they were healthy again. Servants who spoke against their masters were to be strictly punished. Hostility between servants was also to be avoided; upper-level servants were specifically ordered not to treat those under them too harshly.[12]

Recognizing that the problems they perceived in regard to servants could not be dealt with by restrictions on servants alone, city councils began to regulate the conduct of employers as well. In Strasbourg, as long as the first master provided well enough, no one was to coax a servant away from a master with "more pay, tips, beer, money, or other devices," under penalty of a fine of ten gulden. Promises of marriage were not to be used with female servants, unless they were legitimate and did not first involve a period of employment in the future husband's home.[13] In the Duchy of Württemberg, no employer was to give a servant more than one glass of wine a day, even on festive occasions.[14] In Munich, masters found to be "entirely too strict and harsh" were to be punished.[15] Municipal oversight of domestic servants thus extended to what went on within a household as well as in the public marketplace.

In some ways this was no different than guild or municipal

regulations pertaining to apprentices, journeymen, and masters; all of them restricted activities in a household workshop, and guild regulations were motivated by moral as well as economic considerations. Guild leaders were caught up in the increased concern with propriety and decorum in the same way that municipal authorities were; in many cities, of course, guild leaders were the municipal authorities.

Cities' attempts to control servants extended not only into the household but into the family as well. Parents were forbidden to give their children shelter or aid if they had left a position without notice or to take their children out of one place of employment and put them in another. The 1665 Strasbourg ordinance went much further than that:

> Numerous complaints have been made that some widows living here have two, three, or more daughters living with them at their expense. These girls go into service during the winter, but during the summer return to their mothers partly because they want to wear more expensive clothes than servants are normally allowed to, and partly because they want to have more freedom to walk around, to saunter back and forth whenever they want to. It is our experience that this causes nothing but shame, immodesty, wantonness, and immorality, so that a watchful eye should be kept on this, and, if it is discovered the parents as well as the daughters should be punished with a fine, a jail sentence, or even banishment from the city in order to serve as an example to others.[16]

Young women were thus to be prevented from living with their own mothers if they were not needed in the household, as the council felt the mothers could not control them as well as an employer could. Even the family itself was not as important as propriety and decorum in the city, at least in this case.

The "freedom to walk around" mentioned in the Strasbourg ordinance was particularly disturbing to civic authorities. The Munich ordinance from 1580 forbade anyone to coax servants away from their masters, not only with promises of gifts or money, but also with promises of "more freedom."[17] This was expected to lead to "shame, immodesty, wantonness, and immorality," and also might make servant more resentful of all control by their employers, causing them to leave domestic service and search for employment elsewhere. This was unthinkable, in the view of city authorities, because it would remove young single people, and particularly young single women, from the control of respectable, and generally male, heads of household.[18] Cities responded to the threat by forbidding all city residents to rent rooms to single men or women who were not in service somewhere, or to keep their trunks or possessions. Any unmarried man or woman servant who would not take a position but tried to live on his or her own as a day laborer was to be banished, as were the people who house them, even if they were public innkeepers.[19]

In the case of women, this included those who had a trade with which they had formerly supported themselves. Unmarried spinners in Augsburg, for example, were ordered to live with a weaver and not independently, so that their living arrangements were analogous to domestic service, even though their actual work continued to be thread production.[20] Servants who married and set up their own households but were then not able to find enough work to support themselves and their families were also to be banished "so that such young people will first think over how they will support themselves and their children before they get married."[21]

By the end of the sixteenth century, the regulations regarding domestic service served three distinct purposes. The first was economic. In this period of inflation, city authorities attempted to control wages and prices. They could regulate the prices of most things only to a degree: those of foodstuffs and raw materials were largely outside their control, though they tried fiercely to limit them. The wages of servants and day-laborers could be held down more easily, though the frequency with which such regulations were repeated indicates that the limits were often being broken.

The second was social. City governments wanted social distinctions clearly observed, even if this meant forbidding upper-class employers to give gifts to their servants or bring their maids along to private parties. This was also the period of the hardening of sumptuary clothing laws, which made the distinction between master and servant immediately visible because of fabric color and quality, or style of apron and headgear.[22]

The third was both social and ideological. City governments viewed male-headed households as the best instrument of social control and strengthening them the best means to assure order, decorum, morality, and stability. Whenever possible, all unmarried individuals, especially unmarried women, were to be placed under the control of a male-headed household. This even applied to women who had long supported themselves independently, though city governments often justified such moves with a note of paternalistic concern for these women's well-being. It also applied to unmarried women who were living with their own mothers, if the conduct of the young woman was deemed to be unacceptable.

Cities achieved greater control of domestic servants and attempted to achieve greater control of all unmarried individuals by broadening their concepts of what the public good demanded. Servants themselves continued to be considered as part of that "public," however, for even the harshest restrictions allowed a servant to leave a violent master and allowed employment agents to refuse to send servants to such individuals. As long as servants were safely within orderly households, they fit into city authorities' vision of the ideal community and thus deserved protection.

PUBLIC BROTHELS

The relationship between prostitution and the "public good" was an ambiguous one for city authorities. During the medieval period, prostitution had been viewed by both church and secular authorities as, at worst, a necessary evil or, at best, as an Ulm ordinance put it, as "enhancing the good piety, and honor of the whole community."[23] This changed during the sixteenth century, and brothels were closed with justifications couched in exactly the same language as this Ulm ordinance. This involved a change in attitude about the city's responsibility to provide outlets for male sexuality, and about the role of prostitutes, displacing them from the margins of the community to a position totally outside of it.

The first step in regulating prostitution was opening an official municipal brothel (*Frauenhaus*). Although the founding of

186

the brothel was not usually announced publicly, by the fifteenth century, nearly every major city in Germany and most of the smaller ones had an official house of prostitution.[24] All prostitutes were ordered to either move into the brothel or leave the city. Many of these houses, such as one in Frankfurt and one in Mainz, actually belonged to bishops or religious houses; the bishop of Mainz complained at one point that the house was not getting enough business.[25]

Ordinances were passed to ensure that the brothels would serve the community as planned, but inadvertently they also protected the prostitutes against excessive exploitation. Though the prostitute's status in the community was marginal, their health and safety were regarded as important. Because the brothel was frequently visited by foreign dignitaries and merchants, a dilapidated building, undernourished or ill-dressed prostitutes, and violent brawls all reflected badly on the city. The brothel was a very visible municipal institution and thus warranted and received close attention. Beginning in the fifteenth century, lengthy brothel ordinances were passed in many German cities.

Some clauses in the ordinances were designed to reflect the prostitutes' marginality. No daughter of a citizen was to live in the brothel, and only women who had been prostitutes elsewhere were supposed to be taken in, a rule that was obviously not always followed as then no woman would have been eligible. In 1548 in Nuremberg, a citizen's daughter was found working as a prostitute; the brothel manager was given a light fine, but the poor woman was held in the city jail for five years.[26]

Their distinction from "honorable women" was reinforced by the requirement that prostitutes wear special clothing. Prostitutes in Strasbourg were to wear a shorter coat than was customary, with a yellow band of cloth somewhere on their clothing.[27] Yellow bands or veils were a common way of identifying prostitutes. They could not wear any elaborate jewelry, have silk or fur trim on anything, or leave their hair uncovered in the fashion of other young unmarried women. They were often forbidden to have a maid servant accompany them when they went out; if two prostitutes went somewhere together, they were ordered to walk side by side, not one behind the other, lest people even think one were a maid.[28]

The location of the brothel (or brothels) also reflected the prostitutes' marginal status. Often they were set up just inside one of the city's gates, on a small street away from the general flow of traffic, so that people were not constantly reminded of their presence. In 1469 in Strasbourg, prostitutes were found to be living throughout the city, to the dismay of "decent and honorable people"; the council gave them a week to move into the section of the city in which "women such as these have always lived." It also took a survey of the women, finding eight to be living in the official brothel with the manager, and fourteen others "living alone" or "living with two, three, or four others," which makes one suspect that these were women who ran small, unofficial houses. In addition, there is a list of sixteen names with the note "these do not want to be considered public prostitutes [*offen huren*]." Several members of the city council were sent to examine the houses where these women were living, to make sure they were "appropriate for such use," and reported that at least twenty-five or thirty houses in the approved area could be used by prostitutes, along with the official brothel.[29] Apparently this still was not enough, or at any rate the women did not want to move into these houses, for the council repeated its warning that they were not to live among "honorable people," but only in one area of the city. It increased the fines and threats of punishment in 1471, 1493, 1496, 1501, and on into the sixteenth century.

The Strasbourg city council was also troubled by women who made their living in a "dishonorable" way, yet claimed they were not really prostitutes but had another occupation or craft. These women as well were to move to the approved area of the city "and not protect themselves with the argument that they do not carry out such sinful work in their houses." Not only admitted prostitutes, but any woman "who serves a priest or layman and lives with him publicly without marriage" was to wear the short coat and yellow band identifying her as dishonorable. No excuses that she was simply a housekeeper or practiced another craft were to be tolerated, as long as it was "widely known and recognized" that she was really "that sort of woman."[30] There was to be no grey area between women who were honorable and those who were not.

Despite, or perhaps because of, their marginal status, throughout the fifteenth century prostitutes appeared often in public. A chronicle from 1471 reports on the stay of Emperor Friedrich III in Nuremberg:

> [The Emperor] rode behind the grain houses and
> looked at the weapons and the grain, and while he
> was leaving the grain houses, two whores caught
> him with a silver chain and said "Your Grace must be
> captured." He said "We haven't been captured yet
> and would rather be released," and gave them one
> gulden. Then he rode to the *Frauenhaus* where
> another four were waiting and he gave them another
> gulden.[31]

Although chroniclers often exaggerate, this may not have been
far from the truth. Prostitutes were allowed to come to dances at
the city hall in Nuremberg whenever they wished for another
twenty-five years.

In Frankfurt, prostitutes brought flowers to the city council
at their yearly festive meal and were then allowed to eat with the
councilors until 1529, though the council members' wives were
not invited. After this, the prostitutes still received a free dinner
from the council, brought to them in the brothel. The Würtzburg
fire ordinance required prostitutes to help put out the fires that
broke out in the city until 1528; and in Frankfurt, they gave
flowers and congratulations to newly married couples.[32] In Memmingen, they, along with the city's midwives, were given a special
New Year's gift every year.[33]

The ambivalence of official attitudes toward prostitution in
the fifteenth century is reflected in city councils' attempts to draw
women out of the brothel to more "honorable" callings; at the
same time, they tolerated them at or even invited them to public
events. In many cities, anyone who married a prostitute was
given free citizenship, as long as the couple maintained an
"honorable way of life." In Nuremberg, an endowed fund was set
up by Conrad Khunhof to provide support each year for four
women who wanted to leave the brothel and join the sisters at the
nearby convent at Pillenreuth. After the Reformation, when the
convent at Pillenreuth was forbidden to take in any new women,
the city council decided to continue support for the women who
were already there but in the future to look into other ways to use
the money that would correspond with Khunhof's aims. Two
years later, it finally decided to provide dowries of twenty gulden
annually to each of four women from the brothel who had

worked in the city's main hospital. The council also used some of Khunhof's money for a quite different purpose, setting up a stipend fund of fifty-two gulden a year for university students.[34]

The same kind of opportunities were offered in other cities by "Magdalene houses," small houses specifically set up to provide homes for prostitutes who had decided to give up their former lives or were too old to work. Most of these were similar to Beguinages, so that the women did not take actual vows, and many of them were endowed by women who felt this was a particularly appropriate form of charity for a woman.[35]

Many of the clauses in early brothel ordinances were included to prevent violence and bloodshed in the house. The innkeepers in the area around the houses in Nuremberg were limited to the amount of wine they could sell, either to the women or their customers.[36] In 1478, the Frankfurt city council put two iron bands in the brothel for imprisoning men who had gotten out of hand and specifically allowed the manager to carry a knife in order to defend himself or the women. Men who had beaten up or injured prostitutes were supposed to be given longer jail sentences than those given for normal assault.[37] In Nuremberg, the council also forbade women to have favorite customers for it felt this brought "clamour, indignation, discord, and displeasure" and could lead to fights, though the men often identified one of the women as "theirs."[38]

Customers were also to be protected from disease, so cities made some attempts to guard the cleanliness and health of the women in the brothel. They were to be allowed at least one bath a week and, in some cities, had a special separate bathing room at the public baths, another indication of their marginal status. In Ulm, a midwife regularly conducted examinations of all prostitutes, both to check if they were pregnant and to make sure they were "fit, clean, and healthy women."[39]

Though promulgated for the benefit of the brothel's customers, these ordinances regarding violence and disease also worked to the women's advantage. Most ordinances also included clauses designed specifically to protect the women from exploitation by their relatives or by the brothel manager. All ordinances forbade parents and other people to place women in a brothel as payment for a debt to a brothel manager; later editions repeat and strengthen these clauses, a clear indication that this was occurring despite the prohibition. The manager also freely traded women who had become endebted to him after coming into the house. A 1488 Munich ordinance forbade a manager to trade away a woman for more than the debt she owed him, and later ordinances from Strasbourg, Nuremberg, and Frankfurt forbade him to sell or trade away any woman no matter how much she owed him. They attempted to take away all temptation to do so by forbidding him to loan the women more than a small amount at any one time. The manager was forbidden to force women into the house as well, though the burden of proof in such cases was on the woman not on the manager.[40]

The women were to pay the manager a designated amount per customer, usually more if the man stayed all night; the amount the customers were to give the women is not mentioned in any of the regulations, though we can assume it was fairly low, as badly paid journeymen were the most frequent customers. The women were to receive two or three meals a day in the house and were not required to pay any rent when they did not have customers, though they still had to pay for their meals. If a woman owed money to the manager or he felt she was not giving him his fair share, he could seize her clothing and personal effects until the case was brought to trial but theoretically could not force her to stay in the house.

The women were to be allowed out of the house whenever they wanted to go to church and were not to be forced to work at any time. An ordinance from Nuremberg reads: "The manager, his wife, or his servants shall not force, coerce, or compel in any way any woman who lives in his house to care for a man when she is pregnant or menstruating [*mit weiblichen Rechten beladen*] or in any other way unfit or want to hold back from bodily work."[41] In Munich, menstruating women were to have their normal meals augmented by a couple of eggs, as this was felt to ease any pain that might accompany a menstrual period, a good example of what anthropologists term *sympathetic magic*."[42]

The city councils also set minimum age limits for women in the brothels. Usually the minimum age was fourteen, although the treatment of girls found to be too young was hardly gentle. A regulation from Strasbourg in 1500 notes: "Whichever daughters are found whose bodies are not yet ready for such work, that is who have neither breasts nor the other things which are necessary for this, should be driven out of the city with blows and are to stay out under threat of bodily punishment until they reach the proper age."[43] Apparently the city council saw no contradiction in its judgment that these girls were too young to be prostitutes but old enough to be banished out of the city on their own.

The city of Ulm went the furthest in protecting its prostitutes. All of the money that the women made went into a common box and was then distributed each week by a woman who was not herself a prostitute, according to the needs of each woman. This box had three separate locks, with one key held by the manager, one by one of the prostitutes, and the third by this outside woman, so that no one could get money from it illegally. Ulm also had a second fund, into which all prostitutes and the manager paid a portion of their incomes, which was supposed to be used to support prostitutes who were too old or sick to work longer.[44] In return for this old-age pension, the women were required to spin two spindles of yarn every day for the manager. They did spinning in other cities as well, but the amounts and purposes were never specified.

Toward the end of the fifteenth century, city councils became more uncomfortable with the idea of municipally sanctioned prostitution and attempted to hide prostitutes from public view. In 1472 and 1478, Frankfurt prostitutes were ordered not to sit at the door of their house and call out to prospective customers.[45] In Strasbourg, the women were not to sit directly in front of the altar at church, for they often spent the time talking or turning around so that their faces were visible to those behind them. If they were found there, they were to be followed when leaving the cathedral, their coats or shawls taken from them, pawned, and the money given to the poor; the council recognized that they were probably too poor to pay a fine outright. They were also forbidden to come to dances where honorable women were present, with the additional proviso that there would be no punishment for anyone who attacked the prostitute or the person who brought her, unless the attack led to a serious wounding or death.[46]

In Nuremberg, the first restrictions came in 1508, when the brothel manager was ordered to keep all women of the street in their "whore's clothing"; if they went to church or elsewhere they were to wear a coat or veil. Later, the brothel was closed until noon every day and at sunset on Saturday night and the eves of holidays. In 1544, on a complaint of the neighbors, the council ordered a special door to be built on the brothel so that no one could see inside and held the manager responsible to make sure it was always shut. Two years later, prostitutes were no longer to be allowed at public dances or at the wine market; if a number were found out of the house, the manager was to be thrown in jail. The neighbors grumbled again that they had to walk by and "bear their [the prostitutes'] annoying and unsightly presence," so the door was ordered locked shut during the day. It was to be opened only at night, so city officials could go in easily if there was a problem.[47]

Guilds were also growing more concerned about the conduct and morality of their members and increasingly forbade all contact with prostitutes. In 1521 in Frankfurt, all masters and journeymen were forbidden to dance with prostitutes or other "dishonorable" women or even stand next to them in a public place. Similar clauses were added to many guild and journeymen's ordinances throughout Germany beginning at about this time, a trend that resulted from guild attempts to limit memberships in a period of declining opportunities. Children born out of wedlock, children of parents with "dishonorable" occupations, such as gravediggers and executioners, and those who had contact with prostitutes were all denied membership, as were those who married women "tainted" by these factors. The guilds could thus keep their numbers down for economic reasons, while claiming to be upholding the honor and morality of the guild. The fustian weavers in Frankfurt went one step further, forbidding their members to dance with or give drinks to women who were simply suspected of being dishonorable. By 1546, under pressure from the guilds, the city council in Frankfurt had agreed to forbid the burial of prostitutes in hallowed ground; a special cemetery was opened for them near the city's gallows.[48] Even in death, honorable citizens were to be protected from contact with prostitutes.

By the middle of the sixteenth century, city councils determined that the public good demanded closing the brothels not just trying to hide or ignore them. Augsburg led the way in 1532—it had always had the most stringent limitations on the conduct of prostitutes—with Basel following in 1534, Nordlingen in 1536, Ulm in 1537, Regensburg in 1553, and Frankfurt in 1560.[49] No provision was made for the women or the manager; the Augsburg manager asked the city council where he should go now with the women but received no answer.

We can best trace the arguments for and against the closing of a city brothel in Nuremberg, which was always cautious about doing anything that might bring more harm than good. Not until 1562 did the city council begin to ask for opinions as to whether the house should be closed "or if it were closed, if other dangers and still more evil would possibly be the result."[50]

The discussion among the jurists and theologians is very interesting. Augsburg had reported an increase and spread in unchastity since it closed its brothel, so the jurists asserted that the closing could cause journeymen and foreign workers to turn to the masters' or landlords' wives and daughters. The theologians urged the council to think of Nuremberg's reputation as the leading free imperial city and not allow it to break "the word of God" just because of the complaints against the closing of the house by foreigners who visited or lived in Nuremberg. One argued that the brothel caused young men to have impure thoughts about women; those who had no opportunity and were never introduced to sex wouldn't chase other women.[51] In this, he agreed with Johannes Brenz, who wrote, "Some say one must have public brothels to prevent greater evil—but what if these brothels are schools where one learns more wickedness than before?" Brenz, incidentally, goes on to say that if men were the more rational creatures and women the more sensual, as everyone believed in the sixteenth century, why shouldn't women also have brothels? "If the authorities have the power to allow a brothel and do not sin in this, where not only single men but also married men may go, and say this does no harm. . . . Why do they not also permit a women's brothel where women who are old and weak and have no husbands may go?"[52] Brenz was not advocating this, of course, but using the turnabout to point out the absurdity of the arguments for the brothels.

The spread of syphilis was also given as a reason: "If the house isn't closed in a short time, then it will be necessary to build three syphilis clinics instead of just one."[53] The council recognized early that women in the brothel were more likely to get syphilis and pass it on to other people than the population as a whole. It usually attributed this to moral rather than medical reasons, however. When syphilis first swept through Nuremberg in 1496, a special clinic was set up for syphilitics, and prostitutes were readily taken in, though other noncitizens were not. Other cities were not so enlightened. In 1498 in Munich, journeymen stormed the brothel and tried to kill the manager because they were angry about the introduction of syphilis. Thirty-five armed men had to watch the brothel day and night for a month and a half before things quieted down again.[54]

The Nuremberg council wanted an exact report from Augsburg of the number of illegitimate children before and after the closing of the brothel, to see if the numbers had actually increased. It rejected the argument that closing the house would lessen the opportunities for men to perform meritorious services by marrying prostitutes; closing the house would also "pull the women out of the devil's jaws." Another jurist realistically noted that, since there were only ten to twelve women in the brothel, they couldn't possibly be taking care of the sexual needs of all the city's unmarried men, so the closing wouldn't make that much of a difference.[55]

Those arguing for the closing were more persuasive, and the council decided to follow the example of Augsburg and others:

> On the recommendation written and ready by the high honorable theologians and jurists, why the men of the council are authorized and obliged to close the common brothel, it has been decided by the whole council to follow the same recommendation and from this hour on forbid all activity in that house, to post a guard in the house and let no man enter it any more. Also to send for the manager and say to him that he is to send all women that he has out of the house and never take them in again. From this time on, he is to act so blamelessly and unsuspiciously that the council has no cause to punish him. When this has been completed, the preachers should be told to admonish the young people to guard themselves from such depravity and to keep their children and servants from it and to lead such an irreproachable life that the council has no cause to punish anyone for this vice.[56]

Unfortunately for the council, its final words were not heeded. The house was closed, but a short time later the council found that "adultery, prostitution, fornication and rape have taken over forcibly here in the city and in the countryside," and wondered whether its move had been a wise one.[57]

The closing of the official brothels obviously did not end prostitution in early modern European cities, for many women continued to make their living this way, often combining prostitution with piecework or laundering or with theft and other crimes. What it did end was the city council's ambivalent attitude toward prostitutes. For a short period of time, from the first laws protecting them from being sold or pawned to the closing of the brothels, the welfare of prostitutes was a concern of the city government, though they never totally lost their "dishonorable" status. Once the brothels were closed, however, their well-being was no longer viewed as part of the general well-being of the city, and they could be treated like any other criminal. Indeed, they were perhaps worse than other criminals, for they seduced honorable citizens from a life of *Zucht*, the moral order that city councils all were trying to create in the sixteenth century. The public good now demanded that they be punished, not protected, for the paternalistic wing of the city government no longer sheltered them.

CONCLUSION

Throughout the Middle Ages, city governments addressed a wide variety of concerns when they considered the "public good": health and hygiene, consumer protection, security from invasion, fair business practices, just wages and prices, fire protection, to name a few. Though moral considerations entered into their discussions and are often included in the introductions to ordinances or regulations, greater emphasis was placed on economic growth or stability and physical security. During the sixteenth century, these emphases were reversed, and ordinances also were passed solely out of concern for decorum, order, and morality. Paternalistic concern for the good of the community now demanded a still wider range of legislation.

City councils recognized that they could not possibly enforce this moral legislation by themselves and enlisted the assistance not only of lesser officials but also of heads of households, whom they viewed essentially as the lowest level officials in the city. Masters were to control their apprentices and journeymen, employers their servants, parents their children; the proper moral order was strictly hierarchical. Individuals who did not normally fit into a hierarchy, such as unmarried young adults, were to be forced into one and, more important, one that successfully controlled its subordinate members. Lax households were not functioning as agents of the moral order, and so were chastised and could even have their servants or children removed and placed elsewhere. Lenient heads of household or disobedient servants were still considered part of the community, however, and actions taken to control them viewed as contributing both to the public good by promoting public decorum and to their own private moral development by convincing them to change.

Prostitution was initially handled in the same way. The opening of public brothels put prostitutes under the care of the brothel manager, who controlled their conduct and that of their patrons. Concerns for health and hygiene, security, and fair business practices extended to the residents of these somewhat unusual households. As city councils came to regard prostitution as morally unacceptable in and of itself, regulations or restrictions no longer sufficed in their considerations of the public good. A well-run, orderly brothel was still a brothel. Unruly domestic servants could be brought under control and disturbed public order and decorum only by their actions. Prostitutes could not be fit into any hierarchy that reflected an ideal moral order and disturbed the authorities' sense of propriety by their very existence. The only solution was banishment from the city, thus removing them physically from the community from which they had already been ideologically excluded.

N O T E S

The research for this article was supported by grants from the American Council of Learned Societies, the Deutscher Akademischer Austauschdienst, and the Regents of the University of Wisconsin. Some of the material has also been included in my book, *Working Women in Renaissance Germany*, (New Brunswick, N.J., 1987) and is included here with the permission of Rutgers University Press. All translations are my own unless otherwise noted.

1. Nuremberg Staatsarchiv (hereafter NB) Amts- und Standbücher, no. 101, fols. 558-67; Munich Stadtarchiv (hereafter MU) Gewerbeamt, no. 1569 (1580); Strasbourg, Archives Municipales (hereafter AMS), Statuten, vol. 18, fols. 30-34 (1557).

2. Ibid.

3. Ann Kussmaul, *Servants in Husbandry in Early Modern England* (Cambridge, 1981).

4. AMS, Statuten, vol. 10, 1628 Gesindeordnung.

5. AMS, Akten der XV, 1587, fol. 168b.

6. AMS, Grosse Ratsbuch, vol. 1, no. 150; a similar clause is in MU, Zimilien no. 29, Eidbuch 1688.

7. NB, Ratsbuch 6, fol. 59 (1499); NB, Ratsbuch 9, fol. 48 (1508).

8. Frankfurt Stadtarchiv (hereafter FF), Bürgermeisterbücher, 1604, fol. 29.

9. AMS Statuten, vol. 18, fols. 30-35.

10. Dress that obscured or confused status distinctions was viewed as very threatening in early modern society, as a clear sign of social disorder. The author of the English pamphlet *Hic Mulier* (1620) criticized women who dressed like men not only because they broke down gender distinctions but, even more, because class distinctions among women were lost when they all dressed in similar men's clothing. See Mary Beth Rose, "Women in Men's Clothing: Apparel and Social Stability in The Roaring Girl," *English Literary Renaissance* 14 no. 3 (Autumn 1984):367-91.

11. Stuttgart, Württembergische Haupstaatsarchiv (ST), General-reskripta, A-39, Bu. 3 (1562).

12. MU, Gewerbeamt, no. 1569 (1580).

13. AMS, Statuten, vol. 18, fol. 30.

14. ST, Generalreskripta, A-39, Bu. 3 (1562).

15. MU, Gewerbeamt, no. 1569 (1580).

16. AMS, Statuten, vol. 33, no. 61 (1665).

17. MU, Gewerbeamt, no. 1569 (1580).

18. Gordon Schochet has discovered these same opinions among authorities in England. See *Patriarchalism in Political Thought: The Authoritarian Family and Political Speculations and Attitudes Especially in Seventeenth-Century England* (Oxford, 1975).

19. Grethe Jacobsen has discovered similar legislation in Malmø, Denmark, in a city ordinance that "demanded that all self-supporting maidens should take work as servants or be exiled from town." See "Women, Marriage, and Magisterial Reformation: The Case of Malmø, Denmark," in *Pietas et Societas: New Trends in Reformation Social History, Essays in Memory of Harold Grimm*, ed. Kyle C. Sessions and Phillip N. Bebb (Kirksville, Mo., 1985), 76.

20. Claus-Peter Clasen, *Die Augsburger Weber um 1600: Leistung und Krisen eines Textilgewerbes* (Augsburg, 1983), 130-133.

21. MU, Gewerbeamt, no. 1569 (1580).

22. *Frankfurt um 1600: Alltagsleben in der Stadt*. Kleine Schriften des Historische Museums, vol. 7 (Frankfurt, 1976); Ingeborg Köhler, "Bestimmungen des Rates der Reichsstadt Nürnberg über die Kleidung seiner Bürgerinnen" (Zulassungsarbeit, Univ. of Munich, 1953); Kent Greenfield, *Sumptuary Law in Nuremberg*, Johns Hopkins University Studies in History and Political Science, vol. 36, (Baltimore, 1918).

23. Quoted in Lyndal Roper, "Discipline and Respectability: Prostitution and the Reformation in Augsburg," *History Workshop* 19 (Spring 1985):4.

24. Iwan Bloch, *Die Prostitution* (Berlin, 1912), 740-45.

25. Max Bauer, *Liebesleben in deutschen Vergangenheit* (Berlin, 1924), 148.

26. NB, Ratsbuch 24, fol. 128 (1548); Ratsbuch 26, fol. 356 (1553).

27. AMS, Statuten, vol. 2, fols. 75, 78.

28. Ibid., fol. 130; vol. 29, fol. 154; Werner Danckert, *Unehrliche Leute: Die verfemte Berufe* (Bern/Munich, 1963), 150.

29. AMS, ibid., vol. 2, fol. 70; vol. 29, fol 34 (1469).

30. AMS, ibid., vol. 2, fol. 137 (1497).

31. *Die Chroniken der fränkischen Städte* (Leipzig, 1874), vol. 4 328.

32. Anton Kriegk, *Deutsches Bürgerthum im Mittelalter* (Frankfurt, 1871), vol. 2, 322; Helmut Wachendorf, *Die wirtschaftliche Stellung der Frau in den deutschen Städten des späteren Mittelalters* (Quackenbruck, 1934), 120.

33. Memmingen Stadtarchiv, Ratsprotokollbücher, December 19, 1526.

34. NB, Ratsbuch 19, fol. 252 (1539); Ratsbuch 20, fol. 255 (1541).

35. K. A. Weith-Knudsen, *Kulturgeschichte der europäischen Frauenwelt* (Stuttgart, 1927), 173.

36. NB, Ratsbuch 1b, fol. 324 (1455): Ratsbuch 7, fol. 59 (1499).

37. Kriegk, *Deutsches Bürgerthum*, vol. 2, 306; FF, Bürgermeisterbücher, 1510, fol. 19b.

38. Joseph Baader, "Nürnberger Polizeiordnungen aus dem XIII, bis XV. Jahrhundert," *Bibliothek des Litterarische Verein Stuttgart* 63(1861):119-20.

39. Kriegk, *Deutsches Bürgerthum*, vol. 2, 308.

40. MU, Zimilien 41, Eidbuch 1488; AMS, Statuten, vol. 3, fol. 4 (1500); FF, Bürgermeisterbücher, 1545, fol. 47; Baader, "Polizeiordnungen," 119-20.

41. Baader, "Polizeiordnungen," 119-20. Similar clauses in AMS, Statuten, vol. 3, fol. 4.

42. MU, Zimilien 41, Eidbuch 1488.

43. AMS, Statuten, vol. 3, fol. 5.

44. Kriegk, *Bürgerthum*, vol. 2, 316; Bauer, *Liebesleben,* 134.

45. Kriegk, ibid., 306; Bauer, ibid., 133.

46. AMS, Statuten, vol. 2, fols. 75, 78.

47. NB, Ratsbuch 9, fol. 17 (1508); Ratsbuch 19, fol. 342 (1542); Ratsbuch 20, fol. 44, 87 (1544); RB 23, fols. 202, 205 (1546).

48. Danckert, *Unehrliche Leute*, 150.

49. Kriegk, *Deutsches Bürgerthum*, vol. 2, 340; Bauer, *Liebesleben*, 159.

50. NB, Ratsbuch 31, fol. 316 (1562).

51. NB, Ratschlagbuch 34, fol. 137-53.

52. Quoted in Roper, "Discipline and Respectability," 12-13.

53. Karl Sudhoff, *Die ersten Massnahmen der Stadt Nürnberg gegen die Syphilis* (Leipzig, 1912), 109.

54. MU, Ratsgeschaft, 1498.

55. NB, Ratschlagbuch 34, fols. 137-53.

56. NB, Ratsbuch 31, fol. 350 (1562).

57. NB, Ratsbuch 36, fol. 15 (1577).

Joyful in Exile?
French-speaking Protestants in Sixteenth-Century Strasbourg

LORNA JANE ABRAY

I n the course of the sixteenth century, war and persecution drove tens of thousands of people from their homelands. For reformers and their followers in France, Lorraine, and the southern Netherlands, the free imperial city of Strasbourg soon became one of the preferred havens: more than 1700 Protestants found shelter there between the 1520s and the 1590s.[1] Historians have long been familiar with the importance of this Germanic city to the development of reformed Protestantism—not least because John Calvin himself spent three years in Strasbourg—but few attempts have been made to study the French-speaking refugee community as a whole in order to determine who came, why, and what kind of life they lived in exile.[2]

French-speaking religious dissidents began to use Strasbourg as a place of refuge in 1525.[3] The first to arrive were clergymen in trouble for preaching the new doctrines: men like François Lambert, a defrocked monk from Avignon; Jean Vedaste, on the run from prison in Metz; and Guillaume Farel. That same year the first group reached Strasbourg: Lefèvre d'Etaples arrived with four companions from the circle at Meaux. Lay aristocrats began to appear in 1534, after the Affair of the Placards.[4] By the end of the 1530s, the migration broadened to include ordinary families, followers rather than leaders of the new faith. Through the 1540s and 1550s, the community remained fairly compact, able to worship in "a small little place"; refugees from nearby Metz dominated it, and many of them had received permission to settle permanently.[5] With the outbreak of religious war in France, the community began to grow rapidly—in 1562 the magistrates counted over 750 people—and changed in character, becoming a transient population dominated by subjects of the king of France.[6] By the 1580s, the community was dissolving, and very few new arrivals appeared in the 1590s. Perhaps the last person to take shelter here was François le Froid, a Parisian admitted for a few months in 1595.[7]

Just over 1000 adults among the refugees can be identified with a reasonable degree of certainty.[8] The overwhelming majority of these people came to Strasbourg in groups, accompanying a spouse, a child or children, with other kin, or with friends—256 households were linked to other refugee groups by blood, marriage, or business ties. The most common household forms were nuclear families, with or without servants (32 percent and 20 percent of the total, respectively).

The refugees spanned the full range of social classes and occupational groups. Great nobles sent their families to safety: Madeleine de Mailly, the prince of Condé's mother-in-law, brought his young children here in 1562, while Gaspard de Coligny's wife and children were in Strasbourg in 1568.[9] About 4 percent of the refugees were aristocrats, and another 3 percent had held royal or municipal offices, chiefly in Champagne. Proportionately more important than aristocrats or officials were the intellectuals and professional men—preachers, teachers, lawyers, medical men, printers, and the like—who made up about 10 percent of the community, outnumbering merchants by roughly three to one. Some 29 percent of the men were skilled workers and a handful (about 1 percent) were laborers. The largest single occupational category, approximately 30 percent of the population, consisted of servants and apprentices. Mistresses of households made up a quarter of the population, and some of them shared their husbands' work as well as managing the family home.[10] The community also included people who were too old or too sick to work and widows burdened with young children.

About 60 percent of the refugees whose place of origin can be identified came from the kingdom of France, chiefly from the north, with Champagne, Paris, and Burgundy particularly well represented. Lorrainers, mostly from Metz and its environs, made up another 30 percent of the adults. Refugees from the southern Netherlands were much rarer (about 6 to 7 percent of the total) and a very few refugees came from Savoy and the Franche-Comté.[11]

While there is no mystery about what drove these people from their homes, what drew them to Strasbourg deserves comment. The role of the Strasbourg Reformers in the diffusion of Protestant ideas into Lorraine, France, and the Low Countries was an early attraction. Wolfgang Capito and Martin Bucer took an active interest in developments outside their walls, as the welcome they extended to the "Groupe de Meaux" in 1525 demonstrates. Capito kept in touch with people in reforming circles in France, including Marguerite de Navarre, while Bucer acquired contacts in the Netherlands.[12] In cooperation with Strasbourg's printers and with some of the refugees themselves, Capito and Bucer undertook to translate German writings into Latin editions, which enterprising pedlars smuggled across the Vosges, along with books printed in French for export.[13] In 1542, for example, a Strasbourg printer was engaged in trying to supply the Protestants of Metz with six hundred copies of a prayer book and hymnal, John Calvin and Clément Marot's *La manyere de faire prières*.[14] Thus, at a time when Geneva was still obscure, Strasbourg was making a name for itself among religious dissidents to the west and north.

Those who ventured to the city found a warm welcome and, after 1538, a parish of their own.[15] Its first pastor was John Calvin, and the little church he organized was the original mother church of the reformed faith.[16] For a quarter of a century, this parish was a magnet for French-speaking Protestants in flight from their homes. One young refugee wrote home to describe the tears of joy and relief that overcame him the first few times he worshipped with the congregation.[17] But, starting in the 1550s, the parish was wracked by quarrels among its elders and ministers; in 1563 the magistrates, weary of having to referee these squabbles and under mounting pressure from their Lutheran clergy who had come to consider Calvinism heretical, fired the pastor and closed the church. Five years later, after repeated pleas from refugees seeking permission to worship in their own language, the magistrates relented a little and allowed them to hold prayer meetings in private homes, as long as no one celebrated the sacraments at these gatherings. This decision was reversed in 1577, but the new ban on prayer services was not fully enforced until 1597, at which time residents of Strasbourg were also forbidden to attend Calvinist services outside the city.[18]

The closing of the refugee church in 1563 certainly made Strasbourg less attractive to refugees. Nicolas François of Baccarat decided to move his family away in 1564, since there was no longer a functioning congregation in Strasbourg.[19] Yet, most of the refugees stayed on and newcomers continued to pour into this increasingly Lutheran city. In part, this must be attributed to the attitudes of the same magistrates who had closed the French parish. In the 1530s and 1540s, they had pressured Frances I and the authorities in Lorraine, as well as the emperor who ruled over the Low Countries, to tolerate dissent, and the beginnings of the religious wars to the west and north reinforced their determination to help their suffering fellow Protestants.[20] In 1562, recognizing the deteriorating situation in France, they withdrew a decision made five years before to limit the number of foreigners they would allow to live in their city and braced themselves to assist the waves of unfortunates they knew would soon and long be upon them.[21] Over the next decades, they rarely refused to shelter religious refugees. Caught between the exigencies of their pro-Huguenot foreign policy and their clergy's insistence that Strasbourg must condemn Calvinism and keep out of the wars, Strasbourg's rulers usually managed to create compromises that enabled them to continue to protect refugees.

The year 1538 had witnessed not just the birth of the refugee church but also the foundation of what was to become a celebrated Latin school, which, under the direction of rector Johann Sturm (1538-1581), proved powerfully attractive to foreign teachers and students.[22] A refugee himself, Sturm took an active part in the direction and defense of the French parish, kept up a wide correspondence in France, and welcomed such notable refugee jurists and theologians as Charles Dumoulin, François Baudouin, François Hotman, Peter Martyr Vermigli, and Girolamo Zanchi into the ranks of his faculty. Hubert de Bapasme, eager to learn Latin in the 1540s, happily enrolled in Sturm's school, as did other boys and young men seeking the finest humanist education available to Protestants in the sixteenth century.[23]

Sturm, like Capito and Bucer, attracted people who knew him personally or by reputation, and other prominent figures in Strasbourg also had contacts abroad. Jean Gonthier d'Andernach, once the personal physician of Frances I, vouched for the character of Jean de Ferrières, Vidame de Chartres, when he appeared seeking admission to the city in 1563; the printer-publisher Josias Rihel spoke up on behalf of a preacher, François Pithius Cappella, in 1568; Johann Nervius, one of the city's legal advisers, intervened on behalf of a colleague, Charles Maucler, in 1587.[24] The magistrates, too, were in touch with both fellow rulers and informants outside Strasbourg and welcomed some of these people, like Gaspard de Heu of Metz and Georges d'Authy of France, when they had to flee.[25] Of course, as refugees settled in Strasbourg, they sought to bring in their relatives and friends, as did Nicolas Morel, who petitioned on behalf of five families in 1559.[26] Refugees who returned home during one of the periodic lulls in the fighting, as many did, spread the word about the Strasbourg refuge, and sometimes a second generation, drawing on family memory, imitated parents and came to the city seeking its safety for themselves.[27] In some cases, personal contacts with Strasbourgeois reinforced other attractions: Nicolas d'Harracourt came to Strasbourg as a boy to study and returned as an adult with his wife and children; his family was related to a local branch of the Rathsamhausen clan.[28]

No refuge is of any use unless it can be reached. The long-established trade route from Paris across northern France into the empire channeled people towards Strasbourg, which controlled the most northerly bridge across the Rhine.[29] The route was fairly easy going and crossing the Vosges far simpler than penetrating the mountains around Geneva. For Lorrainers, the choice of Strasbourg was almost automatic, since it took only three days travel to reach Strasbourg from Metz.[30] Long before religious refugees began to make their way along the trade routes, merchants had been on the move between France, the Low countries, Lorraine, and Strasbourg; the way was well known and no doubt, in the sixteenth century, contacts with merchants and pedlars decided some refugees on their choice of a destination.[31]

For some of those drawn to Strasbourg the city's physical and cultural position on the Franco-imperial border sang a siren's song. The magistrates' policies combined with geography to make Strasbourg a rendezvous for the bankers and recruiters of the Protestant armies in the second half of the century, so that anyone who wished to get in touch with these circles did well to settle here. Madeleine de Mailly, countess of Roye, half-sister of Coligny and mother-in-law of Condé, was such a person. No

sweet granny seeking only a quiet place for herself and her grand-
children far from the wars, Madame de Roye was the accredited
financial and diplomatic agent of the Huguenot chiefs, and she
made Strasbourg the base for her energetic campaigns on their
behalf.[32] The flow of news through the city undoubtedly aided
her; so, too, it must have comforted other, more obscure men
and women who yearned for reports of the fate of the relatives
and friends they had left behind and craved news of the longed-
for peace that might allow them to end their exile.

More than anything, according to the refugees themselves, it
was Strasbourg's reputation for charity and toleration which
drew them. In the war-torn villages and towns of France, Lorraine, and the Low Countries, a city that fought its religious battles
with pen and paper rather than with swords and stakes exercised
a powerful lure. Jean Masure and Rainolt Megin, who arrived on
the run from the Duke of Alba in 1570, claimed that Strasbourg
was the best place in all of Germany for Gospel-loving victims of
persecution, and their words were echoed the following year by
"a poor persecuted preacher," Franciscus Actopeus; as he put it,
"the mercy of this city . . . is daily celebrated" among Protestants
in the Netherlands.[33] Pastor Guillaume Holbrach, who had been
sacked by the magistrates in 1563 when the French church was
closed, returned in 1572. He had traveled widely in the interven-
ing decade, seeing how things were done in other jurisdictions.
Holbrach intended no irony when he cited Strasbourg's reputation for toleration and mercy.[34]

Primed by tales of the city's charity to the afflicted, refugees
flocked to Strasbourg's gates. The first task for new arrivals was to
secure permission to stay in the city. To do that, they needed to
establish their identity and status before the magistrates, perhaps
by presenting letters like the one Condé had given to the family of
pastor Mathieu Virel.[35] In the 1560s, when the number of refugees
began to peak, at least one local lawyer made a specialty of
representing them in their dealings with the magistrates.[36] In the
first half of the century, refugees were often given a kind of permanent residency permit; but, in later decades, they were usually
granted only short-term permits. Thus Virel's wife and children
were originally admitted for only fourteen days, although they
were told this could be extended.[37] Once given permission to
stay, the refugees had to find a place to live, in principle in an inn
or with a local family, as the magistrates preferred to keep for-

eigners under the scrutiny of trustworthy burghers.[38] In mid-November 1568, fifty-three refugees were living with burghers and another 161 were the guests of innkeepers.[39] In practice, however, many families managed to set up independent households.

Many of the newcomers arrived penniless, having fled in haste or having had their property confiscated by their former rulers. The refugees tried to assist each other as much as possible. Hubert de Bapasme, one of the fortunate ones with some ready cash, told his uncle that, "I can think of no better way to use my money than by helping poor widows." He meant what he said, for he took in two children of the widowed Barbe de Vicery.[41] When the refugees could not cope on their own, the magistrates might step in, as they did to help the Hutmacher children, both of whose parents had fallen ill.[42] By the middle of the century, the refugees were having more and more difficulty taking care of their own poor, and the administration of the parish alms became the subject of bitter disputes.[43] Luckily for those in need of charity, the magistrates were prepared to offer large-scale relief. In 1565-66, they produced more than £410 in cash and 650 *viertel* of grain for the refugee poor, raising the contributions from the city's remaining Catholic foundations.[44]

Once over the original shock of flight, some of those accustomed to a more than comfortable standard of living managed to live on credit extended by local merchants, running up debts on which they frequently ran out at the end of their stay. Madeleine de Mailly's debts remained a sore subject long after her departure in 1563, but the gullible continued to support other worthless debtors, like the seigneur of Dompmartin in the 1580s.[45] Clergymen, lawyers, and officials had little hope of finding work in Strasbourg, although some showed a perhaps surprising willingness to accept a decline in status if they could thus support themselves. Michel Billet, before 1562 the king's "contrôleur du grenier de sel" in Châlons, by 1586 had learned to weave, and worked beside his second wife, Claude Mauclerc.[46] Other refugees needed to make no such adjustment. Merchants, if they had managed to bring cash or goods into exile with them, could continue to trade from their new base. Pierson Matthis, Hans Odinot, and Jean and Didier de Nays were active wine merchants in the 1550s.[47] The magistrates encouraged artisans to join the local guilds, and about 90 percent of them exercised their trades while in Strasbourg.[48] Servants and housewives, who together accounted for about half the refugee population, of course, had brought their work with them into exile.

Surprisingly little information has survived about how the refugees and their hosts coped with the language barrier, which was real for all but the highly educated minority who could communicate among themselves in Latin. The low German known to some Netherlanders was useless in Strasbourg, but possibly refugees from Lorraine had enough Alemannic to manage the basics of daily life.[49] Likewise, some of the local people, accustomed to catering for hundreds of French speakers during the annual summer fair, must have had some grasp of French.[50] For all that, the struggle to get across ideas and needs must have been exhausting and isolating for most. Possibly, the struggle itself became a bond among the unilingual. Marguerite de Lodieuse, a noblewoman who left France, her husband, and her children to arrive alone in Capito's home in 1536, somehow managed to make friends with Wilbrandis Rosenblatt and Elizabeth Silbereisen, although the three women had no common language.[51]

Fortunately for the unilingual, Strasbourg could offer a range of services in French; and, as the community grew, it may have become fairly self-contained. Girls and boys too young or otherwise unsuited for the Latin school could be placed in French school.[52] The refugee community included medical men: surgeons, physicians, and apothecaries. Most of the married women were of child-bearing age and not a few arrived in the last stages of pregnancy; it is easy to imagine their relief at finding Cleonie, a French-speaking midwife, practicing in the city in the 1560s.[53] After 1548, there were a few French printers working in Strasbourg, and along with German publishers, they produced books that were comforting or edifying.[54] Hubert de Bapasme noticed that every member of the French congregation in the mid-1540s had a hymn book, which could have been either the Calvin and Marot *Manyere de faire prières* or Marot's *Cinquante Pseaumes*, published here in 1545. Confessions of faith by Calvin and by Jean Garnier were available in the 1550s. One book that must have found a ready market was the anonymous *Traicté de la croix et affliction des enfans de Dieu, utile á tous pour le temps de persecution*, published in 1563. News accounts and histories of the Reformation and the origins of the religious wars in France and the Low Countries were also on sale to those seeking to make some sense of the catastrophes that had shattered their lives.

208

From 1538 until 1563, when the French church was open, the refugees had no difficulty in worshipping in their own language and according to their own rites. Hubert de Bapasme wrote glowing accounts of the French services he attended.[55] The hymn singing by the men and women of the congregation thrilled him; Jean Garnier's sermons were "marvellously beautiful to hear"; indeed, the whole service was "very lovely to see." The usual order for the service was to sing a psalm, say prayers, hear a ninety-minute sermon, and then sing again. Every two weeks, Garnier celebrated communion at a table placed in the center of the church and covered with a cloth but without "candles or other baggage." Garnier also conducted a second Sunday morning service for the youngsters, at the end of which he questioned them individually on their catechism.

Pronouncing himself "joyful in exile" de Bapasme clearly found life in Strasbourg deeply satisfying. Free at last to practice his religion as he thought fit, this idealistic young man stressed the "repose of conscience" enjoyed by the refugees. It was not just the church that made his life sweet.[56] The professors in the Latin school were kind and conscientious, and he was overjoyed when one of them, Peter Martyr Vermigli, allowed him to move into his home, an exceptional honor, as he excitedly told his uncle. It was expensive to live in Strasbourg, he admitted, but money was a small price to pay for safety and godliness. Among his fellow refugees were some who had abandoned large fortunes for their faith, and yet, he claimed, they "greatly praise the Lord who called them hither."

In many ways, de Bapasme was the luckiest sort of refugee. Young, single, none too happy with the life he had abandoned in Lille—he had doubts about the propriety of the merchant's career for which he had been preparing—blessed with a bit of money, and profoundly serious about his religious duties, he lived in Strasbourg at a time when the Calvinists had not yet been disowned by the local Lutherans. The refugees who followed him found themselves to be second-class Christians even in their place of refuge, barred from holding public worship and forbidden to receive the sacraments from their own pastors. The refugees were allowed to meet privately in their homes to worship after 1568 and pastor Jean Grenon's responses to a series of charges brought against him by the Lutheran clergy in 1575 give some sense of the way those meetings were conducted.[57] Sermons remained an important part of the service, as did the instruction of children; Grenon modelled his liturgy on the common practices of the churches in France. His flock had to turn to the Lutheran clergy to have their children baptized. The Lutherans refused to do this in French, but as a concession, they used Latin as well as German.[58] Likewise for communion, the refugees were supposed to attend a Lutheran church, although many of them preferred to journey the ten miles to Bischweiler, where there was a Reformed parish, even though it, too, conducted its services in German.[59]

Besides these problems, refugees in the second half of the sixteenth century also had to confront a mounting prejudice among the local laity. By the 1580s, things had come to such a pass that some Strasbourgeois were organizing protests against the "Calvinist and Zwinglian" influences they thought they saw infiltrating their government and the Latin school.[60] Meanwhile, since the 1550s, the magistrates had been nervous about the growing number of French-speaking foreigners, whom they saw as a threat to the city's imperial allegiance and Germanic culture.[61] Therefore, they became reluctant to grant citizenship or permanent residency in Strasbourg, but undoubtedly most of them would have preferred to be able to control the timing of their departures. Instead, they were admitted either "at milords' pleasure" or for short terms. Milord's pleasure could change abruptly, as it did in 1569. The Guiscard Duke of Aumale had an army in the field near Strasbourg and the magistrates, fearful that he would deliberately mistake the refugees for Hugenot soldiers and then use their presence as an excuse to attack the city, ordered all the able-bodied men of military age to quit the city immediately.[63] Refugees admitted on short-term permits had to reapply, perhaps several times a year, if they wished to remain in Strasbourg. To add to their anxiety, the permission to remain was not always forthcoming.[64]

Life in Strasbourg thus grew steadily less pleasant for French-speaking refugees in the latter half of the sixteenth century. Yet, the difficulties they met within the city walls were minor indeed compared to the horrors in the homelands they had fled. As long as the wars and the persecutions continued, the Strasbourg refuge would endure, troublesome and dangerous to its hosts, imperfect but necessary to its guests. Only when the wars and persecutions ebbed at the end of the century did it lose its raison d'être, and no one mourned its passing in the 1590s.

Although the refugee community cannot be understood outside its violent context, the essence of the refuge was peace and security. For seventy years, against a backdrop of prejudice, persecution, and painful death, the refugees could live an abnormal form of normal life. People came and went, contracted marriages, welcomed babies, plied their trades, mourned their dead, and prayed for the day of their homecoming from exile. Joyful in exile? Probably only rarely. Grateful in their hearts and bones? Continually, and with reason.

NOTES

Earlier versions of this paper were read to the Canadian Society for Presbyterian History and to the Huguenot Heritage Society of Toronto. All manuscripts are held by the Archives municipales de Strasbourg (AMS) RP, minutes of the Senate and XXI. N, parish registers.

1. The principal lists of French-speaking refugees are AMS III/271/12 (published by Rodolphe Reuss, *Bulletin de la société de l'histoire du protestantisme français* 28[1879]:303-305), AMS II/84b/56 (partially published by Christian Wolff, *Bulletin de la société de l'histoire du protestantisme français* 103[1956]:167-71), AMS II/84b/48, AMS III/64/1 and AMS III/64/2. Many more people can be identified through scattered references in, for example, the minutes of the Senate and XXI. References like "and his household" or "and their children" make impossible an accurate head count, and the wildly varying spelling of French names by German scribes further compounds the problem of identifying individuals. Not all the French-speaking residents of the city were religious refugees. A reasonable guess at the maximum number of refugees who sojourned in Strasbourg in the sixteenth century might be 2500.

2. Christian Wolff, "Strasbourg, cité du réfuge," in *Strasbourg au coeur religieux du XVIe siècle*, eds. Georges Livet, Francis Rapp, and Jean Rott (Strasbourg, 1977), 321-30 is the best such overview. Roger Zuber studied one important contingent in "Les Champenois réfugiés à Strasbourg et l'église réformée du Châlons: Echanges intellectuels et vie religieuse, 1560-1590," *Mémoires de la société d'agriculture, commerce, sciences et arts du département de la Marne* 79(1964):31-55, and "Strasbourg, réfuge des Champenois," in *Strasbourg au coeur religieux*, 309-19. Leon E. Halkin, "Protestants des Pays-Bas et de la principauté de Liège réfugiés à Strasbourg," in ibid., 297-307.

3. Rodolph Peter, "Strasbourg et la réforme français vers 1525," in *Strasbourg au coeur religieux*, 269-83.

4. Jean Rott, "L'église des réfugiés de langue française à Strasbourg

au XVIe siècle: Aperçu de son histoire, en particulier de ses crises à partir de 1541," *Bulletin de la société de l'histoire du protestantisme français* 122(1976):528-29.

5. AMS II.84b/3 (1552) and RP 1553, fols. 366v-367v.

6. AMS II/84b/56.

7. RP 1595, fols. 249v-250r.

8. To be exact 1063. The community also included a minimum of 450 children.

9. RP 1562, fols. 259v-260v and AMS AA 1855, fol. 56r.

10. For example, Claude Mauclerc, see note 46.

11. The city also sheltered Italians, Swiss, Spaniards, and some Marian exiles from England.

12. Olivier Millet, *Correspondance de Wolfgang Capiton (1478-1541). Analyse et index* (Strasbourg, 1982), 112-14. J. V. Pollet, *Martin Bucer: Etudes sur les relations de Bucer avec les Pays-Bas, l'electorat de Cologne, et l'Allemagne du nord,* 2 vols. (Leiden, 1985), vol. 1, 70-79.

13. Miriam Usher Chrisman, *Lay Culture, Learned Culture: Books and Social Change in Strasbourg, 1480-1599* (New Haven and London, 1982), 29-30.

14. Published by Johann II Prüss, the shipment was confiscated in Metz. Henri Tribout de Morembert, *La réforme à Metz,* 2 vols. (Nancy, 1969-1971), vol. 1, 133-34.

15. Rott, "L'église des réfugiés"; Lorna Jane Abray, *The People's Reformation: Magistrates, Clergy, and Commons in Strasbourg, 1500-1598* (Ithaca, N.Y., 1985), 126-39.

16. Richard Stauffer, "L'apport de Strasbourg à la réforme française par l'intermédiare de Calvin," in *Strasbourg au coeur religieux,* 285-95, is a recent contribution to the extensive literature.

17. Philippe Denis, "La correspondance d'Hubert de Bapasme, refugié lillois à Strasbourg," *Bulletin de la société de l'histoire du protestantism française* 124(1978), letter IV, late 1545-early 1546.

18. RP 1563, fol. 329r; AMS II/84b/49, RP 1568, fols. 560v-561r. RP 1577, fols. 94r-99r. RP 1597, fols. 592r-593r. For places where prayer meetings were held after 1577, see RP 1585, fol. 281v and AMS II/84b/82.

19. RP 1564, fol. 312v. Halkin, "Les protestants des Pays-Bas," 303.

20. For interventions prior to 1555, see Hans Virck, Otto Winckelmann, J. Bernays, Harry Gerber, W. Friedensburg, eds., *Politische Correspondenz der Stadt Strassburg im Zeitalter der Reformation,* 5 vols. in 6 (Strasbourg, 1882-1889; Heidelberg, 1928-1933). For the city's support for the Huguenots after 1562, see Abray, *The People's Reformation,* 93-103.

21. RP 1557, fols. 53r-54r and AMS II/93/5. RP 1562, fols. 260v-264v.

22. Anton Schindling, *Humanistische Hochschule und freie*

Reichstadt: Gymnasium und Akademie in Strassburg, 1538-1621 (Wiesbaden, 1977). Jean Rott, "Le recteur strasbourgeois Jean Sturm et les protestants français," in *L'amiral de Coligny et son temps* (Paris, 1974), 407-25.

23. Denis, "La correspondance," letters I, II, and VII.

24. RP 1563, fol. 413v. AMS III/64/1. RP 1587, fol. 318v.

25. Tribout de Morembert, La réforme à Metz, vol. 1, 178. RP 1585, fols. 444v-445r; AMS III/64/2.

26. AMS V/5/71, 1559.

27. Matthieu de Coignet, RP 1587, fol. 29v; RP 1562, fol. 440r.

28. RP 1570, fols. 132v and 136v; RP 1587, fol. 11r.

29. As Wolff notes, the bridge was an attraction in itself, allowing easy flight farther east, should that become necessary, "Strasbourg, cité du réfuge," 322.

30. Denis, "La correspondance," letter IV. As Pierre de Chastenay, a Lorrainer, told the magistrates, he came to Strasbourg because it was close, RP 1585, fol. 525v.

31. Miriam Usher Chrisman, *Strasbourg and the Reform*, (New Haven, 1967), 4-5.

32. "Correspondance de Madeleine de Mailly, comtesse de Roye, avec le duc Christophe de Wurttemberg (1562-1563), *Bulletin de la société de l'histoire du protestantism français* 25(1876):349-61 and 506-18.

33. AMS V/13/31; RP 1571, fol. 1015r-v.

34. RP 1572, fols. 905v and 910r-911r. Church president Johann Marbach, a man often described as an unrelenting bigot for his role in Holbrach's dismissal, now joined Johann Sturm in recommending him to the magistrates.

35. AMS II/84a/44.

36. Wernher Knoderer, RP 1567, fols. 677v and 682v.

37. RP 1574, fol. 366v.

38. AMS III/64/1.

39. AMS II/84b/64.

40. AMS II/84b/56.

41. Denis, "La correspondance," letters VII, IX, XII, XIII, and XVIII.

42. RP 1557, fol. 60v.

43. AMS V/5/2.

44. AMS II/44/8; compare RP 1568, fols. 321r-323r.

45. AMS AA 1855, fols. 38r-39v; RP 1588, fol. 305v.

46. AMS III/64/1. RP 1586, fol. 19r-v. RP 1587, fols. 20v-21r and 77v.

47. RP 1552, fols. 148r-v.

48. AMS III/64/1, fols. 13v-14r. RP 1562, fols. 378r-v. RP 1568, fol. 398v.

49. Denis, "la correspondance," letter II.

50. RP 1580, fols. 335v and 340r. RP 1582, fol. 339v.

51. Millet, *Correspondance de Wolfgang Capiton*, letters 596 and 699.

52. Carl Zwilling, "Die französische Sprache in Strassburg bis zur ihrer Aufnahme in den Lehrplan des protestantischen Gymnasiums," *Festschrift des protestantischen Gymnasiums* (Strasbourg, 1888), 260-61. AMS II/64/2 and RP 1586, fols. 492v and 503r-v.

53. AMS N26, 467.

54. Chrisman, *Lay Culture*, 11-12, and her *Bibliography of Strasbourg Imprints, 1480-1599* (New Haven and London, 1982).

55. Denis, "La correspondance," letters II, IV, and V.

56. Ibid., letters I, III, VI, and VII.

57. AMS II/84b/76. See also his defense of his sermons, AMS II/84b/81.

58. AMS V/18/35. N28b, fols. 67r-68r and N28c, fol. 37r.

59. Rene Bornert, *La réforme protestante du culte à Strasbourg au XVIe siècle (1523-1598): Approche sociologique et interprétation théologique* (Leiden, 1981), 244-45.

60. RP 1581, fols. 201r, 102r-203r. RP 1591, fol. 295r. RP 1597, fols. 542v-543r and 556r-v.

61. RP 1557, fols. 53r-54r and AMS II/93/5.

62. RP 1567, fols. 632v-633v. The decisions to grant or withhold citizenship often seem to have been made quite arbitrarily. Compare RP 1581, fols. 117v and 207r, and RP 1582, fol. 178r.

63. RP 1569, fols. 101v-103r and 110r-v. AMS II/84b/70 and 72.

64. RP 1560, fols. 385r and 486v.

CONTRIBUTORS

Lorna Jane Abray is associate professor in the University of Toronto's Scarborough College. She is the author of *The People's Reformation: Magistrates, Clergy and Commons in Strasbourg 1500-1598* (1985).

Phillip N. Bebb is co-editor of *Occasional Papers for the Society for Reformation History* (1977) and of *Pietas et Societas: Essays in Memory of Harold Grimm* (1985), as well as author of articles in German reformation history.

Thomas A. Brady, Jr., a Missourian, is author of *Ruling Class, Regime and Reformation at Strasbourg* (1978) and *Turning Swiss* (1985). He is professor of history in the University of Oregon.

Mark U. Edwards Jr. is professor of the history of Christianity at the Divinity School of Harvard University. Author of several books on Martin Luther, Edwards is now working on the presentation of Luther and Luther's theology in the vernacular press of the sixteenth century.

Jerome Friedman received his doctorate from the University of Madison-Wisconsin, and is the author of *Michael Servetus: A Case Study in Total Heresy* (1978); *The Most Ancient Testimony: Sixteenth-Century Christian-Hebraica in the Age of Renaissance Nostalgia* (1983), and *Blasphemy, Immorality and Anarchy: The Ranters and the English Revolution* (1987). He is currently completing a volume concerning street literature published during the English civil war.

Hans R. Guggisberg is professor of history at the University of Basel. His main fields of interest are the Reformation, humanism, and the history of religious toleration, but he has also written on U.S. history. At present he is the European editor of the *Archive for Reformation History* and working on a biography of Sebastian Castellio.

R. Po-chia Hsia, associate professor of history at the University of Massachusetts, Amherst, is the author of *Society and Religion in Munster 1535-1618* (1984), *The Myth of Ritual Murder: Jews and Magic in Reformation Germany* (1988), and editor of *The German People and the Reformation* (1988).

Susan C. Karant-Nunn is professor of history at Portland State University and the author of Luther's Pastors: The Reformation in the Ernestine Countryside (1979), and *Zwickau in Transition, 1500-1547: The Reformation as an Agent of Change* (1987).

Ellis (Skip) Knox received his doctorate from the University of Massachusetts at Amherst in 1984 and is currently Coordinator of Microcomputing at Boise State University. He teaches part-time for the History Department there, and is preparing his dissertation on the guilds of Augsburg for publication.

Sherrin Marshall is the author of *The Dutch Gentry 1500-1650: Family, Faith, and Fortune* (1987); she is also editor of *Women in Reformation and Counter-Reformation Europe: Public and Private Worlds*, forthcoming in 1989. Marshall is currently engaged in a study of Protestants, Catholics, and Jews in the Dutch Republic.

Jean Rott is the author of numerous articles and books on almost all aspects of Early Modern Europe and Strasbourg. A two-volume collection of his most significant writings has recently appeared: *Investigationes Historicae: Eglises et Société au XVIe siécle. Gesammelte Aufsätze zur Kirchen und Sozialgeschichte*, ed. Marijn de Kroon and Marc Lienhard (1986).

Merry Wiesner is an associate professor of history at the University of Wisconsin-Milwaukee. She is the author of *Working Women in Renaissance Germany* and a number of articles on social history in early modern German cities. At present she is working on a study of women's defense of their public role in the Renaissance.

Phillip N. Bebb is Associate Professor of History and Director of the history tutorial program at Ohio University. Sherrin Marshall is Associate Dean for Academic Affairs at Plymouth State College, Plymouth, New Hampshire. Miriam Usher Chrisman was for nearly twenty-five years a member of the history department, University of Massachusetts, Amherst; her many other accomplishments include service as President of the Society for Reformation Research, and American editor of the *Archive for Reformation History*.